THE LIFE AND REIGN OF THE EMPEROR LUCIUS SEPTIMIUS SEVERUS

BY

MAURICE PLATNAUER, B.A., B.Litt.

FORMERLY HONORARY SCHOLAR OF NEW COLLEGE
OXFORD
ASSISTANT MASTER AT WINCHESTER COLLEGE

GREENWOOD PRESS, PUBLISHERS
WESTPORT, CONNECTICUT

Originally published in 1918
by Oxford University Press, London

First Greenwood Reprinting 1970

Library of Congress Catalogue Card Number 79-109822

SBN 8371-4313-6

Printed in the United States of America

IN MEMORIAM

AMICI ET QUONDAM PRAECEPTORIS

GEORGI LEONARDI CHEESMAN

PREFACE

THIS book, or the substance of it, was written between the years 1911 and 1914, and submitted in the summer of the latter as a thesis for the degree of Bachelor of Letters in the University of Oxford. The work of preparation for the press was begun immediately afterwards, but was interrupted by the outbreak of war in August, and thereafter, until quite recently, neither time nor inclination admitted of its prosecution.

The Preface to every book should be in the nature of an apology, for every book throws, as it were, an *onus legendi* on some one who may consider that he does not get an adequate return for the time and trouble he takes in reading it. My only reasons for publishing at so unseasonable a time are an exhausted patience and the finding of myself at last in a position where time could be made, if not found, for the correction of the proofs. For publishing at all I can only plead that the reign of Septimius is an important, if not a crucial, one in the history of the later Roman Empire, and that so far no account has appeared in English of one whom Bacon, with some show of reason, has called 'the ablest Emperour almost of all the liste'.

The extant monographs on the reign are, as far as I know, only six in number. Of these, three, the work respectively of two German historians, Fuchs and Schulte, and of the well-known French author Duruy (writing in the *Revue historique*), are of comparatively early date and have received from me no more than a cursory inspection. The three latest books on the subject are those of Höfner, Ceuleneer, and Hassebrank. Höfner's essay, published in 1875, is a painstaking piece of work—erudite, exhaustive, and, on the whole, sound. It is, however, marred by a want of order that amounts to chaos, and disfigured with foot-notes of such magnitude that one can scarcely bring oneself to read so much 'excellent matter' nor, on the other hand, afford to neglect it. Ceuleneer's monograph, which appeared some five years later in the *Mémoires couronnés* of the Belgian Academy, is a much better digested and more mature piece of work. The author has dealt with his subject thoroughly and systematically, and the whole essay can boast some charm of style and grace of exposition, though at times these qualities degenerate into something perilously like diffuseness. The good use made of original sources by both Höfner and Ceuleneer did not seemingly inspire Hasselrank to do the same, though in other respects this writer is imitative enough. His brochure, published in 1890-1, is a worthless production, written without the least attempt to get back to the ultimate authorities—or at least evincing no trace of any such attempt. Wirth's *Quaestiones Severianae* contains some valuable essays on various obscure points in connexion with the dynasty of the Severi, but it is not in any sense a history of Septimius.

My thanks are due to Professor Haverfield for many valuable suggestions, in the light of which my essay has been somewhat modified in its present form. To Mr. P. E. Matheson of New College I am indebted for help in reading the proofs, and to Mr. C. E. Freeman for the investigation of various points which absence from England prohibited my clearing up for myself. A tribute of thanks his eyes will never see is owed to Professor Bormann of Vienna: the kindness with which he threw open to me the resources of the University and Seminar libraries is a pleasant subject for contemplation in a day of universal hate.

What the death in action of Mr. G. L. Cheesman of New College means to the study of Roman history in England only those who enjoyed the privilege of his friendship can say. It is one of the keenest of my regrets that I can never thank him, on the completion of a task, for the constant interest he took in its inception and progress.

My father read through the chapters of this essay as they appeared in manuscript, and to his wide knowledge and broad sympathies I am indebted for such assistance as a specialist in the subject could scarcely have given.

M. P.

B. E. F.
April 27, 1918.

CONTENTS

CHAPTER I

THE LITERARY SOURCES

The literary sources for the reign of Septimius Severus classify themselves obviously, if perhaps illogically, under two headings: contemporary, or nearly contemporary writings, original in that their sources are the eye or the ear of the writer, or, at furthest, current gossip or archival statement; and secondly, a *réchauffé* of such original histories, put together, as a rule, with more care for picturesqueness of narrative than for the truth of fact. This division is, as has been suggested, not logical, inasmuch as it is one of degree and not of quality; for all history must in the Platonic sense be at least once removed from truth, and a dualistic classification of such infinitely variable removals is clearly arbitrary. For practical purposes, however, it may serve.

Into our first division enters but one author—Herodian. Of his private life and circumstances we know but little: he seems to have been born about the year 170, possibly at Alexandria.[1] That he was in Rome by 204 we know from his remark that he saw the *ludi saeculares* exhibited there that summer.[2] We should infer from his method of writing that he was of good social standing: possibly, as Ceuleneer suggests,[3] a senator, or possibly an imperial procurator.[4] The year of his death we can only fix as after 238, the date at which his history ceases.

[1] Sievers, 'Ueber das Geschichtswerk des Herodianus', *Philologus*, xxvi. 29–43, 253–71, points out that he is more *au fait* with Eastern than with Western affairs. He may, as the article in Pauly-Wissowa suggests, have been born at Antioch.

[2] Herod. iii. 8. 10.

[3] *Essai sur la vie et le règne de Septime Sévère*, p. 4, Mémoires couronnés de l'Académie royale de Belgique, Bruxelles, 1880.

[4] Sievers, *op. cit.* Of his own position he says (i. 2. 5) ἐν βασιλικαῖς ἢ δημοσίαις ὑπηρεσίαις γενόμενος, and Domaszewski goes so far as to consider him no more than an imperial freedman (*Archiv. f. Realwsch.* xi. 237 **

As an historian, Herodian occupies now a very different position
in the opinion of the learned world to that held by him a century
or less ago. ' Erst unsere Zeit hat mit Herodianus gründlich
gebrochen,' says Höfner.[1] The causes of this waning popularity
are not far to seek. We live in a scientific, not a humanistic age :
accuracy of statement, exactitude of chronology, are to us everything, nor are we to be led away from the truth by the voice of
style, charm it never so wisely. Now Herodian was, or thought
he was, a stylist, and the humanist is as ready to pardon, or
rather overlook, inaccuracies in a stylist, as is the average man
to do the same by stupidity in a pretty woman. It was,
consequently, not until a scientific and archaeological test had
been applied to the littérateur Herodian that his statements
began to be taken in a more critical spirit. In spite of his
boasted exactitude[2] Herodian is constantly at fault both in
chronology and geography ;[3] he omits much of importance,[4]
and makes up for it by the insertion of long, tedious, and
pointless speeches in imitation of his Greek models. But besides
this, he succeeds in leaving in the reader's mind a general sense
of confusion, a sort of intellectual haze which is more easily
experienced than described. A typical instance of his slovenliness
is to be found in his account of the British war, where he is at
pains to shroud his complete ignorance of events and places
by vague generalizations, only too liable to escape notice by their
unobtrusiveness.[5]

---

[1] Höfner, *Untersuchungen zur Geschichte des Kaisers Septimius Severus,*
p. 25, Giessen, 1875.

[2] i. 1. 3 μετὰ πάσης ἀκριβείας.

[3] Various instances are quoted in Pauly-Wissowa (art. Cassius, 40).
One that concerns us is the probable confusion of Arabia Felix with
Arabia Scenitis in iii. 9. 3. For chronological inexactitudes see i. 6. 1,
i. 8. 1.

[4] Cf. Kreutzer, *De Herodiano rerum romanarum scriptore,* Diss. Berl.
1881, xviii. 3. The Maternus incident is a case in point. The latest
work on Herodian is Baaz's *De Herodiani fontibus et auctoritate,* Diss.
Berl. 1909. (W. Thiele, *De Severo Alexandro imperatore,* Diss. Berl. 1908,
also deals with him.)

[5] Herod. iii. 14. 5. Oman (*England before the Norman Conquest,* p. 132)
notes his vague use of the word γεφύραις.

A much less nebulous and much more accurate writer is Cassius Dio Coccianus.[1] Like Herodian, a contemporary of the events which he records, he has, unfortunately, only reached us in an epitomized version, at least as regards that portion with which we have to do.[2] He thus holds a position scarcely compatible with either of our two divisions, debarred from the first by reason of his late and abridged form, and from the second in that he is not, like others of that class, a *contaminatio* or medley of conflated originals.

We are better informed as to the personality of Dio than we are in the case of Herodian. Born in 155 at Nicaea,[3] he came to Italy and entered the senate before Commodus' death.[4] Under that emperor he held the posts of quaestor and aedile, and was appointed praetor by Pertinax in 193.[5] He entered office in the following year. During the reigns of the Severi, Dio seems to have been in retirement from public life, and if we are to attribute this fact to the disfavour of Septimius owing to the historian's too trenchant criticism of Commodus,[6] we cannot but admit that his pages show nothing of that rancour which we might therefore expect. Further than this we are told by Dio himself that his first work—a 'dream book' written expressly for Septimius [7] —won him much favour from that prince. It is doubtless to this period of enforced or voluntary retirement that we should attribute the bulk of Dio's literary work—his 'dream book', his history of the πόλεμοι καὶ στάσεις subsequent on the death of Commodus, and the greater part of his Universal Roman History. The imitator of Thucydides might be gratified were we to be

---

[1] He is better, if less correctly, known as Dio Cassius than as Cassius Dio, and the use of the former, or of Dio alone, needs no apology.

[2] Of the 80 books of his history we only possess 36-60, which cover a period extending from 68 B.C. to A.D. 60 : books 61-80 (of which 78 and 79 are mutilated and 70 entirely missing) exist only in the abridged version of the eleventh-century monk Xiphilinus. Much of the contents of his earlier books is to be seen in Zonaras, while other fragments are not uncommon in the two tenth-century compilations known respectively as *excerpta de virtutibus et vitiis* and *excerpta de legationibus*.

[3] Dio Cass. lxxv. 15. 3.   [4] lxxii. 16. 3.

[5] lxxiii. 12. 2.   [6] So Ceuleneer, *op. cit.*, p. 2.

[7] Dio Cass. lxxii. 23. 1.

reminded of another who ceased from making history in order to write it.

However, unlike the victim of Eion, Dio returned to public service. He accompanied Caracalla [1] during that emperor's Oriental campaign,[2] and was appointed by Macrinus curator of Smyrna and Pergamum in 218 : [3] under Alexander Severus [4] he became *consul suffectus* and subsequently proconsul of Africa. The year 226 saw him governor of Dalmatia; the next year of Pannonia Superior.[5] In 229 he shared a second consulship with Alexander,[6] and it is this year that he chooses as the terminus of his work.[7] An agreeable lucidity, which not even the rough hand of an epitomizer can completely destroy, characterizes the style of Dio. Less diffuse than Herodian, he is nevertheless more complete; less of a littérateur he is more of an historian. A certain childishness is apparent in his interest for shows and his care for portents, but such naïveté is infinitely preferable to the pretentious dilettantism of Herodian ; and the flight of eagles round the capitol, or 'meteor moons and balls of blaze', form as good, or bad, reading as imaginary and inappropriate harangues.

When we pass on to consider our next source we find ourselves at once among the waves of uncertainty. That collection of historic writings known as the *Scriptores Historiae Augustae* forms the battlefield of one of the most keenly waged of modern historical controversies, and in an age when the study of history tends more and more, especially in Germany, to be synonymous with *Quellenuntersuchungen*, we must accord this question a rather larger share of attention. Ostensibly the *Historia Augusta* is a compilation in thirty books, the work of six writers—Spartia-

---

[1] As Mr. Stuart Jones has pointed out, the correct form of this nickname is Caracallus, but perhaps little apology is needed for adhering to the old form.

[2] lxxvii. 17. 18 ; lxxviii. 8. 4.   [3] lxxix. 7. 4.

[4] Schwartz in *P. W.* says 'vor Severus' Tod ', and quotes D. C. lxxvi. 16. 4, where Dio talks about examining Septimius' legislation. If anything this would seem to indicate a period *after* Severus' death.

[5] lxxx. 1. 3 ; xlix. 36. 4.

[6] lxxx. 5. 1, *cos. ordinarius*, this time.

[7] lxxx. 2. 1 μέχρι τῆς δευτέρας μου ὑπατείας . . . διηγήσομαι.

nus, Vulcacius, Capitolinus, Lampridius, Pollio, and Vopiscus, each of whom is responsible for one or more of the imperial biographies. The problems raised with regard to it are: who were these writers?—when did they write?—do we really possess their original biographies or a later recension? If so, of what date is that recension, and how far does its lateness vitiate the authority of the originals; and lastly, and of greatest importance, what are the sources of the work as we possess it? The most obvious answer to the first two questions is that these six names are those of the authors of a joint historical work, a work which we now possess, and which was written by them during a period whose extreme limits are the years 285 and 340. These dates are inferred from the fact that many of the lives contain apostrophes to, or mention of, the three emperors—Diocletian, Constantius, and Constantine.[1] This fact in turn helps us towards an answer of question number three. Every composite work argues the existence and activities of a 'Redaktor', or editor; and a book, the composition of whose various parts extends over at least twenty years,[2] one cannot suppose to have flowed together without any external help. Nor again does the hypothesis that one of the six contributors was deputed by his colleagues to edit the compilation find universal favour in the opinion of the critics.[3] It is argued, not unreasonably, that had this been the case the apostrophes to Diocletian and Constantius would have been expunged and the whole work dedicated in its entirety to Constantine.[4]

[1] A full list of citations may be found in the index to Peter's edition, Leipzig, 1884: three may be mentioned—an apostrophe to Diocletian in Spartian's life of Helius (i. 1); of Constantine by Capitolinus (Vit. Clod. Alb. iv. 2); and a mention of Constantine by Pollio (Claud. iii. 1).

[2] I am reckoning from the retirement of Diocletian (305) to the reunification of the empire under Constantine (324).

[3] Yet this theory—to the merits of which we shall return later—has its supporters: e. g. Peter (Script. Hist. Aug, p. 103) and Lécrivain (Études sur l'Hist. Aug., p. 26) suggest Capitolinus, Giambelli Lampridius, and Wölfflin Vopiscus.

[4] The relative dates of the writers (presuming for the present the genuineness of the Caesar apostrophes) are hard to determine. From the fact that Pollio and Vopiscus make no mention of Constantine we might

In consideration of this difficulty many critics have supposed that at some date after the completion of the individual biographies a later hand edited them in the form of a single book.[1] The theory is plausible enough, but difficulties arise when we try to determine the date of this editor and to estimate the extent of his influence on the original text. It must at once be confessed that the only means of answering these questions lies in an examination of the text itself—that is to say, that all arguments and conclusions are and must be based on stylistic grounds,—and that all arguments from style are notoriously

conclude that they were the earliest. The mention by an author writing under Constantine of Diocletian or Constantius is quite intelligible, but we do experience some surprise at finding apostrophes by Capitolinus both to Diocletian (Vit. Marc. xix. 12) and to Constantine (Vit. Clod. Alb. iv. 2). Possibly that historian wrote his *Marcus Aurelius* in the reign of Diocletian, and at the time of his final recension under Constantine rewrote his *Albinus*.

[1] e. g. Dessau in *Hermes*, 1889, of whom more in detail later; also Otto Schulz, *Kaiserhaus der Antonine* (Leipzig, 1907). Seeck (*Neue Jahrb. für Philologie und Pädagogik*, 1890) goes so far as to set the final recension under Constantine, the Gallic tyrant (407-411). At this point might be enumerated at least some of the literature devoted to the subject. The controversy may be said to have been opened by Dessau in the above-mentioned article. This was answered by Mommsen in *Hermes*, 1890, pp. 270 sqq. Dessau printed a counter-reply in *Hermes*, 1892. Besides these we have Peter, *Historia critica scriptor. hist. Aug.*, as early as 1860: also in *Philologus*, 1884, and again in the *Jahresbericht* of 1906 (an article on recent works, 1893-1905, itself containing a full bibliography). Articles in the *Rhein. Mus.* by Richter, Rühl, and Klebs (1888, 1890, 1892). Plew, *De diversitate auct. hist. Aug.*, 1869, and *Kritische Beiträge zu den S. H. A.*, 1885. Enmann, in *Philologus*, 1884, an article dealing mainly with the question of sources of the *S. H. A.* and postulating a *Chronicon imperiale* of incredible accuracy and value. Various Italian critics, among whom may be mentioned De Sanctis (*Rivista di Storia antica*, 1895) and Tropea (ibid., 1897). Their conclusions are generally of a more conservative character than those of the Germans. Finally, Lécrivain, *Études sur l'Hist. Aug.*, perhaps the most level-headed and satisfactory of all the monographs on the subject. (For English the most up-to-date and complete statement of the controversy is to be found in Crees's *Emperor Probus*, 1911, pp. 23-58 : he appends a useful bibliography.) I have purposely left unmentioned many books and articles.

uncertain. We must therefore accept all such views with reserve, if not scepticism.

It may not here be out of place briefly to examine the hypo-thesis put forward in the most recent book on the subject—Otto Schulz's *Kaiserhaus der Antonine und der letzte Historiker Roms.* He postulates a 'sachliche Verfasser' of senatorial stand-ing and noble family, born in Egypt about the year 136, probably at Pelusium,[1] where he lived until the age of fifteen or sixteen, when he went to the university at Alexandria. After his course of study there he came to Rome and entered the study circle of Marcus Aurelius. Previous to this, it is suggested, he had had some connexion with the household of Antoninus Pius.[2] During the reign of Commodus he was a stranger to court life, to which he returned under Pertinax. Possibly from then on he started his series of biographies, concluding with that of Cara-calla, and he died about the year 220. For nearly a century his production lay undisturbed, when it was worked up by what we might call an historical syndicate whose names were those which now stand as denoting the authors of the complete history as we possess it. The work of these men was to epitomize and, by the addition of fresh biographical detail, to render more readable the work of the 'sachliche Verfasser'. These six writers lived and worked during the reigns of Diocletian, Con-stantius, and Constantine; so that the imperial apostrophes, which we have already had occasion to mention, are genuine, and not, as some have held, later interpolations inserted by a fourth-century editor for the purpose of simulating a compara-tive nearness to the events chronicled by him.[3] We must suppose further that they wrote the remaining biographies (xiv-

[1] Schulz, p. 115, quotes ten passages from the *scriptores* containing references to Egypt and Egyptian affairs.

[2] *Op. cit.*, p. 22. Schulz notes the detailed account of the death of Antoninus Pius, and gives as the reason the fact that this, being the first imperial decease in the experience of the youthful 'sachliche Verfasser', must have created in his mind a strong impression. He even (p. 212) suggests the latter's identity with the tribune mentioned on that occasion (Vit. Ant. P. xii. 6).

[3] This is Dessau's view. He would, as we shall see, assign the entire work to the last third of the fourth century.

xxx) on the same model and added them to the corpus.[1]   Thus
before the middle of the fourth century we have a collection of
biographies containing an early third or late second century
source, excerpted, worked up, and added to by early fourth or
late third century hands.   In spite, however, of the addition of
biographical detail, the work was considered of insufficient
piquancy to suit the literary taste of a generation later, and
a new edition was demanded to meet popular requirements.
This new edition, the work of Schulz's 'Schlussredaktor', came
out in the reign of the Emperor Theodosius (379–95), and the
method of the editing was as follows.   Much uninteresting
(i.e. true) material was expurgated:[2] new scandal was plenti-
fully introduced, and, on occasion, pure fiction was unblushingly
interpolated.[3]   If we ask why this latest editor left in the apostrophes of his predecessors we are told that he did so in order
to strengthen his claim to historical accuracy by means of their
authority.   Our next question is, not unnaturally, what are the
arguments from which Schulz draws such hard and fast conclusions ?

We have seen that there are three strata in our present text :
the 'sachliche Verfasser', Spartian and his contemporaries,
and lastly the 'theodosianische Schlussredaktor'.   Of these,
two—the first and last—have left their traces on the text.   The
S. V., we are told, is characterized primarily by his interest for
the provinces, being himself, as we have seen, a provincial.
Thus we are to see his work in any passages concerning Roman
foreign or colonial policy.[4]   But besides this general tendency,
his hand is to be recognized by the use of certain words and

---

[1] As this is a question which concerns only the later biographies we
shall not deal with it here.   See Crees, op. cit., for a full discussion.
That Schulz presupposes a 'vitae Sammlung der Herren Spartianus u. s. w.'
is a point to which we shall return.

[2] Schulz quotes as an instance Vit. Sept. Sev. xvii. 5 'Et quoniam
longum est minora persequi, huius magnifica illa . . .', where the minora
form the 'sachliche Darstellung' and the magnifica are borrowed from
Aurelius Victor (Caes. xx).

[3] Especially in Vulcacius' life of Avidius Cassius, whose author Klebs
calls a deliberate 'Fälscher'.

[4] e. g. Vit. Ant. P. vi. 1, vii. 7, vii. 11, x. 7, xii. 3, etc., etc.

expressions, e. g. *sanctum gravemque*;[1] *respuit*;[2] *imperium*, as opposed to *tyrannis* (the latter a Schlussredaktor word);[3] *de iure sanxit*;[4] *ambo imperatores*;[5] *summovere*,[6] etc. The 'theodosianische Schlussredaktor', on the other hand, betrays himself chiefly by a characteristic 'biographische Unbestimmtheit;[7] the use of superlatives;[8] demonstrative pronouns.[9] His favourite words and phrases are: *fuit*, beginning a sentence;[10] *clemens, iactare*, etc.;[11] *ut supra diximus* (inserted in the original text to connect the passage with a previous insertion);[12] *male loqui*;[13] *parcus*.[14]

Not only may we discover by this method the traces of the Theodosian editor, we may further catch a glimpse by the same means of his chief source—Marius Maximus.[15] Marius Maximus

---

[1] Vit. Ant. P. iv. 3; Vit. Iul. i. 7 *sancte ac diu*.

[2] Vit. Ant. P. x. 1; Vit. Marc. vii. 1; Did. Iul. iv. 5; Sept. Sev. ix. 11.

[3] Two occurrences of this word (*tyrannis, tyrannicus*), which occur respectively in Vit. Hadr. iv. 3 and Vit. Car. v. 2, are attributed by Schulz (following Kornemann, *Kaiser Hadrian und der letzte grosse Historiker von Rom*, 1905, p. 14, note) to an 'Überarbeitung'.

[4] Vit. Ant. P. xii. 1.

[5] For use of *ambo* cf. Vit. Marc. viii. 1, xii. 7, xii. 8, xii. 14; Vit. Veri, iv. 3.

[6] Vit. Hadr. x. 7; Ant. P. v. 4; Comm. iii. 1 and iv. 7; Did. Iul. iv. 6; Sept. Sev. x. 3 and xv. 2.

[7] e. g. Vit. Marc. xii. 2 *Nullorum*, xii. 3 *quendam Vetrasinum*.

[8] Vit. Sept. Sev. xviii. 3 *bellicosissimis ... securissimam ... fecundissimum*. I take this instance not from those quoted by Schulz: it is further noteworthy that *securus* is itself called typical of the Schlussredaktor (Schulz, *op. cit.*, p. 141).

[9] Vit. Hel. vii. 4 *haec sunt, quae* . . .; Pesc. Nig. ix. 1 *Haec sunt, . . . quae*, etc.

[10] Vit. Ant. P. ii. 1; Avid. Cass. iii. 4, etc.

[11] Vit. Hadr. xiv. 8, xvii. 8, xxi. 2; Hel. vi. 2; Avid. Cass. x. 10; Car. v. 9; Getae, iv. 1, etc.

[12] Cf. Vit. Marc. iv. 1, where it is used to refer back to the 'Theodosian', section 10 of ch. i.

[13] Vit. Pert. xiii. 5; Cl. Alb. ii. 3, etc.

[14] Vit. Ant. P. vii. 11; Marc. v. 8; Comm. xvi. 8 (*parcissimus*); Pert. viii. 10; Sev. iv. 6 (twice), xix. 8; Pesc. Nig. i. 4, vi. 6; Cl. Alb. xi. 4.

[15] We shall have more to say about Marius Maximus later. Suffice it here to state that this is neither the usually accepted, nor, in my opinion, the correct view as to the position of the writer.

was, we are told, fond of his little joke. Hence all passages containing such words as *ioci, iocare,* etc., are to be attributed to Marius Maximus as grafted on to the text by the ' Theodosianischer '.[1]

We can accord the ingenuity of this theory much admiration —and how much credence ? We notice first of all that although our text is said to have passed through two stages besides the original, yet traces of only one of them is discovered.

Granted that ' fuit ' sentences, the use of superlatives, and the rest of it characterize a later recension, why call this recension Theodosian rather than Diocletianic or Constantinian ? Secondly, though the existence of an original biographer is not improbable, why make his work end with the life of Caracalla ? True, the later lives are as a whole inferior productions to the earlier ones,[2] still it needs a keen eye to detect a generic difference between, say, the biographies of Septimius and Alexander Severus. Thirdly, the truth of all Schulz's stylistic arguments rests on the absence of negative instances : hence when a cursory glance down the first page of the life of Aurelian discovers *sanctus* (a word which we were told characterized the ' sachliche Verfasser ') in the sixteenth line, our faith is somewhat shaken. Incidentally, too, the same life contains the so-called ' sachlich ' word *imperium* (xxxvii. 6), whereas *tyrannis* (in the genitive, coupled with *coniurationis*) is used in quite another sense. Further, so full is this life of *ioca* and *frivola* that Vopiscus excuses himself therefor on three different occasions (iii. 1, vi. 6, x. 1). Now the jocular Marius Maximus died not later than A. D. 230. He could not, therefore, have written a life of Aurelian : hence these jokes do not come from his pen. Why then should we see a causal connexion between *ioca* and Marius Maximus ? Why again is the final edition called Theodosian ?

Here we come to the articles by Dessau in *Hermes,* for he it was who first formulated and upheld the hypothesis of a Theodosian Schlussredaktor, or rather writer—for he goes as far as to

---

[1] e.g. Vit. Hadr. xii. 4, where M. M. is mentioned, xvii. 6 ; Sev. xiv. 13 ; Getae, iii. 3 ; Ant. P. xi. 8 ; Marc. xv. 1 ; Veri, ii. 9 (in a ' fuit ' sentence), vii. 4.

[2] Schiller, *Geschichte der röm. Kaiserzeit,* vol. i, p. 700.

consider the whole corpus a fourth-century forgery.[1] He comments on the strangeness of the dedication by Capitolinus of his
Marcus Aurelius and *Albinus* respectively to Diocletian and Constantine—a point noticed above. He then throws doubt on the
veracity of Vopiscus, who, in his life of Aurelian,[2] details a con-
versation between himself and Tiberianus, the city prefect :
this interview is said to have taken place at the Hilaria
(March 25th), whereas Tiberianus only held the prefecture
between the dates September 14, 303, and January 4, 304.
Traces of fourth-century reference are next discovered in such
names as Toxotius, given in the *S. H. A.* as second husband of
Junia Fadilla, wife of Maximus the younger,[3] Dessau holding
this to be an exclusively (?) fourth-century name and quoting
inscriptional evidence for it dating about the year 378.   The
supposition is that ' Capitolinus ' gave him this name in order
to flatter the fourth-century family.   A similar argument is
brought forward with regard to Ragonius Celsus,[4] Clodius
Celsinus,[5] and Aetius.[6]   The ' prophecy ' in the twenty-fourth
chapter of the life of Probus is supposed to refer to the famous
Sextus Petronius Probus, consul with the younger Gratian in
371.[7] Yet another trace of fourth-century origin is to be seen
in the statement that Maximinus was the son of a Gothic father [8]
and an Alan mother, for, says Dessau, these two peoples did
not live together until Theodosius settled them in amity in the
Balkan peninsula after the year 375.   Lastly, the many

[1] So too Czwalina, *De Epistolarum actorumque fide*, pt. i.

[2] Vop. Aur. i. 1.

[3] Cap. Max. xxvii. 6.

[4] Spart. Nig. iii. 9. *CIL.* vi. 1759, 1760, xiv. 138, 139 are quoted as
showing the lateness of this name (A.D. 380).

[5] Mentioned in the life of Septimius (xi. 3). Dessau supposes this to
have been the name of the father of the praef. urb. of 391 (*CIL.* ix. 1576,
vi. 1712).

[6] This Aetius is mentioned in Spart. Sev. viii. 1. Dessau sees in him
a reference to Servius Aetius, procurator of Achaia (396–401) and prefect
of Constantinople in 419.

[7] He compares with this Claudian's poem on the two sons of Probus,
ll. 11–13, etc. Cf. Crees, *op. cit.*, p. 49, note.

[8] Cap. Max. i. 5.

references to Byzantium are held to be pointless before the transformation of that city into Constantinople.

As to the undoubted likenesses obtaining between the *S. H. A.* and Eutropius, Dessau considers that the former copied from the latter.   Now Eutropius, as we know, wrote his *Breviarium* during the reign of the Emperor Valens (365–78),[1] which fixes the date of the histories as posterior to the year 378.   It will be seen that Dessau's hypothesis differs from that of Schulz in that he attributes the whole corpus to the pen of a fourth-century forger who made use of anachronous Caesar apostrophes to give an air of antiquity to his book.   Schulz's view, on the other hand, is not incompatible with the genuineness of the apostrophes.

In his reply in *Hermes*, Mommsen wrote ostensibly in support and amplification of Dessau's theory, but in effect he left so little of that theory unchanged that he may be considered as belonging to the opposite camp.   He points out that the reference to the *Hilaria* may be in reality to the lesser festival, which took place on November 3 during the Isis feast—not the March one, which formed part of the seven-day Cybele celebration [2]— a suggestion which had been actually anticipated by Dessau himself.[3]   As to the fourth-century character of particular names the argument rests wholly on negative evidence and carries its inconclusiveness on its face.   Nor is it unimpeachable as it stands : the name Ragonius, for example, occurs in the third century, for one L. Ragonius Quintianus was consul in 289,[4] while there was a bishop of Thessalonica, by name Aetius, during the reign of Constantius.   That the Probus prophecy refers to Sextus Petronius Probus is a pure and unwarranted assumption, and there is no reason for disbelieving the statement about Maximinus' parentage even prior to the conflation of the

---

[1] Baumgarten-Crusius, preface of edit., p. 4.   The most striking of the parallel passages are perhaps Vit. Marc. xvi. 3–xviii. 3 and Eutrop. viii. 11–14.   The likenesses in the *S. H. A.* and the *Caesares* of Aurelius Victor (A. D. 360) are similarly explained by Dessau.

[2] A second suggestion was to alter *non. Ian.* to *non Iun.* in the list of prefects.

[3] p. 345.

[4] Liebenam, *Fasti Consulares*, p. 32.

Gothic and Alan races. References to Byzantium are not over-numerous,[1] and might be more so without our being justified in regarding that city as the centre of the empire. As to the parallelisms between the histories and Eutropius we can either presume a common source or—the orthodox view [2]—suppose Eutropius rather to have copied the *S. H. A.*

We may finally examine the view of Lécrivain. Accepting Mommsen's solution of the Tiberianus difficulty he concludes that the Caesar apostrophes are genuine, and that, somewhere about the year 325, Capitolinus united into one volume the biographies of Spartian, Lampridius, Vopiscus, and the rest, adding to the collection smaller lives such as those of Albinus, Pertinax, and Macrinus. As to the date of the compilation, he carries the war into the enemy's country by producing fairly conclusive evidence for a third-century origin. In the mention of Albinus' 'Ceionian descent' [3] he sees a reference to C. Ceionius Rufinus Volusianus, consul in 311 and 314 and praetorian prefect in 321; in that of Hannibalianus to the consul of 292.[4] More conclusive are the arguments drawn from civil and military titles, among which he finds nothing definitely post-Constantinian, whereas for the most part they are pre-Diocletianic.[5]

[1] Peter only mentions eleven instances in his index.

[2] Cf. Bury's *Gibbon*, 1896, vol. i, p. 447.

[3] Cap. Alb. i. 1.

[4] A city prefect Ceionius is mentioned in a (? forged) letter (Vit. Aur. ix. 2): a Nummius Albinus held this post in 256, and he may be the same as M. Nummius Ceionius Annius Albinus, *cos. ord.* in 263 (*CIL*. vi. 314 *b*). Hannibalianus occurs in Vit. Prob. xxii. 3: cf. Liebenam, p. 32. Another instance adduced is Herennianus (Vit. Prob. xxii. 3), who occurs in a third-century inscription (*CIL*. iii. 10174).

[5] The use of *dux* he rightly attributes to slovenly translation from some Greek author, probably Herodian. The *legio VI Gallicana* mentioned in the life of Aurelian is post-Diocletianic. More difficulty—not faced by Lécrivain—is to be seen in Vopiscus' *leg. III felix* (Vit. Aur. xi. 3; Vit. Prob. v. 6), whose name probably implies the prior enrolling of a *prima* and *secunda legio felix*. The *Notitia dignitatum* indeed mentions a *secunda felix* only under Valens. Vopiscus may be referring to *leg. III Gallica*: *felix* was often added to legions as a second title. There is indeed an inscription attesting this occurrence in the case of this legion (*CIL*. ii. 2103). The *catafractarii* mentioned in Vit. Aur. xi. 4 are all right as they date back to Hadrian; cf. *CIL*. ii. 5632.

So, too, in the matter of coinage. With the exception of a passage in the life of Alexander Severus[1] we always find reference to the *aureus*, not to the post-Constantinian *solidus*. And finally the treatment of Christianity in the histories clearly points to a pagan age, in which the writer mentioned the matter when need were and referred to it in what terms he liked. Vopiscus, for instance, makes no attempt to hide his contempt for the Christians, while post-Constantinian pagan writers, such as Victor and Eutropius, maintain a discreet silence on the subject.[2]

The truth of the matter is that our evidence is far too meagre to admit of any conclusion which shall be either detailed or authoritative, and until fresh light is shed upon the subject externally we shall never rise above a mere working hypothesis. The very ingenuity and seeming completeness of such theories as those of Dessau or Schulz should lead us to view them with extreme suspicion. A less robust faith must be content with less, and the only conclusions at which we can arrive with anything like an assurance of their correctness are ones which would probably strike a German *Quellen-forscher* as vague to the point of uselessness. Our view then is somewhat as follows: The biographies are the work of those authors whose names are appended to them. They were written towards the end of the third and at the beginning of the fourth century. Some later hand collected them, and possibly tampered in places with the text, though the evidence does not warrant our making any definite statement on this point. The time of this final recension was probably the first third of the fourth century: its author unknown, though there

---

[1] Lamprid. Alex. Sev. xxxix. 9–10. Cf. the *folles aeris* in Lamprid. Elag. xxii. 3.

[2] Schulz (p. 91) holds that the use of *antiquitas* ('et omnia, quae aede sacrata decrevit antiquitas') in Vit. Marc. xviii. 8 is a proof that this passage was written by a Christian (i. e. or Theodosian) hand. A glance at the pages of Orosius or Origen does not lead one to suppose the early Christians mealy-mouthed enough to refer to the Roman religion as *antiquitas* (a word, incidentally, always used with a good connotation). So far from being absurd in the mouth of a Diocletianic author it would be almost inconceivable in that of a Theodosian.

is some reason to believe that it was one of the six joint authors. There is also, I believe, fairly conclusive evidence for the existence of a dual stratum in the text. A close examination of any of the lives reveals the fact that many 'doublets' occur,[1] the presence of which can only be explained by supposing them to be culled from different sources. These two strata show respectively a chronological and a biographical character: the first revealing an accurate and well-informed writer through and in spite of its abridged form, the second possessing neither credibility nor value. It is of course possible that this useless gossiping material was introduced by the Schlussredaktor, but in default of more definite evidence it is perhaps as well to treat a completer solution merely as an hypothesis.[2] The value of the *S. H. A.* as an historical document rests of course on the question not of the date or origin of the composition, but of the sources used by the compilers, and to this question we now turn.

The main sources of the *Scriptores* we do know inasmuch as they themselves tell us.[3] They are:

[1] Several are quoted by J. M. Heer in his article in *Philologus*, Supplementband IX, pp. 1-208, 'Der historische Wert der Vita Commodi', p. 123.

[2] The theory of the dual stratum, besides its appearance in the above-quoted article of Heer, is to be found not only in Schulz's *Letzte Historiker* but also in his *Beiträge zur Kritik unserer litterarischen Überlieferung für die Zeit von Commodus' Sturze bis auf den Tod des M. Aurelius Antoninus* (Leipzig, 1903). Examining the lives sentence for sentence on Heer's principle (Heer, p. 4) he concludes (Schulz, *Beiträge*, p. 122) that the 'sachlich-historischer' part is the best source for the period, not excepting Dio himself, while the biographical section was put in by the Theodosian Schlussredaktor and contains sometimes that editor's pure inventions, sometimes statements drawn from sources contemporaneous with the events. Heer (pp. 6, 123, 145) comes to much the same conclusions, adding the fact that the chronological epitome was a contemporary record, written in Latin, and of annalistic form. It is not, he holds, to be identified with the work of Marius Maximus (p. 145, etc.).

[3] Caution has in general to be exercised in accepting the *Scriptores'* statements as to authorities. Vopiscus may have gathered his materials from the Ulpian library, as he claims (e. g. Vit. Aur. viii. 1 'Inveni nuper in Ulpia bibliotheca inter linteos libros epistolam divi Valeriani...'). There is little doubt that, as Peter has shown, Pollio's citations are

(1) Marius Maximus. The *Scriptores* contain ten direct references to this writer.[1] He was a contemporary of Severus, possibly *praefectus urbi* under Macrinus,[2] and, in the world of letters, continuer of Suetonius.[3] Of the character of his history we can tell little, nor was the opinion of antiquity at all decided on the point. Ammianus tells us that he was much read;[4] Vopiscus calls him 'homo omnium verbosissimus',[5] and accuses him of omissions; while Spartian[6] seems to testify to his verbosity by his use of the adverb *copiose*. It seems probable that he was not the similarly named general of Severus,[7] and that he did not slavishly follow the memoirs of that emperor.[8]

forgeries. Lampridius' citation from Marius Maximus concerning the 'acclamationes senatus' on the occasion of Commodus' death (Vit. Comm. xviii. 3) has earned the scepticism of Schulz, who calls it 'historisch unbrauchbar' (Schulz, *op. cit.*, p. 145).

[1] Höfner, *Untersuchungen zur Geschichte des Kaisers L. Sept. Sev.*, gives the references: Vit. Sev. xv. 6; Clod. Alb. iii. 4, ix. 2, ix. 5, xii. 14; Getae, ii. 1; Heliog. xi. 6; Alex. Sev. v. 4, xxi. 4, lxv. 4.

[2] Dio. Cass. lxxviii. 14. 3, lxxviii. 36. 1. It is uncertain whether M. M. the city prefect is identical with M. M. the historian or with M. M. the general, or whether all three are the same. Cf. below, p. 82, note.

[3] His work comprised eleven lives: viz. those of Nerva (schol. Iuv. iv. 53), Trajan, Hadrian, Antoninus Pius, Marcus Aurelius, Commodus, Pertinax, Julian, Severus, Caracalla, and Heliogabalus (Lamp. Elag. xi. 6). Müller reconstructs him in *Büdinger's Untersuch. zur römischen Kaisergeschichte*, vol. iii, pp. 19–200). The reconstruction is ingenious, but fantastic and wild to the last degree: saner is J. Plew's *Marius Maximus als direkte und indirekte Quelle der S. H. A.*, 1878.

[4] Amm. Marc. xxviii. 4. 14.   [5] Vit. Firm. i. 2.

[6] Vit. Getae, ii. 1.

[7] Müller, *op. cit.*, p. 170, etc. Peter, *Hist. rom. frag.*, pp. 332–9, thinks historian, prefect, and general identical. So too *Prosopogr. imp. rom.*, vol. ii, pp. 346, 347.

[8] So Höfner, *op. cit.*, p. 5, arguing from Vit. Clod. Alb. iii. 4 'Nec negari potest, quod etiam M. M. dicit, hunc animum Severo primum fuisse, ut, si quid ei contingeret, Pescennium Nigrum et Clodium Albinum sibi substitueret'. Höfner is at some pains to prove (pp. 6–14) that little credence can be placed in Marius as an historian, and that, as a matter of fact, 'überhaupt verdient Cassius Dio mehr Vertrauen, als Marius Maximus'. Any such comparison is rendered at once of most uncertain value in that (*a*) we do not know, except where Marius is mentioned by name, where a statement in the *S. H. A.* can be attributed

(2) These memoirs of which we know little except that they existed.[1] We are ignorant even of the language in which they were written.[2] Severus was possibly helped in their composition by Antipater of Hieropolis,[3] and seems to have had for his object the clearing of himself from the charges of cruelty which had been brought against him.[4] We may suppose them to have been written after February of the year 197, as, previous to his summary treatment of Albinus' followers, there was little or no cruelty to complain of. As we might expect, an autobiography written from so *ex parte* a standpoint commanded little credibility with contemporary historians. Dio, indeed, draws a sharp distinction between Severus' account and the

to him, and (*b*) we have a similar cause for hesitation when we remember that we do not, strictly speaking, possess Dio at all, but only Xiphilinus' epitome. By disregarding these two facts much can be done. For instance, Höfner attributes the remark of Dio (lxxiv. 3. 1) to the effect that Faustina prepared the bridal bed of Septimius and Julia (an obvious blunder, since Faustina died in 175—Dio Cass. lxxi. 29. 1 and below, p. 52, etc.—and Septimius' marriage with Julia was probably in 187) to Xiphilinus : Dio, he says, wrote ' Μαρκίαν, and Xiphilinus altered it to 'Ιουλίαν'. On the other hand, he introduces, as illustration of the untrustworthiness of M. M., the following two passages : Vit. Alex. Sev. v. 4 ' ut Marius Maximus dixit... Severus ... non magni satis loci duxit uxorem ' ; Vit. Getae, iii. 1 ' Severus uxorem duxerat . . . iam optimi in re p. loci '. Now there is not the least reason in this second case to suppose that Spartian was at this point quoting Marius Maximus. Hence the only person proved inaccurate by this comparison of passages is the Schluss-redaktor, who ought to have seen that Lampridius and Spartian agreed on this point. A similar objection may be raised to the attempt both on the part of Ceuleneer (*op. cit.*, p. 9) and of Höfner (p. 13) to prove the feebleness of Marius' geographical knowledge from the statement (Vit. Sev. v. 1) that Severus was acclaimed emperor at Carnuntum by the German legions.

[1] Dio Cass. lxxv. 7. 3; Herod. ii. 9. 4; Vit. Sev. iii. 2, xviii. 6; Vit. Pesc. N. iv. 7, v. 1; Vit. Clod. Alb. vii. 1, x. 1, xi. 5; Aurel. Vict. Caes. xx.

[2] Vossius and Müller say Greek. *Gerardi Ioannis Vossii de historicis Graecis libri tres*, ed. A. Westermann, p. 279; Müller, *Frag. hist. Graec.* iii. 657 (ed. Didot).

[3] Vit. Soph., p. 109 (ed. Kayser).

[4] Vit. Sev. xviii. 6 ' Vitam suam . . . composuit ad fidem, solum tamen vitium crudelitatis excusans '.

C

truth; [1] while even the credulous Spartian commences a
characterization of Niger with the cautious 'si Severo credi-
mus '.[2] Aurelius Victor alone seems to have taken the emperor
at his word.[3]

Other sources of the *Scriptores* are :

(3) Herodian ; [4]

(4) Aelius Maurus, who wrote a history of the reign of
Severus ; [5]

(5) Aelius Junius Cordus, whom Capitolinus accuses of the
pursuit of *frivola* in one place [6] and of undue attention
to the obscurer emperors in another ; [7] and probably

(6) Dio Cassius, though this historian is never expressly
mentioned by name.

The smoke of the battle waged over the *Scriptores Historiae
Augustae* is often so thick that it obscures the real issue. The
only point which interests us, or should interest us, as historians,
is this : how far can we depend upon the *S. H. A.* as the purveyors
of historical truth ? When the question is put in this bald
form it must be confessed that all the results of *Quellenuntersuchungen* appear of little value. Writing some hundred years
after the events they chronicle, the authors used such sources as
they could readily lay hands on : some of these sources were good,
some bad, nor—and this is our real difficulty—have we any means
of knowing when the *Scriptor* is employing credible and when
fallacious evidence. That such writers cite a sound and trustworthy eyewitness such as, say, Marius Maximus, is an indication
rather of a desire on their part to pose as credible historians than
of their having drawn their material from the source stated.
On the other hand, obstinate scepticism is unwarranted and

---

[1] lxxv. 7. 3 λέγω γὰρ οὐχ ὅσα ὁ Σεουῆρος ἔγραψεν, ἀλλ' ὅσα ἀληθῶς ἐγένετο.

[2] Vit. Pesc. Nig. v. 1.

[3] Aurel. Vict. Caes. xx 'idemque (Severus) abs se gesta ornatu et fide
paribus composuit'.

[4] Quoted by name five times: Vit. Clod. Alb. i. 2, xii. 4; Vit. Diad.
ii. 5 ; Vit. Alex. Sev. lii. 2, lvii. 3.

[5] Vit. Sev. xx. 1.   [6] Vit. Clod. Alb. v. 10.

[7] Vit. Marc. i. 3. Capitolinus is indeed the only *Scriptor* who cites
Cordus by name.

ridiculous, and to disbelieve a statement merely because it occurs in the *S. H. A.*, and for no further reason, would indeed be pouring away the baby with the bath water.

As a practical conclusion we should say that where a 'fact' given by the *Scriptores* was in disagreement with archaeological evidence we should without hesitation disbelieve the *Scriptores*, while the earlier literary evidence of Dio or Herodian would also weigh more with us than the unattested word of the *S. H. A.*

Further authorities need not detain us long. Such are the fourth-century chroniclers, Aurelius Victor and Eutropius, and the latter's fifth-century follower, Orosius. Of these Eutropius, *magister memoriae* to Valens (365–78), is a trustworthy, if insufficient, guide, whose sources are to be seen in Suetonius, and, after he ends, in the *Scriptores Historiae Augustae*. He further may have used some now lost chronicle of similar character to his own.[1] Victor was governor of Lower Pannonia in 361.[2] The *Caesares* take us as far as Julian: the Epitome, which seems to depend upon the *Caesares* as far as Domitian, there diverges, and is continued as far as Arcadius and Honorius.[3] We do not know his sources: one may have been, as Bury suggests, Marius Maximus.[4] Orosius was a Spaniard and a Christian.[5] He was a disciple of St. Augustine, and had spent some time in Africa.

[1] So Mommsen-Droysen, ed. mai. praef., p. 26 ; cf. Pauly-Wissowa, 8, p. 1523.

[2] Amm. Marc. xxi. 10. 6.

[3] Aurel. Victor ; crit. edit., F. Pichlmayer, 1892 ; new edit. 1911. Into the question of the authorship of the Epitome we need not here enter. It is of course clearly later, and not by the author of the *Caesares*. See Bury, *Gibbon*, ed. 1896, vol. i, p. 447.

[4] There is a confusion between Julianus the emperor and Julianus the Hadrianic jurist in Vict. Caes. xx and in Vit. Sev. xvii. 5 ; but I cannot see that this fact proves Victor to have been a source for the *S. H. A.*, rather than the *S. H. A.* for Victor (cf. Schulz, *Beiträge*, p. 56). He quotes 'Abgarus, Persarum rex' (Vit. Sev. xviii. 1) as another mistake caused by Victor.

[5] Beck, *De Orosii fontibus et auctoritate*, Marburg, 1832; Th. de Moerner, *De Orosii vita eiusque historiarum libris vii adversus paganos*, Berolini, 1844; H. Sauvage, *de Orosio*, Parisiis, 1875.

c 2

Of fifth-century writers we have Zosimus.[1] Little is known of the man himself except that he was a *comes* and *exadvocatus fisci*.[2] We do not even know his provenance, though his careful description of Constantinople[3] makes it pretty certain that some part at least of his life was spent in that city. His history bears traces of incompleteness, and was probably published posthumously.[4] His sources are probably Eunapius and Dexippus,[5] and he is, for us, chiefly important for his oriental history of Severus. Petrus Patricius,[6] John of Antioch,[7] and Zonaras,[8] deserve no more than a passing notice.

---

[1] Mendelssohn, praef., p. vi, etc., of his edition (Lipsiae, 1887), fixes the date of composition as between 425 (date of the death of Olympiodorus, whom Zosimus mentions (v. 27. 1)) and 502, in which year was published the breviary of Eustathius Epiphaniensis (Müller, *F. H. G.* iv, p. 138), who used Zosimus.

[2] Suidas says Ζώσιμος Γαζαῖος ἢ 'Ασκαλωνίτης, σοφιστής, κατὰ τοὺς χρόνους 'Αναστασίου τοῦ βασίλεως. ἔγραψε λέξιν ῥητορικήν . . . But Mendelssohn supposes this to have been another Zosimus (so too Clinton, *F. R.* ii, p. 323, who indeed considered the sophist of Gaza as distinct from the grammarian of Ascalon). The name was a common one, and information regarding Zosimi cannot with any degree of certainty be attributed to the historian.

[3] ii. 30–5.

[4] Mendels., *op. cit.*, p. 7. His anti-Christian attitude may have caused some trouble with the authorities.

[5] Cf. Phot. bibl. cod. 98, p. 84 bk. εἴποι δ' ἄν τις οὐ γράψαι αὐτὸν ἱστορίαν, ἀλλὰ μεταγράψαι τὴν Εὐναπίου, τῷ συντόμῳ μόνον διαφέρουσαν . . . Reitmeier's view of Zosimus as a blend of the *Chronica* and *Scythica* of Dexippus, the *historia* of Eunapius, and the *silva* of Olympiodorus, has been combated by Mendelssohn, who sees grave discrepancies between Dexippus and Zosimus, and who considers that far more than is just is attributed to these sources. He also disapproves of the view that Ammianus was the joint source of Eunapius and Victor's epitome (cf. Martin, *de fontibus Zosimi*, Berlin, 1866).

[6] Sixth century. Source: probably Eunapius (Mendelssohn, *op. cit.*, p. 37); Müller, *F. H. G.* iv. 181, etc.

[7] Seventh century. Sources: Dio and Eutropius up to Commodus, then Herodian (Müller, iv. 535; Köcher, *de Ioannis Antiocheni aetate, fontibus, auctoritate*, Bonn, 1871).

[8] Twelfth century. It seems probable that Zonaras, whose annals are based almost entirely on Dio Cassius, had before him not that writer in his original and entire form but Xiphilinus' abridgement. The similarity

There is another species of literary evidence which also demands a brief mention—rescripts. Such are to be found in great numbers in the Digests and Codices, and have, over and above their value as evidence for legal activity, the advantage of bearing often an exact date and provenance, and further of recording the title of the emperor's colleague or colleagues at the time of publication. Thus, for example, if we possess a rescript dated June 4 (201), coming from Emona and published in the name of the Augusti Septimius and Antoninus and the Caesar Geta, we presume not only that these three persons (or at any rate Septimius) were in Emona on that particular 4th of June, but also that by that date Caracalla had been raised to the dignity of an Augustus, Geta of a Caesar.

At first sight such evidence appears ideal, but two considerations have to be borne in mind. First, these rescripts are not always dated, nor is the provenance given in every case. Secondly, even when both date and provenance are appended, they are by no means invariably to be trusted. Instances of their obvious falsehood are not far to seek, nor indeed are they to be wondered at when we remember the late date of the Theodosian and Justinian codes. Two examples may here be cited. Both Spartian [1] and coins [2] agree that Caracalla did not receive imperatorial insignia until some time after the death of Albinus. This we know to have been early in 197. Yet we get rescripts of 196, and even 195, naming him indiscriminately Caesar and Imperator: one indeed [3] calls him the latter as early as 194. Again, we have no reason to suppose that Severus left Rome between the completion of the Parthian and the beginning of the British wars (202–8): yet we have a rescript of Severus and Caracalla dated July 22, 205, from Antioch.[4] The probable spuriousness of this document (or at least of its date and provenance) is rendered certain by the existence of another

---

of language between the wording of Xiphilinus and Zonaras is often very marked : cf. Dio Cass. lxxi. 8–10 with Zon. xii. 2 (Höfner, p. 19).

[1] Vit. Sev. xiv. 3.
[2] Eckhel (*Doctrina nummorum veterum*), vii. 200.
[3] Cod. Iust. ii. 24. 1.
[4] Cod. Iust. vi. 46. 2.

rescript, dated July 1 of the same year and hailing from Rome.[1]

For the *Kulturgeschichte* of the period Philostratus is by far the most valuable authority;[2] of less account are Plotinus and Porphyrius. Of Christian writers may be mentioned Tertullian, Cyprian, and Origen; the latter is the most worthy of notice as giving the arguments of his heathen opponent, Celsus.

It will easily be seen that our literary authorities, though comparatively numerous, are for the most part bad. More than this, the three most important and most circumstantial, Dio, Herodian, and Spartian (the author of Severus' life in the *Historia Augusta*), exercise almost equal claims upon our credence, so that where these three authors differ, adherence to the opinion of any one of them must be arbitrary. To lay down a rough line of action we may say that where two agree as against the third we shall follow the two, and where all three disagree, or where two disagree and the third is silent, we shall, if later evidence fail to establish the superior correctness of any one, prefer Herodian to Spartian, and Dio to both.

[1] Cod. Iust. ix. 12. 1.
[2] Edit. C. L. Kayser, 2 vols., Teubner, 1870.

CHAPTER II

EPIGRAPHIC AND NUMISMATIC SOURCES

THE conception of archaeology as an integral part of ancient history is to all intents and purposes a modern one. It is true that even so early as the period of the Diadochoi Craterus formed some kind of collection of inscriptions, of which Plutarch [1] made no small use, and that Polybius claims to have studied an inscription set up by Hannibal in South Italy: still, his very mention of the fact attests its exceptional character.[2]

It is not that archaeology is a new science or a new pursuit: it is nothing of the kind: only the relations obtaining between archaeology and history have altered considerably during the last half century. Whereas it was formerly conceded that the pursuit of the former science engendered a lukewarm interest in the latter, much as the study of philately is said to do for geography, it is now seen that a more practical use can be made of it, and that in two ways; we may, to put it roughly, count our inscriptions, and we may read them.[3]

By the latter method I mean that we may obtain evidence from, and base conclusions on, a single inscription; we may use it, in fact, exactly as we use coins—to check, supplement, or

---

[1] e. g. Cimon, vol. ii, p. 486, Teubner edit.

[2] Polyb. iii. 33, 56 ; we must suppose this inscription to have been a sort of Hannibalic *monumentum Ancyranum*.

[3] Some apology is needed for treating archaeology as synonymous with epigraphy. The value of pottery as a means of dating sites has long been recognized, and the works of Dragendorf, Déchelette, Knorr, and others need no more than a mention. Nevertheless, the obviously local character of such evidence, and the impossibility of obtaining therefrom a chronological unit of less than a half-century, make it clear that its employment to illustrate a reign of seventeen years would be tentative and infrequent.

correct literary evidence. To take a special instance: we have
reason to believe from numismatic evidence[1] that Septimius
showed some special indulgence to the city of Carthage, and
we interpret the design on the coin as referring to the construction or reconstruction of an aqueduct or some waterworks by
the emperor. This interpretation is rendered all the more
plausible by the existence in Carthage of a ruined aqueduct
bearing a fragmentary inscription of at least possible reference
to Severus.[2] Again, we are left in some doubt by our literary
authorities as to the exact date of Septimius' birthday, the
alternative days being April 11 and April 8. Dio Cassius and
Spartian alone mention them: the former gives April 11,[3]
the latter[4] the 11th in one MS., the 8th in another. We
should be inclined, this being the case, immediately to accept
Dio's statement as the true one, on the ground of his greater
reliability in general, were it not for the fact that in this very
passage he seems to make a mistake as to the year of Septimius'
birth, while Spartian is correct on this point.[5] But if Dio is
wrong in his year he may be equally wrong in his day, and our
inclinations veer round to Spartian, especially as ' vi idus ' is
the reading of the best MS.,[6] and we might rest content with
the earlier date were it not for some inscriptions which point
conclusively to April 11 as the day of the emperor's birth.[7]

---

[1] Eck. vii. 183, 204 : see below, p. 203.

[2] *CIL.* viii. 891. The actual letters are ' (Sept)IMIVS . . . AR '.

[3] Dio Cass. lxxvi. 17. 4.   [4] Vit. Sev. i. 3.

[5] Dio says Severus lived 65 years 9 months and 25 days : now we know
he died in 211, on the 4th of February. This puts his birth in 145.
But Spartian assures us : ' natus est Erucio Claro bis et Severo coss.,' and
the date of their consulship is known to have been 146 (cf. *CIL.* xiii.
6514, 6728). Has Dio made a mistake with his figures or Spartian with
his consuls ? Surely in this case Spartian is right, for a consular date is
obviously less liable to distortion and error than one given in figures.

[6] Peter adopts this reading in his edition.

[7] *CIL.* i, p. 379 ; cf. vi. 1063, xi. 1322, xiv. 168, 169. These last two are
two dedications from Olbia dated April 11, and clearly referring to some
important happening on that day. The first is part of a fourth-century
calendar of Philocalus giving the birthdays of some of the emperors.
Unfortunately, as we shall see, Caracalla's name does not appear there.

Dio's story of the bald-headed conspirator,[1] a story fantastic enough to make us doubt the word of any but a contemporary, receives undoubted confirmation from an altar set up at Sicca Veneria in Africa in the year 208 by a loyal subject, 'ob conservatam . . . salutem detectis insidiis hostium publicorum '.[2]

We realize from another inscription at Apulum [3] that the uncertainty which shrouds the praenomen of Geta was experienced even by the ancients themselves, the inscription running L. P. SEPT.   Ceuleneer [4] would have us believe that a like doubt hangs over the praenomen of Septimius' father.   He gives the name as Marcus, but adds that Lucius has been suggested.   As a matter of fact it is most probable that his name was Publius.   Such at least is the name found on the base of a statue in Cirta: [5] the notion of Marcus probably arose from the M. FIL. to be seen on many Severan inscriptions, among them on the Arch of Severus in the Forum.   This M., however, though it of course stands for Marci, refers not to the emperor's real father, but to Marcus Aurelius, his preposterously adoptive parent.   Incidentally, this African inscription bears out Spartian's words, 'patri . . . statuas conlocavit'.[6]

As to the quantitative use of inscriptions, the method, that is to say, of basing historical deductions not on particular instances but upon the frequent occurrence of certain types, it is to be noticed that knowledge so obtained is almost invariably knowledge of the state of things obtaining in the provinces, and is all the more valuable in that literary evidence for the same is wofully to seek.   No Roman historian from Tacitus to the scandalmongers of the third and fourth conturies ever wrote imperially.   Their outlook on things was strictly confined within the walls of Rome, sometimes indeed within those of the palace.

Nothing illustrates more decisively our ignorance of provincial affairs than the strange episode of Maternus.   Here was an

---

[1] Dio Cass. lxxvi. 8.
[2] *CIL.* viii. 1628; cf. iii. 427 and below, p. 205.
[3] *CIL.* iii. 1174.
[4] p. 13.   [5] *CIL.* viii. 19493.
[6] Vit. Sev. xiv. 4. Also *uxori*: such a statue was that which stood on the base whose inscription may be seen in *CIL.* viii. 19494.

insurrection which, if we may believe Herodian, spread not only over Gaul and Spain, but disturbed also the peace of Italy; and yet neither Dio nor the *Scriptores* nor Victor nor Eutropius deign so much as to mention it.[1] A passing notice of the Indian Mutiny by one English historian and silence on the part of the rest would be some sort of a parallel.

Being thus left in the lurch by our literary authorities, whose provincial interests are satisfied with the story of a governor's trial for maladministration, we are thrown back upon epigraphy, and bound to draw our conclusions from evidence of a not wholly satisfactory character. That this evidence is not wholly satisfactory is a fact which has to be faced, for it is more than possible to run epigraphy too hard. To base conclusions on the comparative frequency of certain inscriptions is to disregard a great many other elements, a consideration of which would cause us largely to modify those conclusions. To infer, for instance, that Septimius showed greater favour towards, or exhibited more care for, the province of Africa than for those of Britain or the Germanies, on the ground that African inscriptions of his reign are far more common than British or Germanic ones, is to leave out of consideration the difference in mere size between the countries in question, to say nothing of the fact that a southern climate does not produce that deleterious effect on stone that a northern one does, and that man, a still more disturbing element than weather, has in the one case used over and over again the building material he found ready to hand, and in the other withdrawn almost entirely from the scenes of his former habitation. Chance, too, is bound to play no unimportant part in this epigraphic legacy. To take a case in point: it so happens that there is in the north of Italy an altogether disproportionate number of Caracallan inscriptions, but he would be a bold man who would deduce a local popularity of that prince over the plains of Lombardy. To a less extent much the same may be said of Ceuleneer's conclusion [2] that Severus was widely popular among the soldiers,

---

[1] Herod. i. 10 πᾶσάν τε κατατρέχοντες τὴν Κελτῶν καὶ Ἰβήρων χώραν . . . ἐς τὴν Ἰταλίαν παρεδύοντο: cf. below, p. 45. Herodian's account is itself very meagre. [2] p. 171, etc.

since there remain so many inscriptions of a military character dating from his reign. An emperor who, like Severus, threw open a military career to all and sundry, and whose views on the subject of the 'provincialization' of the army were so determined as to give rise to a modern German theory of *Barbarisierung*,[1] is only too likely to have been the soldiers' idol. Besides this we must remember that a very large proportion of the provincials, or at least of the sojourners in the provinces, were military men.

As regards the dates of our inscriptions it is perhaps worth noting that by far the larger portion of datable stones belong to the period 198–201,[2] and we may possibly see within these dates the high-water mark of Septimius' popularity, 198 marking the foundation of his power after the destruction of his two rivals, the latter date stamping the temporal limit in the provincial breast of thankfulness for quiet restored.

Such then is our epigraphic evidence, and such the general[3] conclusions we draw from it: meagre indeed, but perhaps all that we are justified in drawing. Many are the gaps we must deplore; many the districts where we could hope for richer and more numerous finds. One of the most serious of the former is the breaking off of the acta of the Fratres Arvales in the year 193 and the complete disappearance of the same until the year 214.[4] The countries best illuminated by epigraphic evidence are undoubtedly Italy and Africa; Spain, the Danube provinces, and the far East are considerably behindhand, though, relatively with the inscriptions of other emperors, well up to the average. In Gaul,[5] Germany, the Greek provinces of Europe,

---

[1] A discussion of Severus' military innovations must be reserved for a later chapter, as must also the views of Domaszewski on this so-called barbarizing tendency.

[2] I noticed this particularly in the case of inscriptions from Dacia, the Moesias and Pannonias, Noricum, Raetia, etc. Of these four years 198 and 201 seem the commonest, but this must be a mere coincidence.

[3] A more detailed examination of the inscriptions is reserved for the chapter on the provinces.

[4] The last entry is Jan. 12, 193. *CIL.* vi. 2102.

[5] Ceuleneer (p. 176) well suggests that the absence of Severan inscriptions in Gaul is consequent upon that emperor's cruelty towards the supporters of Albinus.

as well as in Egypt and Britain, the paucity of inscriptions of this reign may justify a not unreasonable disappointment, and awaken in us a still more lively expectation of those revelations of archaeology by which alone so many historical problems can be solved.

From its very nature numismatic evidence can seldom be more than complementary. Not that it is untrustworthy : forgeries set aside,[1] no testimony can be surer than that engraved upon stone or moulded in bronze and silver, a text eternally free from interpolation, excision, re-editing, as true a witness now as when it left the mason's yard or an imperial mint. It is not the quality but the quantity of the evidence that is somewhat to seek. Where, however, numismatic and literary authority agree on a point, we may safely believe what the existence of the coin alone might leave ambiguous, or the literary authority unconvincing. We read for instance that Pertinax 'annonae consultissime providit',[2] a statement which we might overlook as a polite commonplace, applicable to any emperor whom his biographer was anxious to belaud (for emperors are black or white : they 'do evil in the sight of the Lord' or 'they do good'), and selected by Capitolinus for Pertinax at haphazard from a store of commendatory tags, were it not for the existence of a coin whereon, together with the design of a caduceus and ears of corn, is inscribed 'saeculo frugifero'.[3] We should have no reason for doubting (indeed we should hazard the conclusion a priori) that Judaea was a faithful adherent of Pescennius Niger, as we are told twice by Spartian;[4] still, we are not insensible to the fortification of our belief by a coin of Niger with the legend COL. HEL. CAP. COMMOD.[5] 'Severus ipse

---

[1] Eck. vii. 157 notes the forgery of many foreign minted coins of Pescennius Niger: especially those with Latin titles in Greek letters, e g. ΙΟΥϹΤΟϹ for ΔΙΚΑΙΟϹ.

[2] Vit. Pert. vii. 5.   [3] Eck. vii. 144.

[4] Vit. Sev. ix. 5 'Palaestinibus ius civitatis tulit, quod pro Nigro diu in armis fuerunt'; xiv. 6 'Palaestinis poenam remisit, quam ob causam Nigri meruerant'.

[5] Eck. vii. 157 ; Cohen, Médailles impériales, vol. iii, Nig. no. 82. (All references are made to the second edition.)

Caesarem suum . . . appellari voluit ',[1] says Capitolinus of Clodius Albinus, a policy of concession or fraud, to whose credibility a coin of Clodius as ' Caesar, cos. ii ' bears witness, while supplying us with the date of that event—194.[2] This last, indeed, is the chief value of coins: they help to date occurrences left dateless or misdated by a slovenly literary authority. A good instance is to be found in the remark of Spartian : [3] ' Inde (i. e. from Parthia) in Syriam redit victor . . . dein cum Antiochiam transisset, data virili toga filio maiori secum eum consulem designavit et statim in Syria consulatum inierunt.' The chronological difficulty here involved will be treated in detail later. Suffice it to say literary evidence supplies too many facts to be forced into a short period of time, and that one method of cutting the Gordian knot is to exclude the last of the series of events—the paying of the Decennalian vows—from the year 202 and to put it in 203.[4] Such a conclusion is directly shattered by an appeal to numismatic evidence, for the decennalian coins are all of the year 202.[5] As an instance of the uncertainty, not of fact, but of interpretation of fact, afforded by numismatic when unsupported and unexplained by literary evidence, may be quoted a coin of not uncommon type[6] with the figure of a seated goddess, a thunderbolt in her right hand, in her left a spear : she is seated in a lion-drawn car by the side of a rock out of which flows water. The legend reads— INDVLGENTIA AVGG. IN CARTH. What evidence are we to extract from this ? The figure can be no other but that of the goddess Astarte.[7] To what does the water refer ? Possibly

---

[1] Vit. Clod. Alb. x. 3.   [2] Eck. vii. 162.

[3] Vit. Sev. xvi. 6–9.

[4] So, e. g. Tillemont, *Hist. des emper.*, iii. 460, note 24.

[5] Eck. vii. 181, 182, 202, 203. ADVENT. AVGG., CONCORDIA AETERNAE, VOT. SUSC. DEC., etc., etc., are such reverses. The tribunicial year is 202 (X for Septimius, V for Caracalla).

[6] Eck. vii. 183, 204. Specimens have been found in England. For a find of twenty-one of these coins cf. *Num. Chron.*, 3rd series, xviii (1898), p. 151.

[7] *Iuno caelestis* of the Carthaginians : originally a moon and star goddess. Her worship was brought to Rome by Scipio after the second Punic war (Serv. *ad* Virg. *Aen.* xii. 841). Inscriptions from Rome, Britain,

merely to the goddess in her character of 'pluviarum pollicita-trix':[1] possibly to the rebuilding of an aqueduct by Severus.[2] The only references we possess throwing light upon an *indulgentia* are the vague notice in Spartian,[3] 'Tripolim . . . securissimam reddidit'; and the passage in Ulpian,[4] 'In Africa Carthago, Vtica, Leptis magna a divis Severo et Antonino iuris Italici factae sunt'.

The coins of Pertinax seem as a class to show forth clearly the relief felt by the world at large at its newly-won freedom from the tyrant Commodus. The corn-head coin has already been instanced, nor is it a solitary example of a people's expression of thankfulness for the inauguration of a new régime. Many of Pertinax' coins bear the figure and inscription 'Liberalitas';[5] many, again, read OPI DIVIN(AE),[6] while others testify to the delight felt at the return to a constitutional and rational form of government.[7] Foreign minted coins of the reign are rare, a first brass of Prusa, a second of Tomi, and a few Alexandrine specimens being alone known. A coin of Mitylene refers to his wife Titiana.[8]

As might be expected the coins of Pescennius Niger are all

and Dacia (*CIL.* vi. 77–80, vii. 759, iii. 993) attest her popularity and the width of her influence. Proconsuls even disdained not to consult her oracles (Tert. *Apol.* 23).

[1] Tert. *Apol.* 23.

[2] As we have seen (above, p. 24) this view is supported by epigraphic evidence.

[3] Vit. Sev. xviii. 3.   [4] *Dig.* l. 15. 8.

[5] Eck. vii. 142: cf. Vit. Pert. vii. 5 'donativa et congiaria, quae Commodus promiserat, solvit'.

[6] Eck. vii. 143.

[7] Eck. vii. 142 MENTI LAVDANDAE: a clear reference by anthesis to the amentia of Commodus. The quasi-deification of Mens is not uncommon: cf. Livy xxii. 10. 11; Cic. *de legg.* ii. 8; Ovid, *Fast.* vi. 241, etc.

[8] Eck. vii. 147. An inscribed gem is known bearing the heads of Pertinax and his wife and the legends ΔIK (= Justus) and TIT (Titiana). No Roman-minted coins bear the name of Titiana, a fact which helps to bear out Capitolinus' statement, 'Pertinax nec uxoris Augustae appellationem recepit' (Vit. Pert. vi. 9). The further statement (v. 4), 'Eadem die . . . et Flavia Titiana uxor eius Augusta est appellata', is not really contradictory.

minted in the East—almost without exception at Antioch. The workmanship is rough, and many irregularities occur in the lettering.[1] The brass has naturally no S. C. mark. It is curious to note the parallelism between the legends on the coins of Pescennius and the contemporary minted ones of Severus, as if, as Eckhel suggests, 'uterque, ut arma armis, sic et numos numis opponebat'.[2] This same tendency is noticeable in the coins of Clodius Albinus, who echoes Septimius' 'saeculo fecundo'.[3] Such coins were of course minted in Gaul,[4] and we can see clearly from them the exact date of the insurrection, inasmuch as the coins up to 195 are inscribed Caesar, a privilege granted by Septimius,[5] those of 196 Augustus.[6]

The coins of Septimius himself form not unnaturally a more complete series, but it cannot be pretended that they much enlarge our knowledge of the events of his reign. His first period of tribunician power lasted from April (or perhaps May) 193 till December 9 of that year. On December 10 he became 'trib. pot. ii', and so on regularly till his death. Of his three consulships only those of 194 and 202 are recorded on coins.[7] Imperial titles are found up to the number of eleven (or fifteen),

[1] e. g. COS. I. and IMP. I. in place of the more usual COS. and IMP. (Coh. iv, p. 8). Inaccuracies in Antioch-minted coins are common enough: e. g. BONI SPES on a coin of Severus (Coh. iv, Sept., no. 62); IMI for IMP on another (p. 13).

[2] Eck. vii. 155. Such legends are 'invicto imp. tropae.', 'boni eventus', 'bonae spei', 'Cereri frugiferae', 'felicit. tempor.', etc. Cf. *Num. Chron.*, 3rd series, xvi (1896), p. 193, for a Severan coin of 193 with the legend VICTOR. IVST. AVG.: here Severus even borrows his rival's name, Justus.

[3] Eck. vii. 194.

[4] Eck. vii. 163: GEN(ium) LVG(duni) COS. II. There is really no evidence in support of the theory that Albinus coined money in London (Haverfield, 'Roman London', *J. R. S.*, vol. i, part 2, p. 152, note 3).

[5] Cap. Alb. x. 3, and above, p. 29.

[6] Cohen, iii, Alb., no. 46; Eck., p. 164: IMP. CAES. CL. SEPT. ALBIN. AVG.—S.P.Q.R. P.P. OB. C. S. Eckhel argues from this coin the existence of a Gallic senate on the analogy of that of Pompey in Greece or Scipio in Africa. Höfner (p. 203) points out that it was not the business of a senate, Gallic or Roman, to coin silver.

[7] Dio (lxxii. 12. 4) tells us that Septimius was one of the twenty-five consuls of the year 190 appointed by Cleander. Spartian (Vit. Sev. iv. 4) confirms this statement; see below, p. 47.

and an examination of them helps us to follow his career of victory and to check its chronology. The first acclamation by the Pannonian troops was in the spring of 193; the second, third, and fourth all fall within the year 194, and can be attributed with certainty to the three victories of Septimius and his generals over Niger.[1] The next three acclamations—v, vi, vii—occur in 195, and find their cause in the defeats inflicted by Rome on the Osrhoeni and Adiabeni. IMP. VIII occurs first in the year 196 and must refer to the capture of Byzantium.[2] The final defeat of Albinus at Lugdunum in 197 is commemorated by the ninth imperial greeting, while the tenth, which occurs in the same year, may be attributed to the retirement of the Parthians from Mesopotamia or the capture of Seleucia and Babylon.[3] The title Parthicus Maximus is found for the first time on the coins of 198 in conjunction with the eleventh imperial acclamation, and we have little or no hesitation in seeing in this combination a reference to the fall of Ctesiphon, the crowning triumph of the Parthian war.[4] Above eleven the imperial greetings, at least on coins, do not go.[5]

---

[1] Wirth, in his *Quaestiones Severianae*, pp. 24–7, has an article *De acclamationibus imperatoris Severi*. His conclusions agree almost entirely with mine (arrived at independently before his dissertation came into my hands). With regard to IMPP. II, III, and IV, he attributes II to the Cyzicus victory, III to that at Nicaea, and IV to Issus. It is true, however, that both a coin (Cohen, Sev., no. 364) and an inscription (*CIL*. vi. 1026) couple IMP. IV with the title Parth. Arab. Parth. Adiab., which was not won by the emperor until the following year (195). We can only suppose these to be errors.

[2] We get, however, several IMP. VIII inscriptions of 195, e. g. *CIL*. viii. 1428, 8835; *CIG*. 3837, 3838, possibly referring to the victory over the Moors mentioned by Spart. (Sev. xviii. 3: cf. Aur. Vict. Caes. xx. 19; Eph. ep. v. 760).

[3] So Höfner, p. 243.

[4] This supposition is strengthened by an appeal to an analogy in Trajan's coinage. This emperor, on his capture of Ctesiphon, αὐτοκράτωρ ἐπωνομάσθη καὶ τὴν ἐπίκλησιν τοῦ Παρθικοῦ ἐβεβαιώσατο (Dio Cass. lxviii. 28. 2).

[5] A considerable amount of confusion shrouds IMP. XII to IMP. XV (existing in inscriptions), which numismatic evidence would do much to dissipate. As far as we know there was no war between 198 and 208, so we might suppose the last four acclamations to have occurred in the

The adoption by Septimius of the name of Pertinax is mentioned in literary and borne out by numismatic and epigraphic evidence, the latter giving us further the exact period during which this title was in use, viz. 193–9.[1] In this latter year the title Pertinax is ousted by that of Parthicus Maximus.[2] Indeed, the two designations overlap, as Parthicus

British war. Inscriptions do not help us much : as a rule, indeed, those after 198 continue to bear the title IMP. XI, even as late as 208 (*CIL*. iii, p. 890). Still IMP. XII is found on several milestones, e. g. *CIL*. viii. 9035 (205), x. 5909 (207), ix. 6011 (210), xi. 5631 (210), vi. 1405 (208), viii. 10337, 10338, 10353, 10358 (of 198), iii. 5735 (200), 4364 (208). Neither IMP. XIII nor IMP. XIIII ever occur, and IMP. XV only occurs twice (*Mél. d'arch.* xiii (1893) 516 ; *CIL*. vi. 32533), dates 208 and 209. Mistakes are by no means rare in inscriptions, and we might not unreasonably call IMP. XII and IMP. XV typographic errors were it not for the fact that the former seems so widespread while the latter hails from Rome itself, and where, if not there, should they know the emperor's title in all accuracy ?

[1] Vit. Sev. vii. 9 'Se quoque Pertinacem vocari iussit : quamvis postea id nomen aboleri voluerit quasi omen'. Herod. ii. 10. 1 Σευῆρόν τε Περτίνακα ἑαυτὸν ὀνομάσας. Vit. Pert. xv. 2 'Severus amore boni principis ... Pertinacis nomen accepit'. Incidentally, some doubt has been felt as to the motive of Septimius in this matter. The question is : did Septimius adopt the name of his own free will or because he was forced to do so ? Spartian (Vit. Sev. vii. 9) and Herodian mention no motive, but Capitolinus, followed by Eusebius, Eutropius, and Orosius, says 'willingly'. This is further borne out by another passage in Spartian (Vit. Sev. v. 4) 'excipiebatur enim (Severus) ab omnibus quasi ultor Pertinacis'. Indeed, the only evidence we have against the willingness of Septimius are the two passages Vit. Sev. xvii. 6 and Aur. Vict. Caes. xx. In both these places the choice of a name is attributed to a 'parsimoniam similem'—a phrase of Victor's, who is clearly copying the older authority. (Spartian had 'non tam ex sua voluntate quam ex morum parsimonia '.) We have two alternatives : either to suppose that Spartian is talking nonsense (incidentally on Schulz' theory the 'sachlich-historische' part ends with chap. xvi), and that Victor copied it uncritically ; or else to suppose a corruption in Spartian which must have crept in before Victor used the text. So indeed Peter, who boldly reads 'voluntate *atque* morum parsimonia '.

[2] There is a coin of 207 which still retains Pertinax ; Eck. vii. 187. However, as it has four other peculiarities, (1) no P. P. or PIVS, (2) titles in full, (3) AVG. for AVGG., and (4) bears the legend 'advent. Aug. Gall.', though the expedition did not start till 208, Eckhel concludes

Maximus is, as has been said, found on coins of 198.[1] The
title Parthicus alone affords yet another crux. Spartian says
distinctly that the emperor refused it: 'excusavit et Parthicum
nomen, ne Parthos lacesseret.'[2] Setting aside the question
whether the Parthians would be any better pleased with Parthicus
Maximus, we are faced with the fact that Parthicus is by no
means unknown on coins and inscriptions. Notable among the
last is the inscription on the Arch of Severus in the Forum,
which reads PARTICO ARABICO PARTICO ADIABENICO.
A coin[3] of 195 bears a similar legend, while PAR. AR. AD.
occurs in another of 198.[4] As another instance may be cited
the inscription from Saepinium of 195, which gives Severus the
Parthian title.[5] The title Parthicus Maximus itself lapses at
the beginning of the third century : Eckhel indeed says it is
only found on coins of 199 and 200, though he himself instances
a coin of 201 with this lettering. Cohen[6] mentions one of the
year 202. Other titles need not detain us long: *pontifex
maximus* is of course regular from 193 onwards, *pater patriae*
from 194. *Pius* occurs first in 195 on coins celebrating
Septimius' self-adoption as the son of Marcus and the brother
of Commodus,[7] and after 201 is usually found in place of
Parthicus Maximus.[8] Arabicus and Adiabenicus are first found

that it is a forgery. As to the fourth point we may perhaps ask the
meaning of that 'Victoria' mentioned on at least two inscriptions of
207: *CIL*. iii. 4364, 11081.

[1] And even on one of 196: Cohen, Sept. Sev., no. 374, p. 41. Surely
a forgery?

[2] Vit. Sev. ix. 11. The use of *excusavit* in the sense of 'refusing' is
peculiar, but any other meaning is impossible. (Cf. Tac. *Ann.* i. 44
'reditum Agrippinae excusavit ob imminentem partum'.)

[3] Eck. vii. 172.   [4] Eck. vii. 177.

[5] *CIL*. ix. 2444. See Schiller, *Kaisergesch.*, i. 712, 5; 720, 2.

[6] iv, p. 13; Sept. Sev., no. 100.

[7] Dio Cass. lxxv. 7. 4 τοῦ τε Μάρκου υἱὸν καὶ τοῦ Κομμόδου ἀδελφὸν
ἑαυτὸν ἔλεγε. Vit. Sev. x. 6 'Severus ipse in Marci familiam transire
voluerit'.

[8] Eck. vii. 179. The coins of 201 are in general of a 'domestic'
character: heads of Caracalla (given the *toga virilis* that year) and of
Geta are frequent, as well as such legends as 'perpetua concordia'.
They show clearly the attempts of the *pacator orbis* to put his house in
order.

in 195: Britannicus and Britannicus Maximus not until 210.[1]

From a strictly historical point of view, however, the coinage of Severus offers few puzzles and little information. For the first four years of his reign the metal was poor and the minting careless; coins of Julia Domna are constantly found cracked, and such letterings as PERCT. and PRTE.[2] for PERT., FORT. RDEVC., FORT. REDVG., FORTA. REDVC. for FORT. REDVC. (i. e. *fortunae reduci*)[3] are no rarities. That such were struck in the East (mostly at Antioch) is more than a probable supposition, and is rendered the more likely by the fact that coins bearing the stamp of the eighth imperial greeting are some of them of rough, others of good, workmanship: the former were those minted at Antioch at the end of the year 196, the latter at Rome at the beginning of the year following. Many of the early coins, those especially of 193, bear the names of legions: some fifteen kinds of these are known, and it is a probable inference that the legions so mentioned had declared their adhesion to the new emperor.[4]

We are told by Spartian that one of Septimius' first cares in his war against Niger was to safeguard Africa, lest the eastern general should put Vespasian's plan into execution and starve Rome into surrender by cutting off her main corn supply.

---

[1] For Brit. cf. Eck. vii. 188.
[2] Eck. vii. 167.   [3] Cohen, iv, p. 22.
[4] Probable, but not certain, as revolted generals were not above minting coins declaring the loyalty of legions which had at the best remained neutral. There is no reason, for instance, to suppose that Carausius had the support of leg. XXX Ulpia victrix, though coins of his with the name of this legion have been found. Did the British pretender impose also on Mr. Rudyard Kipling to the extent of making him believe that this legion was quartered in Britain? (see *Puck of Pook's Hill*, p. 157, edit. 1906, Macmillan). The legions mentioned on the coins are:

I adi.	III Ital.	XI Claud.
I Ital.	IV Flav.	XIII gem.
I Min.	V Mac.	XIV gem.
II adi.	VII Claud.	XXII prim.
II Ital.	VIII Aug.	XXX Ulp. vict.

Eck. vii. 168; Cohen, iv, p. 31.

A coin of 194, with the lettering AFRICA. S. C., bears out this statement.[1] Another of the year 197, bearing the legend MVNIFICENTIA AVG. and the figure of a mailed elephant, illustrates the remark of Herodian and others that games were given by the emperor prior to his start for the East in the course of that year.[2]

Herodian again, followed by Zosimus, does not pass unnoticed the secular games of 204, and were confirmation of such statements necessary it could be found in certain coins minted at the time.[3] We shall in a later chapter deal with the attitude of the emperor towards religion, but it may here be mentioned that Dio's statement with regard to Septimius' special care for Hercules and Bacchus is borne out by the existence of coins bearing these deities' heads, while Juppiter Ammon and Minerva on others indicate further imperial favourites.[4]

The coins of Caracalla, Geta, Julia Domna, and Plautilla offer scarcely any points of interest. The number of 'colonial' coins of Julia—Cohen (vol. iv, p. 127, etc.) mentions nineteen places of minting—is just what we should have expected, thirteen of the nineteen cities being Asiatic. Little light is thrown by coins on the praenomen of Geta, both L(ucius) and P(ublius) being found: on the whole, however, P. tends to supersede L. on the later coins. There is known a coin of Caracalla of the year 209 which, if not throwing light on, at least attests the credibility of, a statement in Herodian which we have had occasion to mention before.[5] Septimius, says Herodian, during his British campaign, built bridges over marshes. We might be inclined to accept this as a rhetorical commonplace, like so

[1] Vit. Sev. viii. 7 'Ad Africam legiones misit ne . . . occuparet ac p. r. penuria rei frumentariae perurgeret'. Eck. vii. 171.

[2] Herod. iii. 8. 9; Vit. Sev. xiv. 11 ; Eck. vii. 176. Other coins of this year read PROFECTIO AVG.

[3] Herod. iii. 8. 10; Zos. ii. 4, 3 ; Eck. vii. 185. To this same year belong the coins celebrating the erection of the arch in the Forum and inscribed ARCVS. AVGG. S.C.

[4] Eck. vii. 171; Cohen, iv. 190. The Juppiter Ammon coin may probably be ascribed to the year 201, when, as we know, Septimius visited Egypt and its shrines.

[5] Herod. iii. 14. 5.

many of Herodian's remarks, were it not for the existence of
this coin which bears on its reverse the legend TRAIECTVS
PONTIF., and the design of the emperor and his troops crossing
a bridge of boats.[1]   Where this bridge was is a question
impossible to answer: the combination of literary and numismatic evidence is enough to attest the fact; the locality must
still remain a problem.[2]

[1] Eck. vii. 209.

[2] Prof. Oman, *England before the Norman Conquest*, p. 132, suggests
the Solway Firth and the Forth estuary below Stirling, only to reject
both : the former on the ground that there already existed a solid road
leading north to Birrens, the latter because the Romans could not have
held land so far north during so early a period of the war. It is possible,
though, as Prof. Oman further suggests, that the Maeatae and Caledonians
withdrew north of the Forth when they sued for peace (Herod. iii. 14. 1).
Cf. below, p. 135.

CHAPTER III

EARLY LIFE

FROM the year of his birth to that of his accession Septimius may be said to have lived the ordinary life of the provincial Roman of the upper classes. His ancestors had belonged to the equestrian order, but two of his great-uncles (on his father's side) had been consulars.[1] A maternal uncle,[2] one Fulvius Pius, seems to have incurred the censure of Pertinax during the latter's governorship of Africa.[3] In this same province, on the 11th of April, 146,[4] was born, of parents whose names Spartian gives as Geta[5] and Fulvia Pia, the future Emperor Lucius Septimius Severus. His birthplace was Leptis Magna.[6] Of his boyhood we know little save for such accretions of fable as tend to gather round the youth of the great. It seems curious to think of Septimius studying Latin; still more so to hear that, in spite of the proficiency in its literature for which Spartian vouches, he was cursed all his life long with an African accent.[7] His prowess indeed as a scholar is more than doubtful, and Dio Cassius expressly tells us that in this department his aspirations

[1] Vit. Sev. i. 2. One of them, P. Septimius Aper, had been *consul suffectus* to M. Sedatus Severianus, Liebenam, p. 79.

[2] The reversal of 'maternus' and 'paternus' in the text of the *Scriptores* (Vit. Sev. i. 2) is certainly correct, though Peter retains the MS. reading. Casaubon emended it as early as 1671 (ed. Lugd. Batav., p. 589).

[3] Dio Cass. lxxiii. 17. 3, frag. ἐπὶ πονηρίᾳ καὶ ἀπληστίᾳ ἀσελγείᾳ τε ὑπὸ τοῦ Περτίνακτος, ὅτε τῆς Ἀφρικῆς ἦρχε, κατεδεδίκαστο.

[4] See above, p. 24.

[5] His father's full name was P. Septimius Geta (*CIL*. viii. 19493), not M., as Ceuleneer, p. 13. Cf. above, p. 25.

[6] Eutrop. viii. 18.

[7] Vit. Sev. i. 4 'Latinis Graecisque litteris, . . . quibus eruditissimus fuit'. Ibid. xix. 9 'canorus voce, sed Afrum quiddam usque ad senectutem sonans'. So too Aurel. Vict. Caes. xx.

were much in advance of his achievements.[1] A far more congenial
subject to the young statesman must have been the Law. In
pursuit of this study he left the 'nutricula causidicorum'[2] and
came to Rome, abandoning the legal games of his childhood for
the serious business of legal apprenticeship.[3] The exact year of
this journey we do not know, but we may safely take it to have
been between 164 and 170. Once in Rome he set himself to
study under the famous jurist Q. Cervidius Scaevola, and seems
to have had as a fellow pupil the still more.famous Papinian.[4]

The amusements with which he enlivened this period of study
were not of so innocent a character as those which had graced
his childhood, and, if we may believe his biographer, his sedulous
pursuit of 'the broad way and the green' led the young jurist
into serious trouble. The story, however, of his accusation for
adultery and of his acquittal therefrom by the 'proconsul Didius
Iulianus' contains such inaccuracies as to discredit the whole
account; for when Julianus was proconsul of Africa Septimius
was in Pannonia, while, supposing the scene to be in Rome, how
could a proconsul be there at all?[5] Whatever his excesses were
they do not seem to have interfered with his rapid advancement.
Through the influence of his uncle, a man of high standing, he
received from the Emperor Marcus Aurelius the *latus clavus*,[6]
having previously held the equestrian post of *advocatus fisci*.[7]

[1] lxxvi. 16. 1 παιδείας ... ἐπεθύμει μᾶλλον ἢ ἐπετύγχανε.

[2] 'Nutricula causidicorum Africa,' Juv. vii. 148.

[3] It is, typically, from the gossiper Spartian (i. 4) that we get the tale
of Septimius' game of 'iudices'. Characteristically enough the future
emperor arrogated the chief part to himself and left his companions to
carry the fasces and axes.

[4] Vit. Car. viii. 3; for Scaevola cf. Huschke, *Jurispr. antijust.*, p. 342.

[5] Vit. Sev. ii. 1-3. 'Iuventam plenam furorum' is at least credible.

[6] Vit. Sev. i. 5.

[7] Höfner, p. 57, disputes this point with what seems to me very little
justification. He has against him the authority of Spartian (Vit. Get. ii. 4;
Vit. Car. viii. 3), of Eutropius (viii. 18), of Aurelius Victor (Caes. xx).
His only argument seems to be that these statements did not come from
Marius Maximus and that they are therefore useless; both of which suppositions seem to be arbitrary. True, the appointment of Severus to this
office by Antoninus Pius (Vit. Get. ii. 4) is chronologically absurd, while
the passage in the Vit. Car. is held by Mommsen (*Hermes*, xxv, p. 288;

Our knowledge of his subsequent career is spoilt by the fact
that the passage in Spartian dealing with the subject is hope-
lessly corrupt. Peter adopts Hirschfeld's (*Hermes*, iii.
230) emendation and reads 'quaesturam diligenter egit omisso tri-
bunatu militari. Post quaesturam sorte Baeticam accepit.'
This makes good enough sense, but completely ignores the
statement of Eutropius (viii. 18) to the effect that Septimius
was a military tribune. It is, of course, not impossible that
Eutropius is confusing the posts of military and plebeian tribune,
but in the present state of our knowledge on the point any very
definite statement is to be deprecated. Another difficulty is
to be found in the question, what was the exact position of
Septimius in Baetica? Apparently that of quaestor, as we
read that he was transferred from Baetica to Sardinia, where he
certainly held that post. We must suppose, then, that Septimius
held an urban quaestorship, possibly in the year 171, and went
out to Baetica in the year following as a proquaestor.[1] During

also Savigny, *Zeitschr.* xi. 1890, p. 30) to be an interpolation of the
thirteenth century. To the first of these considerations we should
answer that an anachronistic statement may often be correct as to fact;
to the second, that the objection only holds good for the Palatine MS.
(Peter's P.), and that the passage may have been rightly added from an
older MS. Ceuleneer (p. 15) and Hirschfeld (*Die kaiserlichen Verwaltungsbeamten*, 1905 edit., p. 51, note 2) both believe that Şeptimius held this
post. It is, however, worthy of note that the scepticism of Höfner can
claim the support of Domaszewski, who (*Rangordnung des röm. Heeres*,
p. 169) thinks it absurd for a senatorial like Septimius to have held
such an office. So too Dessau (*Prosopogr.* iii, p. 213, no. 346).

[1] An uncommon arrangement, but by no means unknown; e. g.
P. Sestius, quaestor in 63 B. C., who accompanied Antonius next year
to Macedonia as proquaestor. That Spartian speaks of the office as
a quaestorship, not a proquaestorship, is paralleled by the fact that
Cicero (*pro Sest.* v. 13) refers to Sestius' 'quaestura Macedoniae', though
addressing him in a letter (*ad Famil.* v. 6) as P. Sestio, L. f. proq. An
imperial instance of the same occurrence is to be seen in the case of
L. Aquillius Florus, who was first 'quaestor imp. Caesaris Augusti', and
subsequently 'proquaestore prov. Cypri' (*CIL.* iii. 551). This implies
that he was working under a propraetor; but it is quite possible that he
was acting in place of the governor in Baetica or Sardinia, much as the
quaestor Sulla acted for Marius when that general was shelved during
the Jugurthine war (Sall. *Jug.* 103). Sulla, it is true, was a quaestor,

his period of office in Spain Septimius' father died, and Septimius himself journeyed to Africa to set his house in order. In his absence the Moors overran Spain,[1] and Baetica became an imperial province, the emperor taking it in exchange for Sardinia, to which province, accordingly, Septimius betook himself on his return from Africa.[2] He seems to have acquitted himself with peculiar distinction during this period of his official career, and was given as a reward the post of legatus on the staff of the African proconsul, though of his precise duties in the province we are in ignorance, as we are of the exact year in which he fulfilled them. We may suppose him to have governed one of the three main 'dioceses'.[3] We are not told with what success the legate performed his functions, but from his treatment of an old friend whose respect for office was not all that Septimius

not a proquaestor, but the existence of a proquaestor propraetore is not unknown (Cic. *ad Famil.* xii. 15).

[1] Vit. Marc. Aurel. xxi. 1.

[2] Such, at least, is the view of Zumpt (*Stud. rom.*, p. 144). It is accepted by Marquardt (*L'Organisation de l'emp. rom.*, tome ii, p. 61, note, French translation).

[3] Vit. Sev. ii. 5. I can find no justification for Ceuleneer's statement (p. 18) that there were five 'dioceses' in the province of Africa. Dio (liii. 14. 7) says that the proconsul had three legates, and we have inscriptional evidence for the existence of: (1) dioc. Carthaginiensis (e.g. *CIL.* ii. 1262, 4510, xiv. 3599); (2) dioc. Hipponiensis (e.g. *CIL.* ix. 1592, x. 5178—both under Septimius); (3) a vague 'legatus proconsulis' (*CIL.* viii. 7059-7061). The likelihood is that the latter governed Tripolitana, though his sphere of command may have been Hadrumetina. After Diocletian's time there certainly were four dioceses. I suspect that Ceuleneer has included in his 'five' some of the 'tractus' or 'regiones' which were *administered financially* by imperial procurators, but not, of course, *governed* by them (*CIL.* viii. 9 'proc. reg. Thevestinae'; *CIL.* vi. 790: cf. xiv. 176).

On the question of the date it is rash to dogmatize. Our only fixed point is Septimius' praetorship in 178. We do not even know whether the Sardinian quaestorship fell in the same year as the Baetican— Septimius leaving Spain for Africa, say, in March, and Africa for Sardinia in, perhaps, July—or in the next. On the whole the latter is the more probable, and we may suppose, therefore, Baetica, 172, broken into by a visit to Africa; Sardinia, 173; legatus proconsulis Africae, 174.

desired, we should infer that if he erred at all it was not on the side of slackness.[1] One of Spartian's characteristic horoscope stories makes its appearance at this point; otherwise we know nothing of his doings.

On the 10th of December, 174 or 175,[2] Septimius entered upon the office of plebeian tribune. The tribunate now was but a *nominis umbra*;[3] its former powers were vested in the emperor by virtue of his *tribunicia potestas*, and it is typical of its lack of any real importance that a man of twenty-five years of age could hold it, while neither it nor yet the aedileship formed any longer a necessary step between quaestorship and praetorship. But whatever were the duties of the office, they were fulfilled by the future emperor with characteristic vigour and severity.[4]

It was in the course of this year that he married his first wife Marcia, a lady of whom we know very little. Septimius himself, indeed, seems to have been reticent upon the subject in his memoirs, though he had the grace to erect various statues to her after his assumption of the purple.[5]

In 178, that is to say in his thirty-third year, Septimius became a praetor, elected, seemingly, to this office rather than nominated for it by Marcus.[6]

His sphere of duties, however, was not Rome but the province

[1] The story is to be found in Vit. Sev. ii. 6. The friend, a humble plebeian, had embraced his friend Septimius 'praecedentibus fascibus', for which act of affection he was scourged, while a notice was sent round forbidding any possible recurrence of such an incident.

[2] Höfner (p. 55) says the former, Ceuleneer (p. 18) the latter: if we put his African legateship in 174 we may fix on 175 as the date.

[3] Pliny, indeed, suggests at least the possibility that even in his day it was an 'inanem umbram et sine honore nomen' (*Ep.* i. 23. 1).

[4] Vit. Sev. iii. 1.

[5] Vit. Sev. iii. 2, xiv. 4. The record of one such statue is preserved in *CIL.* viii. 19494. It was erected, however, not by the emperor, but by the Colonia of Cirta, as was another statue (19493) to Septimius' father.

[6] Vit. Sev. iii. 3. I entirely fail to follow Ceuleneer's remarks (p. 20) on Spartian's phrase 'non in candida sed in competitorum grege'. Spartian, he says, 'écrivant d'après les usages de son temps, aura employé le mot *in candida* au lieu de celui de *candidatus*': 'candidatus Caesaris' is what Spartian should have written according to him. Both terms seem to me to mean the same. True, originally *in candida* or *in toga candida* denoted an applicant for office.

of Spain, and he was obliged to give the games expected of
a newly appointed praetor during his absence.[1] In Spain his
position was very similar to that held by him previously in
Africa. He was certainly not the *legatus propraetore* of the
province, for in this case, as Höfner and Ceuleneer point out, his
subsequent appointment to the command of the fourth legion
would have been a step backwards in the *cursus honorum*. Spain,
like Africa, was divided for administrative purposes into three
districts, and over one of them, most probably the dioecesis
Tarraconensis, Septimius was set. It was an important post, but
its holder was, of course, answerable to, and under the orders of,
the *legatus propraetore Hispaniae Tarraconensis*.[2]

The next year, 179, saw Marcus Aurelius succeeded by his
worthless son, and Septimius given command of the Syrian
legion, IV Scythica ;[3] but his sojourn in the far East does not

---

[1] Vit. Sev. iii. 5 'Ludos absens edidit'. Certainly as praetor, not as
aedile. The aedileship was at this time an alternative to the tribunate,
and was never held by Septimius.

[2] The legate of Hispania Tarraconensis had under him three *legati*,
often referred to in inscriptions of the second century as *legati iuridici*
(e. g. *CIL*. viii. 2747), or, simply, *legati*. One of these was stationed in
Bracara in the diocesis of Asturia and Gallaecia (afterwards—circ. 216—
Caracalla's 'Hispania nova citerior'): cf. *CIL*. ii. 2408, 2415, vi. 1486,
etc. He seems to have been distinct from the leg. leg. VII gem. stationed
at Leon (*CIL*. ii. 2634).

The second diocesis was that of Tarraconensis. Its governor was called
legatus iuridicus (*CIL*. ii. 4113, 3738, xii. 3167).

The third diocesis was probably that of Cantabria. Strabo (who in
iii. 4. 20, p. 166, gives a full account of the organization of Spain)
explains it as παρόρειον μέχρι Πυρήνης, but as yet no inscriptionary
evidence of its legate is forthcoming.

The Tarraconese diocese seems to me the most likely sphere of
Septimius' activities from the mention in Spartian of the 'templum
Tarraconense' (Vit. Sev. iii. 4).

[3] Vit. Sev. iii. 6. We know that this legion was stationed in Syria
(Dio Cass. liii. 23. 3; Borghesi, *Œuvres compl*. iv. 265; Zumpt, *Comment.
epigr*. ii. 18; Daremberg et Saglio, *Dict. des Antiq*., p. 1081). We know
further that Septimius held at some time an official position in the East
(Vit. Sev. ix. 4), where the people of Antioch are said to have laughed at
him 'administrantem in orientem'; Severus admits that ἐπὶ τὸ . . .
ἀποσκῶψαι ἐπιτήδειοι Σύροι, καὶ μάλιστα οἱ τὴν Ἀντιόχειαν οἰκοῦντες (Herod.
ii. 10. 7). Taking these two facts together we are perfectly justified in

seem to have been of long duration, and we hear of his retirement to Athens 'studiorum sacrorumque causa et operum ac
vetustatum'.[1] Only three years before had died the famous
Herodes Atticus, and we may suppose his pupil and successor,
Chrestus, had at least some share in directing the studies of an
illustrious pupil.[2]

Of Septimius' life as an elderly undergraduate we know little
except the fact that the Athenians succeeded somehow in offending his dignity: conduct for which, if we are to believe
his biographer, the emperor made them atone subsequently by
the withdrawal of certain privileges.[3] Ceuleneer raises the
interesting question whether the retirement of Septimius to
Athens was or was not the result of strained relations between
himself and the government. His Grecian visit certainly seems
to correspond in time to the rule of Perennis in Rome, and his
return to public life is probably to be attributed to the very
year following that minister's death.[4] In this year, 186, Cleander
succeeded Perennis, and Septimius was appointed *legatus propraetore* of Gallia Lugdunensis.[5] His administration seems to
have been just and beneficent; so much so that Spartian assures
us that few governors were ever more popular. The ardour,

rejecting the reading (apparently accepted by Peter) which places this
legion 'circa Massiliam'. Zumpt's emendation 'Orimam' seems to me
quite satisfactory. Orima is probably to be identified with the modern
Orum: it was in Coele-Syria, and formed the head-quarters for leg. IV
Scythica until nearly 400. Oresa seems to have been another name for
the same town.

[1] Vit. Sev. iii. 7.

[2] Philostr. Soph. ii. 10 (Kayser, vol. ii, pp. 92, 94, etc.); Fuelles, *de
Tib. Claud. Attici Herodis vita*, Bonn, 1864, p. 26.

[3] Vit. Sev. iii. 7. The truth of the remark is borne out by *CIG.* 2154,
an inscription recording the liberation by Severus of Sciathus from
Athens.

[4] Perennis was killed in 185 (Dio Cass. lii. 9 ; Herod. i. 9. 6 ; Lampr.
Comm. vi. 2).

I can find no justification for Domaszewski's statement (*Geschichte der
römischen Kaiser*, vol. ii, p. 245) that Severus was 'banished', nor
yet for the remark that he completed his education at Athens and
Massilia.

[5] Vit. Sev. iii. 8 ; Dio Cass. lxxiv. 3. 2.

however, with which Lugdunum subsequently embraced the cause of Albinus may justify our suspicions of the credibility of this passage, especially as there is no epigraphic evidence to back it up.[1]

Two important events in the life of the future emperor occurred during his tenure of this Gallic office: the first was his second marriage, the second the revolt of Maternus. The causes and origins of this revolution are shrouded in mystery:[2] even for any detailed account we are beholden only to Herodian,[3] and yet both the boldness of its design and the extent of its influence should have ensured it a more thoroughgoing treatment. All we know is that somewhere during the years 186 to 188 (the very date is a matter of uncertainty) one Maternus collected a body of deserters and brigands, overran Gaul and Spain, and even penetrated into Italy. Not content with this Maternus planned a deliberate attempt on the life of Commodus, which was to take place during the licence afforded by the spring festival of Cybele and, in the words of Herodian, περὶ βασιλείας ἤδη καὶ μειζόνων πραγμάτων ἐβουλεύετο. Jealousy among his followers, however, betrayed him, and he was captured and executed. Meanwhile Commodus, alarmed at so wide a spread of disaffection, dispatched Pescennius Niger into Gaul to deal with revolt there. In Gaul, therefore, the future rivals met, and Severus seems to have been much struck by the capability and energy displayed by Niger in dealing with the crisis. Not content with writing home to Commodus to the effect that Niger was a man 'necessary to the state', he treasured the memory of Niger's capacity in this and other spheres of office when he himself was emperor, and wrote to one Ragonius Celsus, himself

---

[1] A fragmentary inscription cited by Ceuleneer (p. 22) seems to me very dubious. Renier's restitution is very bold.

[2] I suspect that a recrudescence of the plague just before this time may have been largely instrumental in causing disorder and demoralization. A Norican inscription of 182 mentions three people 'qui per luem vita functi sunt' (*CIL.* iii. 5567).

[3] Her. i. 10. Spartian, in his life of Niger (iii. 4), mentions a revolt of 'desertores', and Lampridius (Vit. Comm. xvi. 2) refers to a 'bellum desertorum'.

governor of Gaul, lamenting an inability to imitate one whom
he has defeated.[1]

A similar uncertainty of date attaches to the celebration of
his second marriage. Caracalla we know to have been born on
April 4, 188,[2] and we have Spartian's word for it that Septimius
' statim pater factus est '.[3] We should conclude therefore that
the marriage took place some time in the year 187. The lady
whom he married was the famous Julia Domna, born at Emesa
on the Orontes, and the daughter of one Julius Bassianus, priest
of Bâl in that city. An interesting and suggestive story is
connected with this incident. Ever prone to superstition, in
spite of his Athenian schooling, the widowed governor of Gaul
found his second wife in one whose horoscope foretold that she
should wed a king, and, though we may suppose a previous
meeting in the East, this seems to have been the chief reason for
his choice.[4]

Of Julia herself we shall have occasion to speak more fully
hereafter : for the present it is enough to say of her what Tacitus
said of Poppaea, that she lacked nothing but virtue.

Septimius' next step in the *cursus honorum* was the proconsulate
of Sicily, during the tenure of which he rendered himself liable
to an impeachment for having consulted magicians, a step which
any creature of Commodus would hasten to consider treasonable.[5]
Cleander, however, who was losing the favour of the emperor,
resolutely acquitted the defendant and had the accuser crucified.
The proconsulship belongs to the year 189, the impeachment
doubtless to the early months of the following year.[6]

---

[1] Spart. Nig. iii. 3-9. It must, however, be remembered that the
genuineness of letters in the *S. H. A.* is more than questionable.

[2] See appendix at the end of the chapter.   [3] Vit. Sev. iii. 9.

[4] Vit. Sev. iii. 9 ; Spart. Getae, iii. 1.   [5] Vit. Sev. iv. 2-4.

[6] I am not altogether disinclined to doubt, with Wirth (*Quaest. Sev.*,
pp. 21, 22), the historicity of this impeachment story, for the following
reasons :

   (i) A comparison of Jul. ii. 1 with Sev. iv. 2-4 makes it seem at least
      probable that the Septimius impeachment is but an echo of the
      Julianus one—the latter an indisputable fact (Dio Cass. lxxiii.
      11. 2). An obvious cause of confusion is supplied by the fact
      that the accuser of Julianus bore the name Severus.

On the 1st of April, 190, Septimius became *consul suffectus*,
with Apuleius Rufinus as his colleague, but he seems to have
made no greater mark on history in his first tenure of this office
than the other twenty-four on whom Commodus thought good
to bestow the doubtful honour.[1] We cannot suppose Septimius'
consulship to have lasted for more than a month, and so from
about the beginning of May until the end of the year he
remained without office; he was, in fact, to quote his biographer,
'anno ferme otiosus'.[2]

The next post which he held was, thanks to the influence of
the praetorian prefect Laetus, that of legatus of Pannonia, where,
with three legions at his disposal and with Carnuntum for his
head-quarters, he had the duty of holding the line of the middle
Danube.[3] Here then, for two years and more, Septimius remained

(ii) With the exception of the (?) spurious letter (Vit. Clod. Alb. ii, cf. xiii)
there is no evidence of hostility between Septimius and Commodus.
(iii) Would Commodus have continued Septimius (even though acquitted) in his career of office? How explain the latter's consulship that very year? There was no magnanimity about
Commodus.

[1] Dio Cassius (lxxii. 12. 4) and Lampridius (Comm. vi. 9) tell us that
Commodus appointed twenty-five consuls this year. Spartian contradicts
himself about Septimius' colleague. In Vit. Sev. iv. 4 he gives the name
as Apuleius Rufinus, in Vit. Get. iii. 1 as Vitellius. In the latter passage
Spartian is giving the date of the birth of Geta: 'Natus est Geta Severo
et Vitellio coss. Mediolanii . . . vi. kal. Iunias.' As a matter of fact Geta
was born in 189, probably at Rome: Spartian, in another passage (Vit.
Sev. iv. 2), says that it occurred during the Sicilian proconsulship, and
this, we have seen reason to believe, was in 189. Liebenam and Wirth
(p. 23), on the strength of the passage in the life of Geta, put Severus'
first consulship in 189, a conclusion which seems to me to be in contradiction to almost all the facts of the case. We may either suppose the
'Severo et Vitellio' to be wrong or else suppose this to have been another
Severus.

[2] Vit. Sev. iv. 4. That this passage affords no justification for a belief
in the theory that Septimius was COS. I in 189 is proved by the word
'ferme'. Had he been consul in 189 and not gone to Pannonia until
191, the period of his freedom from office (say May 189 to January 191)
could not be described as 'ferme anno'.

[3] Two questions arise in connexion with this provincial appointment:
(1) of what province was Septimius governor? Dio Cassius (lxxiii. 14. 3)
says distinctly Pannonia. His statement is supported by the Epitome

settling the province, which had been so shaken by the recent wars under Marcus Aurelius and his son, and doubtless winning by his capable management of, and politic care for, his troops that popularity which was to stand him in such good stead in his bid for empire.

APPENDIX ON THE DATE OF CARACALLA'S BIRTH.

The whole question of the birth of Caracalla demands a more thoroughgoing investigation, the evidence on the matter being more than usually confused and self-contradictory. The problem naturally falls into two parts: (1) when was Caracalla born? and (2) of whom was he born? We will deal with the latter first.

(xix. 2: Savaria, however, takes the place of Carnuntum as the scene of the imperial greeting), by Herodian (ii. 9. 2), and by Zonaras (xii. 7). Spartian, however, says 'proficiscens ad Germanicos exercitus' (Vit. Sev. iv. 5), though he clearly has heard of Severus' Pannonian appointment, and mentions it as occurring between the governorship of Lugdunensis and that of Sicily (Vit. Sev. iv. 1). He also gives Carnuntum as the scene of the acclamation. Aurelius Victor (Caes. xix. 4) gives Syria, which is quite obviously wrong. There can be little doubt but that Pannonia is right, though more writers than one have been led by Spartian's evidence to suppose a joint command of Pannonia and Germany (e. g. Renier, *Mélanges*, p. 163). (2) Was Septimius governor only of Pannonia Superior or of both the Pannonias? The decision here is not so easily made. Spartian (Vit. Sev. iv. 2) says Pannonias, and Herodian (ii. 9. 2) expressly states ἡγεῖτο Παιόνων πάντων (ὑπὸ μιᾷ γὰρ ἦσαν ἐξουσίᾳ). On the other hand, Dio Cassius (lxxiii. 14. 3) and Zonaras (xii. 7) say one Pannonia only: τρεῖς γὰρ δὴ τότε ἄνδρες (i. e. Severus, Albinus, and Niger), τριῶν ἕκαστος πολιτικῶν στρατοπέδων . . . ἄρχοντες . . . Σεουῆρος δὲ τῆς Παννονίας. Now there were three legions in Upper Pannonia, viz.: I adiutrix, X gemina, and XIV gemina. Had Septimius been governor of lower Pannonia as well he would have had in addition leg. II adiutrix, thus making four, not three. We have thus to decide between two contemporary writers, each supported by later literary evidence. It seems to me safest to steer a middle course and to suppose that Septimius possessed some sort of *maius imperium* to that held by the praetorian legate of the lower province. Thus he might be called legatus of both Pannonias and yet have but three legions under his immediate and direct control. Domaszewski, *Rangordnung des röm. Heeres*, p. 173, notes that in provinces governed by praetorian *legati* the legate is generally legate both of the legion and of the province—a second legate being appointed only if the legion leaves the province.

The two candidates for the doubtful honour are, naturally,
Marcia and Julia, respectively the first and second wives of
Septimius. In favour of Marcia we get the following passages:

(1) Spart. Sev. xx. 2 'Bassianum . . . ex priore matrimonio sus-
ceperat et Getam de Iulia genuerat'. (The passage is said to
come from Aelius Maurus.)

(2) Ibid. xxi. 7.'qui novercam suam . . . uxorem duxit'. (I take
the 'matrem quin immo' to be merely a piece of rhetoric.)

(3) Spart. Getae, vii. 3 'matrem Getae, novercam suam'. (The
first chapter of Caracalla's biography also points vaguely to the
fact that Julia had but one son.)

(4) Spart. Car. x. 1 'Novercam suam Iuliam uxorem duxisse
dicatur'.

(5) Aur. Vict. Caes. xxi. 3 'Iuliano novercam . . . uxorem
affectavit'.

(6) Aur. Vict. Epit. xxi. 5 'Qui novercam suam duxit uxorem'.

(7) Eutropius, viii. 20, repeats the Epitome almost word for
word at this point: e. g. both call Caracalla 'impatiens libidinis'
—as does Eusebius.

(8) Orosius, vii. 18. 2 'Novercam suam Iuliam uxorem duxerit'.

(9) Eusebius, *Chron.* (ed. Schoene, p. 177) 'tam impatiens libidinis fuit ut novercam suam Iuliam uxorem suam duxerit'.

Against Marcia and in favour of Julia we have:

(1) Vit. Sev. iii. 8, which says he married Julia when legatus
Lugdunensis and soon became a father by her. (We have had
reason to put this tenure of office at least within the years 186–8,
and shall see further that Caracalla's birth falls within the same
period.)

(2) Dio Cass. lxxvii. 10. 2, speaking of the character of Caracalla,
says he had τὸ πανοῦργον τῆς μητρὸς καὶ τῶν Σύρων.

(3) Ibid. lxxvii. 10. 2 (frag.) says he belonged to three countries,
and had their respective characteristics: two are Syria and Gaul.[1]

(4) Aur. Vict. Epit. xxi. 1 'Bassianus Caracalla . . . Lugduni
genitus'.

(5) Philost. Vit. Soph. ii. 30 (ed. Kayser, vol. ii, p. 121) Ἀντωνῖ-
νος δὲ ἦν ὁ τῆς φιλοσόφου παῖς Ἰουλίας. (Incidentally we may point
out that: (a) Philostratus was a member of Julia's circle and an

---

[1] Other references *ad hoc* in Dio are: lxxvii. 2. 2, lxxvii. 10. 4, lxxvii.
18. 2, lxxviii. 4. 2, lxxviii. 23. 1.

intimate friend. (*b*) He is perhaps the one literary authority
whose text we have no reason to suppose excerpted or corrupted.)

(6) Oppian, *de Venat.* i. 4 'quem magno peperit genetrix
Augusta Severo'. (Oppian was another member of the Julian
circle.)

(7) Herodian (another un-rewritten contemporary) iv. 13. 8
μήτηρ Ἰουλία. Herodian v. 3. 2 Ἰουλίας . . . Ἀντωνίνου . . .
μητρός.

(8) We know that Caracalla's real name was Bassianus (e. g.
Spartian, Car. i. 1); we know also that Julia's father was a
Bassianus (Aur. Vict. Epit. xxiii. 2 'Huius (Elagabali) matris
Soemiae avus Bassianus nomine'). It is therefore natural to
suppose that just as Geta was called after his grandfather or uncle
on the father's side (Spart. Get. ii. 1; Aurel. Vict. Caes. xx. 32),
so Caracalla received his name from his mother's father. Indeed
the Epitome expressly tells us that this was the case: 'Hic
Bassianus ex avi materni nomine dictus est' (Aur. Vict. Epit.
xxi. 2).

(9) Most conclusive of all, indeed decisive to my mind, is the
epigraphic evidence. If Julia were not the mother of Caracalla,
how comes she to be called MATRI AVGG? The double 'g', no
rare phenomenon but the abbreviation generally found, indicates
the plural 'Augustorum', i. e. Caracalla and Geta.

The evidence thus marshalled seems to be overwhelmingly
in favour of Julia; when we have the word of four contemporaries (one, it is true, in a later epitomized form) besides the
testimony of inscriptions we can safely disregard the statements
of fourth-century and later authors. Nor indeed is it hard to
see that these latter get their supposed fact from one vitiated
source: this I consider proved by the appearance of the word
'novercam' in all the pro-Marcia passages.

The second point, viz. the date of Caracalla's birth, is not so
easily disposed of. The passages in our authorities dealing with
the question are as follows:

(1) Dio Cass. lxxviii. 5. 4 τῇ ὀγδόῃ τοῦ Ἀπριλίου . . . ὁ Μαρτιάλιος
. . . ἐπάταξεν. The year of his death was certainly 217: of that
there is no doubt nor ever has been. Further, since Dio is the
only author who mentions the day of his death, we have at least
a possible reason for accepting his statement as true. We have
thus a fixed *terminus ad quem*: viz. April 8, 217.

(2) Dio Cass. lxxviii. 6. 5 βιούς τε ἔτη ἐννέα καὶ εἴκοσι καὶ ἡμέρας τέσσαρας, τῇ γὰρ τετάρτῃ τοῦ Ἀπριλίου ἐγεγέννητο, καὶ αὐταρχήσας ἔτη ἐξ καὶ μῆνας δύο καὶ ἡμέρας δύο. Working this out from (1) we get : Born April 4 (it is noteworthy that the date agrees with the previous statement), 188. Began to reign February 6, 211.

(3) Spart. Car. ix. 1 'Bassianus vixit annis quadraginta tribus ; imperavit annis sex'. This puts his birth in the year 174 (accession date as Dio, 211).

(4) Eutrop. viii. 20 'Defunctus est . . . anno imperii vi mense ii vix egressus aetatis XLIII annum'. We can safely disregard this as it is a mere echo of Spartian or of Spartian's source. In both authors the phrase 'Funere publico elatus est' follows the notice of his death.

(5) Aurel. Vict. Epit. xxi 'Vixit annos fere triginta'. He agrees, that is to say, with Dio.

(6) Spart. Car. vi. 6 'die natali suo, octavo Idus Aprilis', i.e. April 6.

(7) Spart. Sev. iv. 6 says Caracalla was quinquennis while his father was setting out for the command of the Pannonian legions, i.e. in 191. This points to 186 as the year of his birth.

(8) Spart. Sev. xvi. 3 'Bassianum . . . qui Caesar appellatus iam fuerat, annum xiii agentem participem dixerunt imperii milites, Getam quoque . . . Caesarem dixerunt'. The date of raising of Caracalla to the rank of Augustus and of Geta to that of Caesar may with tolerable certainty be stated as 198 (cf. p. 21). This gives us as the date of Caracalla's birth the year 185, of which we only say that it approximates more nearly to 188 than to 174, and that it shows up fairly conclusively the unreliability of Spartian as a chronological authority.

(9) Zonaras xii. 12 ζήσας ἔτη ἐννέα εἴκοσιν, αὐταρχήσας δ' . . . ἐνιαυτοὺς ἐξ καὶ δύο μησὶ καὶ ἡμέραις τισί.

The other literary sources are unimportant. Herodian merely mentions a six years' reign (Herod. iv. 13. 8): so too Aurelius Victor (Caes. xxi. 5). Eusebius (Chron., p. 176) and Georgius Syncellus (p. 672) say seven years ; the former, following Spartian, gives his age as forty-three. Orosius (vii. 18) says 'non plenis septem'; Joannes Malalas (p. 295) gives the reign as seven years twelve days, and his age when murdered as forty-seven: according to the Chronicon Paschale (p. 497) he died in 219 at the ripe age of sixty.

The lateness and badness of most of these sources justify our rejection of them, so far as the year of Caracalla's birth is concerned. We have to weigh against each other Dio (with slight support from the Epitome) and Spartian (with the reduplication of Eutropius and others). Our conclusion must certainly be in favour of Dio, and the subject could be considered as settled were it not for a mysterious passage in Dio himself. That we must now examine. Dio Cass. lxxiv. 3. 1 μέλλοντι δ᾿ αὐτῷ τὴν Ἰουλίαν ἄγεσθαι ἡ Φαυστῖνα . . . τὸν θάλαμον . . . παρεσκεύασεν.

Now Faustina, wife of Marcus Aurelius, died in the year 175. Dio (lxxi. 29. 1) and Capitolinus (M. Aur. xxvi. 4) do not mention the precise date, but state that the death occurred in the East. The exact year is fixed by the fact that coins and inscriptions of 175 are the first to refer to her as DIVA (e. g. Eck. vii. 80 ; CIL. ix. 1113). If, therefore, we are to believe that Faustina prepared the bridal chamber of Julia and Septimius we must modify considerably our views on the date of this marriage, and must concede that, placing the wedding in 173, the theory that Caracalla was born in 174 receives some support.

It has been usual to suppose that Marcia should here be read in place of Julia. Höfner (p. 10, note 18) suggests that the error springs from Xiphilinus, who, he considers, wilfully substituted the well-known second for the lesser-known first wife of the emperor. There seems to me no reason for crediting either Dio with crass carelessness or Xiphilinus with conscious fraud. The most superficial reading of the passage convinces one that Dio never stated and never meant to state that Faustina assisted at this marriage. The whole tale is a dream, and is given as one of the σημεῖα with which the chapter deals. So far, indeed, are Dio or Xiphilinus from wilfully misleading the reader that after the next episode (said to have taken place in Lugdunum) they add the reminder ὄναρ φημί.

This being the case we may with comparative certainty adopt 188 as the year of Caracalla's birth. For the day we prefer Dio's word to Spartian's, that is to say April 4 to April 6, while the statement of Dio, which makes his reign begin on February 6 instead of February 4, must be regarded as a slip on the part of the historian or his epitomizer.

Our final conclusions, therefore, are : That Caracalla was the son of Septimius and Julia Domna; that he was born at Lyons on April 4, 188, ascended the throne February 4, 211, and died April 8, 217, at the age of twenty-nine.[1]

[1] It seems to me a not improbable theory to suppose that, just as modern readers have been misled by Dio, so too Spartian, or his source, was misled, and took the story of Faustina and Septimius' marriage as sufficient justification for attributing Caracalla's birth to the earlier date. Wirth, in his article 'Quo anno Caracalla natus sit' (*Quaest. Sev.*, pp. 19–21), prefers 186 as the date of Caracalla's birth on what appears to me entirely inconclusive evidence. He starts by impugning the accuracy of Dio as to dates in general, instancing several cases where that historian is proved (?) wrong by an appeal to other evidence. Six passages are adduced: of these only one (or perhaps two) contains an actual self-contradiction in the text of Dio himself, three disagree with Suetonius, four with the *S. H. A.*, while in the last the historian expressly states his uncertainty as to the date—thus affording, one would have thought, a strong supposition in favour of his accuracy in such matters. Thus of the nine cases certainly five can be discounted, for—special pleading set aside—it is a mere paradox to prefer the testimony of the *S. H. A.* to Dio, epitomized though he is.

His other two arguments are:

(1) If there is only one year between the births of Caracalla and Geta (who was certainly born May 27, 189), why is there an interval of three years between their respective first consulships (202 and 205) and of four between their co-optations 'inter pontifices' (Caracalla in 197, Coh., Car., no. 53, etc.; Geta in 201, Occo, *Imp. rom. num.* 300)?

To this we would answer: The would-be founder of a dynasty is prepared to shock public opinion by heaping honours upon an immature eldest son; but he has no interest in risking unpopularity by so acting in the case of a second child.

(2) Why did not the *S. H. A.* comment upon the so speedy investiture of Caracalla with the consulship after his receiving of the *toga virilis*, as they did in the case of Commodus (Lamp. *Comm.* ii. 4)?

The answer is that the *S. H. A.*, so far as they thought at all, believed Caracalla to have been born in 186; hence, for them, there was no need to remark upon the early bestowal of such privileges.

Another verdict in favour of 186 is that of Liebenam, p. 110, who follows Wilcken in *Hermes*, 1885, p. 473.

CHAPTER IV

THE WAR OF ACCESSION

WE have now reached the point at which the fortunes of Septimius are synonymous with those of the empire, but before we follow them farther we must turn back and review the state of affairs in Rome, to see in what manner preparation was being made (all-unconsciously) for the reception of a new dynasty.

If material prosperity is in any measure the criterion of a nation's greatness we may not unnaturally see in the reign of Antoninus Pius the zenith of Roman power. Long before the end of his successor's reign storm-clouds had begun to gather on the northern horizon, and neither the brave wars of a philosopher nor the shameful peace of a profligate could do more than postpone the coming danger. Trouble from the peoples from without the empire, seditions within it, a madman at its head—everything called for a new régime; but the daggers of Laetus, Narcissus, and their fellow conspirators offered no more than a very practical piece of destructive criticism.

On December 31, 192, Commodus was murdered.[1] The praetorian prefect, Laetus, was the protagonist in the drama, but he had behind him the firm support of the Senate, whom the insults of the emperor had galvanized, for once, into something more than mere spitefulness. Whether or not Septimius was privy to the scheme seems to me a question which, in default of positive evidence on the point, it is more advisable to shelve than to answer. Each view has, and has had, its supporters: Schulte,[2] and recently Domaszewski,[3] hold Severus to have been implicated, while Ceuleneer[4] and Mr. Stuart

---

[1] Dio Cass. lxxii. 19; Herod. i. 16, 17; Lampr. *Comm.* xvi. 17; Zos. i. 17; Aur. Vict. Epit. xvii; Eutrop. viii. 7.

[2] *De Imp. Luc. Sept. Severo*, Monasterii, 1867, p. 16.

[3] *Op. cit.*, vol. ii, p. 246.   [4] *Op. cit.*, p. 28.

Jones[1] incline to a meticulous acquittal. That Pertinax was not altogether without a shrewd suspicion of what was going to take place, nor entirely surprised by the deputation that offered him the crown on that New Year's morning, is a supposition wanting neither evidence nor probability.[2] The tyrant once dead, the Senate showed its spirit by an order that all his statues and inscriptions should be destroyed, and so thoroughly was this command carried out that even Hercules, with whom Commodus had identified himself, fell, in one instance, a victim to popular fury, real or simulated.[3]

Of Publius Helvius Pertinax, the senatorial nominee in succession to Commodus, there is no need to speak at great length. His origin was humble,[4] but lowly birth had long ceased to be a bar even to imperial honours, and a striking diversity of accomplishments compensated for any deficiency in this respect. Born on August 1, 126, his earliest occupation was his father's, where his assiduity earned for him his cognomen:[5] his next profession, that of a schoolmaster,[6] he relinquished on his appointment to the praefecture of a cohort in Syria. Here he served in the Parthian war of Lucius Verus (162); with some distinction, it seems. On his return he was appointed curator or sub-curator of the Via Aemilia,[7]

---

[1] *The Roman Empire*, p. 236.

[2] Vit. Pert. iv. 4 'interficiendi Commodi conscientiam'. So too Julian, *Caesares*, § 10, 312 c (Teubner, edit. 1875) κοινωνῶν τῆς ἐπιβουλῆς.

[3] So M. Passy in his *Recherches sur une statue colossale d'Hercule, dite Hercule Mastaï* (Mémoires de la Soc. des Antiq. de France, 31). Ceuleneer (p. 28) disbelieves this, but quotes instances of the destruction of 'Commodiana' in Georgia and Armenia.

[4] Dio Cass. lxxiii. 3. 1 πατρὸς οὐκ εὐγενοῦς : his less courtly biographer (Cap. Pert. i. 1) says 'pater libertinus', and states that he was a wood-merchant.

[5] Vit. Pert. xv. 6, i. 1.

[6] Dio Cass. lxxiii. 3. 1 ; Vit. Pert. i. 4. I take the account of Pertinax' pre-imperial career chiefly from Capitolinus, whose remarks seem in the main credible. The mention of his duties in Britain and Moesia (ii. 1) is, of course, chronologically wrong, and must be taken to foreshadow iii. 5 and ii. 10 respectively. No further references to Capitolinus' first four chapters will be made.

[7] In connexion with the 'alimentation' service : Hirschfeld, p. 221.

was subsequently placed in command of the Rhine fleet,[1] and finally made procurator of Dacia. The goodwill of the Emperor Marcus, to which he owed this last post, seems to have been suddenly withdrawn, and a short period of retirement or even disgrace supervened, from which he was rescued by the kind offices of Claudius Pompeianus, son-in-law of Marcus, and possibly a personal friend of his own. He served in the German war in some subsidiary position,[2] was meanwhile given senatorial insignia, raised to praetorian rank, and then put in command of a legion.[3] His sphere of action was Raetia and Noricum. In 175 he was appointed to the consulship, in which office he possibly had Didius Julianus for a colleague.[4] After his consulship he seems to have fought (in what capacity we do not know) against the pretender, Avidius Cassius, in Syria, towards the end of the year 176.[5] His next office was that

---

[1] Generally known as 'classis Germanica': founded by the elder Drusus (Florus, ii. 30). It lasted until well into the fourth century (Hegesipp. *bell. Iud.* ii. 9. 124–7; Eumen. *paneg. Const.* xiii. 1).

[2] Ceuleneer, p. 30, says 'in command of *cohortes veteranorum*'; Vit. Pert. ii. 4 'vexillis regendis'.

[3] This was leg. I adiutrix: cf. Vit. Pert. ii. 6; Jünemann, 'de leg. rom. I adi.' in *Leipziger Studien*, 1894, p. 89. Ceuleneer, without any authority, so far as I can see, puts this in the year 172. If this is the case we might almost see in Pertinax the 'cumulus' of the war, for the year 172, as Schiller (*op. cit.*, p. 647) points out, marks a turning-point: 'Germanicus' and 'Vict. Germ.' appear then for the first time on Marcus' coins (Eck. vii. 59, 60).

[4] So Vit. Jul. ii. 3, but the statement is made in support of a generalization, and we may not unreasonably suspect a confusion between Didius Julianus and one Salvius Julianus who was consul that year (*CIL.* xv. 7240; Lampr. *Comm.* xii. 2).

[5] This raises the vexed question as to the date of Cassius' rising. Dio (lxxi. 22. 2) is vague, also Gallicanus, Cassius' biographer, except that in chap. xi, § 8 a letter speaks of Pompeianus' consulship as in the future. Now Pompeianus was consul in 173 (Liebenam, p. 24): hence some have put the insurrection in 172. So, too, Waddington from archaeological evidence. But (1) this letter in Gallicanus' life is probably not genuine, and (2) the archaeological evidence is purely negative—absence of monuments in the Hauran later than 171. Against this is the express testimony of Ammianus (xxi. 16. 11). This later date is almost certainly right, probably 176–8. So Stout, *Governors of Moesia* (Princeton, 1911), p. 31.

of governor of the two Moesias, then of Dacia, and afterwards
of Syria, where he was at the time of Marcus' death (180).
Ex-governor of four consular provinces, he returned to Rome
in 181 a rich man and entered the Senate an unpopular one.
Perennis typified and voiced this unpopularity, and Pertinax,
bowing before the storm, retired to his native Liguria. On the
death of the minister in 185 he was recalled and sent to Britain,
where he quelled a rebellion of the legions.[1] Presumably in
187 he became *praefectus alimentorum*;[2] then proconsul of
Africa; next *praefectus urbi*, and finally, in 192, consul for the
second time with Commodus.[3]

On January 1, 193, as we have seen, Pertinax exchanged the
consular for the imperial robes; but he was not destined to
wear them long. Nothing is stranger or more indicative of
the precarious position of an emperor than the rapidity with
which his fate overtook one whose accession was hailed with
such universal joy. Like Galba, whom in his short imperial
career he strikingly resembles, he had a senatorial majority at
his back, while the coins and inscriptions of his three months'
reign attest a provincial loyalty not wholly time-serving.[4]
After a vain attempt to thrust the reins of government into
the hands of his old general, Claudius Pompeianus, Pertinax
set himself to remedy some at least of the abuses introduced
by his predecessor. Like Galba, again, his reforming zeal
carried him too far, and Capitolinus expressly notes that the

---

[1] Dio Cass. lxxii. 9. 2. Hübner, 'Die röm. Leg. in Brit.', *Rhein. Mus.*
xx, p. 62.

[2] Not 'curator', as Ceuleneer says. The curators of the third and end
of the second centuries were merely local officials, such as was Pertinax
himself in earlier years. To have been made *curator alimentorum* after
being governor of a consular province would have been a degradation :
cf. Hirschfeld, p. 218.

[3] *CIL.* xiii. 7325.

[4] He was *princeps senatus* (Dio Cass. lxxiii. 5. 1), and seemingly of
affable manners. ἐχρῆτο δὲ καὶ ἡμῖν δημοτικώτατα· καὶ γὰρ εὐπροσήγορος ἦν,
says the senator Dio. His biographer is not so flattering (e. g. xii. 1–2),
'verbis . . . affabilis, re inliberalis'; cf. his nickname 'agrarius mergus'
(ix. 5). Apparently he made some definite attempt to restore the
Augustan dyarchy, and with this end in view caused 'princeps senatus'
to be inscribed among his official titles (e. g. *CIL.* ii. 4125).

law concerning praetors earned him much unpopularity.[1] National bankruptcy, too (yet another echo of 69), stared him in the face; and though he sought to meet the emergency by such legitimate measures as the sale of Commodus' instruments of luxury and vice (Capitolinus characteristically gives us a veritable sale catalogue), yet he is not free from the accusation of having had recourse to the less creditable method of raising the wind by means of the sale of offices and appointments.[2] Laetus, we are told, repented bitterly of his choice, and one of the consuls of the year broke into open revolt; nor did the consequent execution of many soldiers on insufficient (i. e. servile) evidence serve to increase the loyalty of the army. To cut a long story short the well-meaning emperor took but two months completely to alienate the sympathies of most of his quondam supporters, whose hatred found expression in the spear of one Tausius, a Tungrian of the guard.[3] The murder took place on March 28, 193.[4]

If the murderers of Commodus had no other constructive scheme than the delegation of the supreme authority to an honest but tactless sexagenarian, how much more unprepared were the next imperial assassins? The empire lay without a master; and, as on the decease of Galba, three candidates, one put forward by the soldiery of Rome, the other two by provinces respectively of the east and the west, were found ready to bid for empire. Once more, as in the year 69, his position enabled the Roman pretender to forestall his provincial competitors, and on the same day as had seen the murder of Pertinax, the rich senator M. Didius Julianus assumed the purple, an honour for which he is said to have paid 25,000

---

[1] Cap. Pert. vi. 10. By this law a real praetor (one, that is, who had actually held office) was ranked above those whom Commodus had 'adlected' in such quantities (e. g. Lampr. *Comm.* vi. 9).

[2] Cap. Pert. ix. 7.

[3] Not, of course, the praetorian guard, but the *equites singulares imperatoris*.

[4] So Dio Cassius, who gives eighty-seven days as the total length of his reign (lxxiii. 10. 3). The usual variants occur: e. g. Aur. Vict. Caes. xviii gives eighty days; the Epitome (xviii) eighty-five; Orosius (vii. 16) six months, etc., etc.

sesterces to each man of the praetorians—i. e. 250,000,000 HS
= £2,500,000—and which he enjoyed for some sixty-four days.[1]
But though Julianus was the successful praetorian candidate he
was not, if we may believe our authorities, the only one. Two
claimants appeared, the other of whom was Flavius Sulpicianus,
the city prefect and father-in-law of the dead Pertinax. He
it was who was acclaimed, or at least on the point of being
acclaimed, emperor within the walls of the praetorian camp,
when Julianus, encouraged alike by his ambition and his family,[2]
approached the walls from the outside and started to outbid
Sulpicianus. How far this extraordinary story of the auction
of the empire is true or not is hard to say. Spartian,[3] untrue
to his character, treats the sensational incident very cursorily,
though giving us a picture of Julianus ' e muro ingentia polli-
centem ' ; and adds that it was not until the latter had warned
the praetorians that Sulpicianus would undoubtedly avenge his
son-in-law's death, whereas himself would restore the Commodan
régime, that the gates were opened to the successful claimant.
Herodian [4] gives a much fuller account, including a picturesque
description of Julianus in a state of intoxication, mounting on
to the wall by means of a ladder; while even the staid Dio [5]
admits most distinctly the fact that some form of sale by auction
did take place. Startling, therefore, though the story is, we are
bound, in face of the evidence, to accept it.

But though money raised Julianus to the throne of the
Caesars, it could not keep him there. The plebs hated him

[1] Dio (lxxiii. 11. 1, etc.) and Spartian (Vit. Iul. xxiv) clearly suppose
the election of Julianus to have taken place the very day of the murder,
nor does there seem any reason to discard this very natural account in
favour of Herodian (ii. 6. 3) or Ammianus (xxvi. 6. 14), who intimate
that an interval of one or two days intervened between the two
occurrences.

[2] Herod. ii. 6. 7. His wife was Mallia Scantilla and his daughter
Didia Clara (Spart. Iul. iii. 4). Both subsequently received the imperial
title (cf. Eck. vii. 150). The daughter was married to one Cornelius
Repentinus, who succeeded Sulpicianus as *praefectus urbi* (Spart. Iul. iii. 6).

[3] Vit. Iul. ii. 4-7.　　　　　　　　　[4] ii. 6. 4-11.

[5] lxxiii. 11. 3-6; e.g. ὥσπερ . . . ἐν ἀγορᾷ καὶ ἐν πωλητηρίῳ . . . ἡ ἀρχὴ
. . . ἀπεκηρύχθη . . . ὠνητίων δὲ ὅ τε Σουλπικιανὸς καὶ ὁ Ἰουλιανὸς ὑπερβάλ-
λοντες ἀλλήλους, ὁ μὲν ἔνδοθεν ὁ δὲ ἔξοθεν.

because they had recognized in Pertinax a possible restorer of
constitutional government, and saw in Julianus the dashing of
their hopes.[1] They evinced, too, a pharisaic inconsistency in
objecting alike to the parsimony of Pertinax and the suspected
luxury of his successor; [2] so unpopular indeed was he that the
soldiers were obliged to escort him to the palace ' holding their
shields over his head, lest any should stone him from the houses '.[3]
The Senate both loathed and feared him, for had he not come,
a second Commodus, to supersede the senatorial Pertinax ?
Dio [4] gives a realistic picture of the nervousness of that august
body when the new emperor entered the Senate-house to obtain
the fathers' ratification of his position, which ratification he
showed himself not unwilling to extract by force of arms should
it be refused. Even the soldiers, as we shall see later, were
unwilling to fight for one who owed his election at their hands
rather to his money than his merits.[5]

Meanwhile, at least one more would-be emperor was not idle.
Whether or not Severus foresaw and worked for his elevation
during Commodus' life, at least the death of Pertinax afforded
him an opening and a pretext of which he was not slow to avail
himself. To pose as the avenger of a constitutional emperor
would win him the affections of both Senate and people, while
with a superior force at his back he had little need to consult
the wishes of the praetorians. Pertinax, as we have seen, fell
on March 28. On April 13 Septimius addressed a meeting of
his troops in Carnuntum, the chief city of Pannonia and his
own head-quarters, told them of the murder, reminded them of
the sterling character of the dead emperor as shown there among
them in the Illyrian wars of Marcus, depicted the effeminacy of
the praetorians, contrasting it with their own hardihood, and
finally, if we can believe Herodian, who of course gives the

---

[1] e.g. Spart. Iul. iii. 7; Dio Cass. lxxiii. 13. 2 ὁ δὲ δῆμος ἐσκυθρώπαζε
φανερῶς.

[2] Spart. Iul. iii. 8.

[3] Herod. ii. 6. 13.   [4] lxxiii. 12.

[5] The pre-imperial career of Julianus is of no great interest or moment.
It is to be found in Spartian's life (i. 2. 3), to the accuracy of which at
least one inscription attests, CIL. vi. 1401.

speech *in extenso*, exhorted them to march on Rome before his rival Niger, of whose defection he must have heard, could cover the longer distance which separated him from the capital.[1] His speech was enthusiastically received, himself acclaimed emperor, and preparations begun for the southern march. And, indeed, he started with fair promise of success. With the exception of Byzantium, which adhered to Niger, and of Britain, which might reasonably be expected to follow Albinus should he dissociate himself from Septimius, all Europe was on his side.[2]

Niger had as yet made no move, and Albinus he had mollified by the offer of Caesarship and the promise of a consulship.[3]

---

[1] Vit. Sev. v. 1 gives 'idibus Augustis', but Baronius' emendation 'Aprilibus', accepted by Clinton (*Fast. Rom.*, p. 192) and by Ceuleneer (p. 35), is certainly right. This gives sixteen or seventeen days for the news to reach Septimius, supposing, as is natural to suppose, that he acted upon it at once. Augustus used to say that a rebel army in Pannonia could reach Rome in ten days (Vell. Pat. ii. 111); and Septimius with his army must have taken only about forty from Carnuntum. All our authorities attest his position as Pertinax' avenger: e. g. 'excipiebatur enim ab omnibus quasi ultor Pertinacis' (Vit. Sev. v. 4; cf. Spart. Iul. viii. 5). Herodian mentions the fact that he called himself Pertinax in Carnuntum and was acclaimed as such (ii. 10. 1, 9)— ἔλεγε δὲ δεῖν ἐπαμῦναι καὶ ἐπεξελθεῖν τῷ Περτίνακος φόνῳ (ii. 9. 8). Two small points arise in connexion with Septimius' title of Pertinax: (1) Herodian says he adopted it in Pannonia; Spartian (vii. 9), though without saying so in so many words, implies that the title was first used at the time of Pertinax' deification in Rome. (2) A strange tradition has crept into the text of the *Scriptores* which pictures the name as thrust on the unwilling Septimius, not as chosen by him. Such a passage is Vit. Sev. xvii. 6 'non tam ex sua voluntate' (the actual text is in a very bad state here); but the contrary view is certainly right: cf. in the *Scriptores* themselves Vit. Sev. vii. 9; Cap. Pert. xv. 2 (see above, p. 33). If Septimius knew in Carnuntum of Niger's revolt, the latter must have been in arms before the death of Pertinax. Between March 28 and April 13 there is not time enough to allow for the one piece of news (Pertinax' death) to reach Syria and the other (Niger's defection) to reach Pannonia.

[2] Dio Cass. lxxiii. 15. 1; Vit. Sev. v. 3. (This passage speaks of Gaul as pro-Severan, since 'Gallicani exercitus' must refer (irregularly) to Gaul proper.)

[3] Dio Cass. lxxiii. 15. 1. See above, chap. ii, p. 29. Besides the above-quoted numismatic we have epigraphic evidence of this Caesar-

Besides his own three legions (or four if we include II adiutrix, the legion of Lower Pannonia, stationed at Aquincum) he could count on the support of the four in Germany, the two in Raetia and Noricum, the two in Dacia, and four in Moesia. The African legion, moreover, was favourable to him, as the event proved.[1]

Leaving some troops (perhaps only auxiliaries) to guard the frontier, Severus hastened to Rome by forced marches: no ship: *CIL.* viii. 1549, 17726, xiii. 1753, xiv. 6. Consulship: Cap. Alb iii. 6, vi. 8; Clinton (sub. 194). Mommsen (*St. R.* ii. 1153—references to the *Staatsrecht* denote the 3rd edit., 1887) even thinks that *trib. pot.* was offered him. True, Eck. vii. 164 and Cohen, iii. Alb. no. 19 are almost certainly forgeries; still there is no other reason to doubt the genuineness of Cohen, ibid. no. 35.

[1] I take this list from Ceuleneer, pp. 36, 37—with emendations. The legions in question are:

leg. I adi. stationed at Brigetio.

(This, it will be remembered, is the legion of which Pertinax was once legatus. For a temple erected in honour of its victorious fighting on the side of Septimius cf. *CIL.* iii. 4364.)

leg. X	¡ gem.	stationed at	Vindobona.	
„ XIV	„	„	Carnuntum.	
„ VIII	Aug.	„	Argentoratum	} Germ. sup.
„ XXII	prim.	„	Moguntiacum	
„ I	Minerv.	„	Bonna	} Germ. inf.
„ XXX	Ulp. Victr.	„	Vetera	
„ III	Ital.	„	Castra Regina. Raetia.	

(Not Augusta Vindelicorum, as Ceuleneer: cf. *CIL.* iii, p. 730, and such inscriptions as *CIL.* iii. 5942, 5950, etc.)

leg. II   Ital. stationed at Lauriacum.   Noricum.

(Not Celeia, as C.: cf. *CIL.* iii, p. 689 and nos. 5681, 5682. Also *Itin. Ant.*, p. 100.)

leg. XIII	gem.	stationed at	Sarmizegethusa	} Dacia.
„ V	Maced.	„	Potaissa	
„ IV	Flav.	„	Singidunum	} Moes. sup.
„ VII	Claud.	„	Viminacium	
„ XI	„	„	Durostorum	} Moes. inf.
„ I	Ital.	„	Novae	

As to the African legion (III Aug.) we know that by 194/5 it bore the title *pia vindex* (*CIL.* viii. 17726: cf. 2527, 2557), which looks as though it had fought for Septimius (cf. Schiller, p. 709). Possibly a *vexillatio* of it was sent to secure Egypt (Vit. Sev. viii. 7). (For medals struck by the legions cf. chap. ii, p. 35.) Besides the legionary troops there are also the auxiliaries to be reckoned: Ceuleneer gives a list of these also.

soldier took off his breastplate between Carnuntum and Rome, says Dio.[1] His route seems to have been that followed by Vespasian's general, Antonius Primus, and he entered Italy by the passes of the Julian Alps, outstripping, so at least says Herodian,[2] the news of his approach. His first success was the defection of the Ravenna fleet and the voluntary surrender of the town.[3] The praetorian prefect, Tullius Crispinus, sent by Julianus to guard against this mishap, arrived too late and was forced to retire.[4]

At this point the emperor seems to have lost his head : first he declared Septimius a public enemy and sent an embassy to recall his troops to allegiance ; many of the embassy seceded, and one, Vespronius Candidus, who remained faithful, barely escaped with his life.[5] Then he endeavoured to ensure the continued loyalty of the guards by enormous bribes, but, as he seems not to have paid up his 25,000 sesterces per man, the money was taken as a debt paid rather than an obligation incurred.[6] He next suggested an appeal *ad misericordiam* by means of a deputation of vestal virgins, but was sharply reprimanded by the augur Plautius Quintillus, who reminded him that he could be no emperor who could not support his claims with the sword.[7] Julianus was, however, averse to violent measures. He appointed a third praetorian prefect, one Veturius Macrinus, a nominee of Septimius ; and, after a preliminary and abortive attempt on Septimius' life, offered to share the empire with him.[8] The one thing he does not seem to have done is to have fought, although certain authorities make mention of

---

[1] lxxiii. 15. 3.　　　　　　　　　　　　　　　[2] ii. 11. 3.

[3] Spart. Iul. vi. 3 ; Dio Cass. lxxiii. 17. 1.

[4] Spart. Iul. vi. 4. He also carried the final senatorial decision to Septimius and was killed for his pains (Spart. Iul. viii. 1).

[5] Dio Cass. lxxiii. 17. 1.

[6] Septimius declared a public enemy, Vit. Sev. v. 5 ; Spart. Iul. vi. 8 ; Dio Cass. lxxiii. 16. 1. The bribe, Herod. ii. 11. 7. Spartian (Vit. Iul. iii. 2) says he paid 30,000 instead of 25,000 ; Suidas follows Herodian.

[7] Spart. Iul. vi. 6. Probably this Quintillus is the consul of 177, the same again (so Hirschfeld, *Hermes*, xxiv, p. 160) who was killed by Severus (Dio Cass. lxxvi. 7. 3) ; cf. *CIL.* xv. 7360.

[8] Spart. Iul. vii. 7 ; Vit. Sev. v. 7 ; Herod. ii. 12. 3· Dio Cass. lxxiii. 17. 2.

a battle at the Milvian bridge.[1] Some martial preparations, however, were made, trenches were dug before the city, and circus elephants were requisitioned for war purposes with the intention of striking amazement into the unsophisticated Illyrian. In this they would probably have succeeded. A detachment from the fleet at Misenum was summoned, but, according to Dio, the sailors were as unused to military discipline as the elephants, and as useless.[2] Laetus and Marcia, two of Commodus' murderers, were next sacrificed, presumably to enlist still further the goodwill of the praetorians.[3] Deserted of men the bewildered emperor had recourse to the gods, or at least to the art of magic, and sought to avert by child-sacrifice the doom prophesied by maniac children.[4] As for Tullius Crispinus, entrusted with Julianus' offer to Septimius of half the empire, he not only failed in his object but also lost his life.[5]

Meanwhile, the disgust at the incompetence and cowardice of the emperor, voiced by Quintillus, found still more definite expression in the desertions of his troops in Umbria and in the consequent throwing open of the Apennine passes to Septimius.[6] Julian's counterstroke was to entrust Lollianus Titianus with the arming of a school of gladiators, and to offer a share of empire to Marcus' old general and son-in-law, Claudius Pompeianus. The latter refused the doubtful honour, pleading old age and defective sight ; and, just when the emperor's cup of sorrows seemed full, the praetorians, his last and only hope, went over to his rival.[7] Hereupon the Senate took action. Notice of

[1] Herodian says he dared not leave Rome (ii. 11. 9), and Dio is silent on the point. Our only authorities for a battle are Aurelius Victor (Caes. xix), Orosius (vii. 16), Eutropius (viii. 9), and Eusebius (175). We cannot believe that Dio would have omitted to mention a battle had there been one.

[2] Dio Cass. lxxiii. 16. 3 ; Herod. ii. 11. 9.

[3] Dio Cass. lxxiii. 16. 5 ; Spart. Iul. vi. 2.

[4] Dio Cass. lxxiii. 16. 5 ; Spart. Iul. vii. 10.

[5] Spart. Iul. viii. 1.   [6] Spart. Iul. viii. 4.

[7] It is quite impossible to be sure of the exact chronology of these events. Spartian alone (Vit. Iul. viii. 3) mentions the arming of the gladiators and the offer to Claudius. For the defection of the praetorians cf. Dio Cass. lxxiii. 17. 3 ; Vit. Sev. v. 9. Neither Herodian

the praetorians' defection had been duly given to the consul Silius Messala, who accordingly summoned the fathers to a meeting in the Athenaeum. Here the unhappy Julian was condemned to death and Septimius declared emperor in his stead.[1]

So on the 1st of June perished the luckless emperor, an example ready to hand for all who would preach on the vanity of riches. His character is difficult to estimate, so quickly is he flashed upon the screen of history and so quickly withdrawn. His vacillation, to call it by no harsher name, cannot be denied, yet a firm and consistent policy in the face of so many difficulties might have been looked for in vain from many a man the world has called hero, had he been situated as was Julian. The morbid interest attaching to the last words of a man of note is one which the historiographers of the late empire ever found irresistible. Those of Julian were, so Dio informs us,[2] καὶ τί δεινὸν ἐποίησα; τίνα ἀπέκτεινα;—a pitiful appeal to the assassin, not a convincing one to the historian : the cry of a negative spirit. Circumstanced as Otho had been, he lacked the resolution of that prince, and cannot like him be said to have atoned for the ineffectiveness of his life by his manner of leaving it.

The Senate had made away with an emperor, and their next care was to welcome his successor. Septimius' pose as the avenger of their representative Pertinax clearly counted for something, but it is more than doubtful whether the governor of Pannonia would have exercised a higher claim than a member of their own body, or even than the popular candidate Niger, had it not been for his actual presence in the peninsula.[3]

(ii. 12) nor Spartian (Vit. Iul. viii) mentions it expressly: Spartian merely says 'desertus est ab omnibus' (Iul. viii. 6).

[1] Dio Cass. lxxiii. 17. 3, 4 (he speaks as an eyewitness); Herod. ii. 12. 5, 6; Spart. Iul. viii. 7; Vit. Sev. v. 9. (Spartian here speaks as though the praetorians rather than the Senate authorized the murder of Julianus; while in Vit. Nig. ii. 1 he says 'Iulianum . . . iussu Severi et senatus occisum'—a striking proof of his carelessness.)

[2] lxxiii. 17. 5.

[3] The seeming popularity of Niger with the city mob is somewhat striking. Spartian (Vit. Iul. iv. 7), Herodian (ii. 7. 3), and Dio (lxxiii. 13. 5), however, all attest the fact.

Conveniently forgetting, therefore, that some week or so ago they had declared Septimius a public enemy, an embassy of one hundred senators set out to meet him. Septimius was at Interamna.[1] The reception accorded them was scarcely encouraging, as they were submitted to a preliminary search for concealed arms, a proceeding which the previous attempt on Septimius' life fully justified and for which he could have found precedent, had he so wished, in the similar action of Vespasian and Claudius.[2] The present of ninety aurei apiece and the offer of a place in his triumphal entry into Rome may have been considered by some as a compensation for the indignity.[3] Three other events seem to have happened prior to Septimius' arrival in Rome. One was the mission of L. Fulvius Plautianus to the capital, with orders to secure Niger's sons as hostages for their father's loyalty to the new emperor; another the appointment of Flavius Juvenalis to the praefecture of the praetorians; and the third, the punishment of that body for their murder of Pertinax. This last occurrence was of a somewhat dramatic character. The soldiers were summoned to the Campus Martius, unarmed and in civilian dress; arrived, they were at once surrounded by the Illyrians and harangued by the emperor. Herodian does not fail to give the speech. He would inaugurate his reign by no bloodshed, yet could not pardon so dastardly a crime: the praetorians might therefore consider themselves as exiles whose lives would be safe if, and only if, they advanced no nearer the city than the hundredth milestone. Thus the king-makers left Rome.[4]

Quite clearly, however, a new guard had to be formed. Of the formation of this guard we find the fullest information in the

[1] Vit. Sev. vi. 2; Herod. ii. 12. 6.

[2] Suet. Vesp. xii; Claud. xxxv.

[3] The donative is only mentioned by Spartian (Vit. Sev. vi. 4) and is doubted by Höfner (p. 107), who argues (1) that such a donative was only given to the soldiers and the city mob; (2) that such unnecessary liberality was essentially foreign to the character of Severus. I confess that such *a priori* arguments do not weigh much with me.

[4] Niger's sons, Vit. Sev. vi. 10; Spart. Nig. v. 2. Plautianus: Ceuleneer (p. 48) calls him Flavius Plautianus here by mistake. He is certainly the future minister of Severus. Juvenalis: Vit. Sev. vi. 5; cf. Spart. Vit. Get., ii. 7. He was of course second praefect.

pages of Dio.[1] According to this writer eligibility for admission
into the guard had been previously restricted to Italians,
Spaniards, Macedonians, and Noricans: this special privilege
was now done away with, and any soldier of the empire, no
matter from what province he came, might be advanced to the
position of a praetorian. This circumstance has been pointed to,
together with certain others, as indicative of a clearly marked
tendency towards the 'Barbarisierung' of the Roman army of
the third century, but with very little justification. The spread
of Roman civilization from Rome itself as a centre to the outer-
most provinces was a mere matter of time, and by the close of the
second century there is no reason to suppose even the Spaniard
more Roman than the Syrian, the Macedonian than the Dacian.
According, then, as this civilization spread, so spread the privileges it entailed. In the time of Tiberius the dignity of the
praetorian guard was reserved for Italians alone, and indeed not
for all of them:[2] the ex-legate of Lower Germany, Vitellius,
was the first emperor to admit soldiers from the distant legions
into that *élite* body,[3] and it is only a natural extension of this
very obvious principle that led Septimius to take the step he did.
If the Roman army was barbarized by this measure then the
Roman Empire was barbarized by Caracalla's gift of universal
citizenship.

Septimius' entry into Rome must have been an impressive
spectacle. The emperor advanced on horseback attired as a
general as far as the gates: here, as Vitellius[4] had done before
him, he dismounted, and entered the city on foot and in civilian
dress. At the gates, too, the Senate met and welcomed him,[5]
while the people flocked round him wearing laurel-wreaths on
their heads. The whole town indeed was decorated with laurel
and with flowers, the streets were packed, one man climbing on
another's shoulders the better to see the new emperor and to
hear his voice. Senators mingled freely with the mob.[6] The

---

[1] lxxiv. 2. 4-6.   [2] Tac. *Ann.* iv. 5.
[3] Tac. *Hist.* ii. 92. He raised the number of cohorts from nine to
sixteen.
[4] Tac. *Hist.* ii. 89.   [5] Herod. ii. 14. 2.
[6] Dio Cass. lxxiv. 1. 3-5.

procession went first to the Capitol, where sacrifice was offered :
then to the palace, the soldiers carrying before Septimius the
standards taken from the disgraced and dismissed guard.[1] The
wildest enthusiasm prevailed, nor were dissentient voices raised
in opposition to the general rejoicing; only a few Christians
refused resolutely to illuminate their houses.[2] It was not until
Severus had been in Rome some days that the populace began
to view the presence of the Illyrian soldiery in the capital with
perhaps not ungrounded suspicion.[3]

On the next day Septimius entered the Senate-house attended
by soldiers and friends. He was tactful enough to swear the
oath sworn by all ' good' emperors, as Dio calls them, to
the effect that he would put to death no senator, though he
never considered himself in the least bound by it in theory or in
practice.[4] Indeed, he seems to have made a very specious oration,
in which, as Herodian tells us, he vindicated his position as
Pertinax' avenger, held out the brightest hopes for the future,
professed an energetic anti-*delatores* policy, and promised to take
Marcus Aurelius as a pattern for all his actions.

One of the new emperor's first acts was the funeral and deification of the murdered Pertinax. The first scene was enacted
in the Forum. Upon a platform, ostensibly of stone, but in
reality of wood, was placed a highly ornamented couch, covered
with purple and gold brocade, on which lay a waxen image
of the dead emperor, as though he were not dead but slept ;
the pretence being heightened by the presence of a beautiful
slave, who, with a fan of peacock's feathers, kept the flies from
off the sleeper's face. When all were assembled, the senators

---

[1] Vit. Sev. vii. 1.   The standards were carried ' supinis, non erectis '.

[2] Tert. *Apol.* xxxv. It is hard to fathom the reason for this refusal
except on the hypothesis that early Christian ' obstinatio ' was invariably
' agin the government '.

[3] Dio Cass. lxxiv. 2. 3 ; Herod. ii. 14. 1. Herodian mentions δέος καὶ
ἔκπληξιν at the entry itself, but he clearly antedates this feeling. Spartian
(Vit. Sev. vii. 3) talks of the ' ingressus Severi' as 'odiosus atque terri-
bilis', but from his own words it is clear that he refers rather to the
subsequent lawless behaviour of the soldiers than to the actual entrance.

[4] Dio Cass. lxxiv. 2. 1, 2. Nerva, Trajan, and Hadrian all took a
similar oath. Vit. Sev. vii. 5 ; Herod. ii. 14. 3.

seated in the open, their ladies in the basilicae hard by, there
advanced a chorus of men and boys singing a dirge for Pertinax.
A strange procession followed—lictors, knights, *imagines* of famous
Romans, after which was carried an altar adorned with gold and
ivory and precious stones. When all had filed past Septimius
ascended the rostrum and delivered an encomium on the murdered
emperor, frequently interrupted by the applause or the tears of
the assembled senators. On the conclusion of the speech the
multitude followed the bier to the Campus Martius, whither it
was carried by the priests and the knights, the emperor himself
bringing up the rear of the procession. Here a gorgeous pyre
had been erected, made of gold and ivory, and decorated with
statues ; on it stood the gilded chariot Pertinax had been wont
to drive. Into this chariot were thrown the funeral gifts, and
on it was placed the couch containing the figure. After Septimius and the relatives of Pertinax had kissed this waxen image,
and the senators had taken their seats on benches provided for
them, the consuls applied torches to the pyre, released from
which, as it burned, an eagle flew up to heaven, thereby typi-
fying the addition of yet another deity to the elastic Roman
pantheon.[1] Other marks of honour were the erection of a temple,
and of a golden statue [2] which was set up in the circus, and the
institution of a religious guild and priesthood dedicated to the
service of the dead emperor.[3] Of Septimius' adoption of
the name Pertinax we have already spoken.[4]

The new emperor had entered his capital : it now remained
for him to see that no rival claimed a like entrance, and to crush

----

[1] Such is the account (shortened) of Dio (lxxiv. 4. 1–5). Spartian
barely mentions the funeral (Vit. Sev. vii. 8, xvii. 5) ; cf. Capitol. Pert.
xiv. 10, xv. 1 ; Aur. Vict. Caes. xx. 1. For consecration coins of Pertinax
cf. Eck. vii. 144 ; Cohen, iii, no. 12, etc.

[2] Dio Cass. lxxiv. 4. 1 ; cf. Eck. vii. 144.

[3] Vit. Sev. vii. 8 ; Cap. Pert. xv. 4 ; Spart. Getae, vi. 6. His own son
was the first priest, and the guild was one originally formed in honour
of Marcus Aurelius, and hence called Marcian. By its renaissance as
Helvian Pertinax was associated with the Antonine family, and, as
Septimius was a 'son' of Pertinax, he too became attached to the same
dynasty, a position on which, as we shall see later, he laid much stress.

[4] See above, p. 33.

Eastern and Western sedition ere either gathered strength and overwhelmed him. But before he could turn his eyes abroad he felt it incumbent upon him, to establish in Rome a position which he himself would have been the last to consider secure. The Senate, it is true, was on his side, but there had been too much sitting on the fence for very much sympathy or mutual trust to exist between the emperor and his advisory board. Those who, at the instigation of Julian, had declared Septimius a public enemy could scarcely be considered loyal adherents of dead or living prince. The city mob, too, were, as we have seen, pro-Nigerian in sentiment, nor was their confidence in Septimius increased when they saw Pannonian soldiers issuing from the barracks in place of the tame praetorians to whom they had grown accustomed. Accordingly, during the brief thirty days spent by the emperor in Rome before setting out for the East, measures were taken by him more completely to secure his position.[1] First of all he sought to win the favour of the populace by means of a *congiarium* [2] and a series of costly games.[3] Further, he bettered the city's corn supply in some way,[4] and showed himself an energetic and a stern administrator of justice.[5] Besides these bids for popularity he endeavoured to crush any sympathy that might still be felt for the cause of Julian by a systematic persecution of that luckless prince's known or suspected adherents, together with an abortive attack on his measures.[6] To secure partisans in high places he gave his two daughters by his first wife Marcia in marriage respectively to Aetius and Probus, whom he also appointed consuls, and the latter of whom he would have made city prefect had not

---

[1] Vit. Sev. viii. 8 'intra triginta dies': Herodian (ii. 14. 5) merely says διατρίψας . . . ὀλίγον χρόνον. The month was presumably from *circ.* June 15-July 15.

[2] Eck. vii. 169.   [3] Herod. ii. 14. 5.

[4] Vit. Sev. viii. 5; Eck. vii. 169 'saeculo frugifero': this may, however, merely refer to the good harvest of the year: so Höfner, p. 127. We know, however, that Septimius did reorganize the corn distribution (see below, p. 177).

[5] Vit. Sev. viii. 4 'accusatos a provincialibus iudices probatis rebus graviter punivit'.

[6] Vit. Sev. viii. 3; Aur. Vict. Caes. xx.

that post been refused with the tactful remark that to accept it after becoming son-in-law of an emperor would be a degradation.[1] The post refused by Probus was bestowed upon Domitius Dexter, who thus succeeded Bassus.[2] All was now ready, and before the end of July Septimius set out against his first rival; but the causes and the manner of his going demand a separate chapter for their treatment.

NOTE ON THE POSITIONS OF LEG. I ITAL. AND V MACED. IN 193.

Leg. I Italica was not, as Ceuleneer (p. 37) supposes, at Troesmis; though there may have been a detachment encamped in that city.[3] The legion was at Durostorum during the first century,[4] but occupied Novae from Hadrian's reign.[5] It was therefore certainly at Novae in 193.

The position of V Maced. is more difficult to determine with certainty.

Inscriptions give us two outside dates. *CIL.* iii. 6169 proves that the legion was still at Troesmis in Moesia inferior during the reign of Marcus Aurelius,[6] while *CIL.* iii. 905 shows conclusively that by 195 it was at Potaissa in Dacia. The question then arises: did Septimius move the legion to Dacia after his accession, or was it there at, and indeed before, the time of that event?[7]

---

[1] *Vit. Sev.* viii. 1. It is only natural to suppose that this Probus is the same as the Probus mentioned by Dio (lxxv. 3. 1, etc.) as taking part in the Parthian war.

[2] *Vit. Sev.* viii. 8.

[3] Cf. *CIL.* iii. 6176; Renier, *C. rendus de l'Acad. des Inscr.*, 1865, p. 273.

[4] Ptolem. iii. 10. 10.

[5] *Itin. Ant.*, p. 221; *Anon. Raven.*, pp. 187, 189. Cf. *CIL.* iii, p. 1349; cf. Beuchel, *de legione rom. I Ital.*, Diss. Lipsiae, 1903, pp. 72, 73. Incidentally this writer, and also Van de Weerd, *Trois légions rom. du Bas-Danube* (p. 256), doubt the station at Durostorum—it rests solely on Ptolemy's word.

[6] Van de Weerd, p. 40, also quotes *CIL.* iii. 7505, evidence drawn from which seems to me inconclusive.

[7] We may disregard the contention of Pfitzner (*Gesch. der röm.*

The old view is that Septimius was the author of the change.
It rests on the following arguments:[1]
(1) That no Dacian inscription of the legion exists prior to that
of 195.

(2) That Septimius was, in Schiller's words, 'the second founder
of Dacia' (p. 732); that he gave Potaissa the *ius coloniae*,[2] and
that the stationing of a legion in the town would be a natural
concomitant to that honour.

The answer to (1) takes the form of a *tu quoque*: viz. there is no
epigraphic evidence of the legion in Moesia after Marcus Aurelius'
principate.   The answer to (2) is that the moving of a legion to a
city is on the whole more likely to precede than to accompany that
city's elevation to colonial rank.   But there is a further consideration.   Dacia underwent a tripartite, in place of a dual, division
under Marcus,[3] at which time the erstwhile praetorian[4] *legatus*
was superseded by a consular one.   Now the existence of a consular [5] *legatus* in an imperial province argues the presence there of at
least two legions—were there only one legion the legate would only
be of praetorian rank.[6]   This second legion (the original one was
XIII gem. at Sarmizegethusa) can be none other than leg. V Maced.
transferred from Troesmis to Potaissa by the Emperor Marcus,
doubtless in consequence of the Marcomannian War.   Did our
belief need further confirmation it might be got from an examination of the Marius Maximus inscription.   From this we learn

---

Kaiserleg., pp. 86 and 162) that Trajan shifted the head-quarters of
leg. V Maced. from Troesmis to Potaissa.   No evidence in favour of the
view exists, and it is directly contravened by *CIL.* iii. 6169.

[1] So Mommsen, *CIL.* iii, pp. 160, 172, 999; 'Die röm. Lagerstädte ',
Hermes, vii, p. 323; Desjardins, 'Voy. arch. et géogr. dans la région du
Bas-Danube', *Rev. Arch.*, 1868, xvii, p. 257.   Ceuleneer (p. 37) holds this
view.

[2] See below, p. 196.

[3] Certainly by 168, *CIL.* iii. 1457.

[4] e. g. M. Statius Priscus, *CIL.* vi. 1523, etc., etc.

[5] Cf. Borgh., *Œuvr. comp.* viii, pp. 471 sqq.   In Cap. Pert. iii. 2 Pertinax
is said to have governed four *consular* provinces: i. e. the two Moesias,
Syria, and Dacia.   For inscriptional evidence of consular governors cf.
CIL. iii. 1457 (in 168), 1153, 1415, 1174, etc.

[6] Domaszewski, *Rangordnung des röm. Heeres*, p. 175.   So Jung, *Fasten
der Provinz Dacien*, p. 17, and Filow, *Die Legionen der Provinz Moesia*
(Leipzig, 1906), p. 78.

that that general was 'dux exerciti (*sic*) Mysiaci apud Byzantium',[1] i.e. during the siege of that town from 193 to 196. But it is just some time in these three years that the supporters of the old view suppose Severus to have moved one 'Mysian' legion to Dacia. Can we then believe that in the event of all the Moesian troops' investing Byzantium one legion would be spared for untroubled Dacia, or that in the event of some of the Moesian garrison's remaining in the province a similar step would be taken?

[1] *CIL.* vi. 1450; see below, p. 82.

CHAPTER V

THE WAR AGAINST NIGER

Of the early life of Gaius Pescennius Niger Justus we are singularly ill-informed. With unusual candour, though with characteristic vagueness, his biographer tells us that 'some represent him of a middle class, others of noble family', and gives us only the names of his father, Annius Fuscus, and his mother, Lampridia. From the same source we learn that one of his grandfathers was curator of Aquinum.[1] Dio assures us that he was of equestrian birth, and an examination of his career bears out the statement. Niger was probably older than either[2] of his rivals, and his birth may be set somewhere between the years 135 and 140. That his position in the official world in and before 193 should be only the same as that of the younger imperial aspirants, i. e. that his advancement was slower than theirs, may be taken as an indication of his comparatively lowly birth.[3] He seems to have held the post of *primus pilus*, and certainly was afterwards three times military tribune.[4] He next held some command in Egypt[5] in or about the year 172 : exactly what his position there was is a matter of some un-

---

[1] Spart. Nig. i. 3. For his surname Justus cf. Eck. vii. 153; Cohen, vol. iii, pp. 404, 405, etc.

[2] Dio Cass. lxxiv. 6. 1 ἐξ ἱππέων. I am much indebted in this section to an article by von Premerstein, 'Untersuchungen zur Gesch. des Kaisers Marcus', in *Klio*, vol. xiii, part i, 1913, pp. 97–104, though I cannot altogether agree with all his conclusions.

[3] Herod. ii. 7. 5 τὴν μὲν ἡλικίαν, ἤδη μετρίως προβεβηκώς in 193; cf. Spart. Nig. v. 1 'aetatis provectae cum in imperium invasit'.

[4] Spart. Nig. i. 5 'ordines *diu* duxit': primus pilus (?), iv. 6.

[5] iii. 7, vi. 10, iv. 4. The date of these posts would be 155/60–70. There is no evidence for his having served in the Parthian war of 161–6.

certainty, but the most probable supposition is that he was
praefectus castrorum of the auxiliary troops stationed in that
province.[1]

The next step was probably a financial procuratorship in
Palestine which Niger may have held some time between 175 and
180, and possibly, too, one in Rome itself,[2] where he is said to
have raised the pay of the *consiliarii*.[3]

Niger now left the ranks of the equestrians and entered the
Senate by means of *adlectio inter praetorios*—a method of which
Commodus is said to have made extensive use. The date of
this advancement[4] cannot be stated with any certainty. It was
of course prior to his consulship, which occurred most probably
in 190 and probably after his term of service in the Dacian war
(*circ.* 183), in which he fought in some equestrian office.[5] After

---

[1] The other possible view is that Niger was prefect of leg. II Traiana.
That he held *some* Egyptian post is certain from (1) the statement of
Aur. Vict. Caes. xx. 9 'dux Aegyptum obtinens' (cf. the *ducatus*
mentioned in Spart. Nig. iv. 4, vi. 10). (2) Spart. Nig. vii. 7—an
anecdote about him 'apud Aegyptum' and the 'limitanei' (i. e. frontier
troops). (3) Ibid. xii. 6—an epigram calling him 'Terror Aegyptiaci
. . . militis, . . . Thebaidos socius'. (4) Eutrop. viii. 18 'Nigrum, qui in
Aegypto et Syria rebellant': both Eutropius and Victor put Egypt as
the province from which the revolt started.

As to the choice between *praef. castr.* and *leg. leg. II Traiana*, we can
only say that so far as rank is concerned the posts were almost equal,
both being ducenarian. We know that Niger was concerned with the
Thebaid and the frontier troops while the legion was stationed at
Alexandria. It seems therefore safer to place Niger with the
auxiliaries in the south. It is at least a possible view that he was
ἐπιστράτηγος of the Thebaid. As to the date, von Premerstein believes
Niger's praefecture contemporaneous with the Bucolici troubles (172)
when the legion was away in Pannonia.

[2] Cf. the anecdote in Spart. Nig. vii. 7.   [3] vii. 6.

[4] Cap. Pert. vi. 10 'adlectionibus innumeris'.

[5] Von Premerstein argues in favour of an early consulship (180-3),
and sends him to Dacia as consular legate. For this there seems to me
to be but little evidence. There was fighting in Dacia about the year
183 (Dio Cass. lxxii. 8. 1, 3. 3; Lampr. Com. xiii. 5; Zon. xii. 4:
Commodus then gained his fifth and sixth imperial greetings), and in
that fighting Niger bore a part (Dio Cass. lxxii. 8. 1), but the only
evidence for his consular legateship is an inscription (*CIL.* iii. 7750)
which reads: 'C. P(escenniu)s (Niger?) leg(atus) Aug(usti) pr(o) pr(ae-

his Dacian command Niger was sent to help crush the revolt of
Maternus in Gaul (circ. 187), and here, if tradition speak true,
he made the acquaintance and won the esteem of Septimius.[1]
In 190 the future rivals both held the consulship. The next
year saw Niger appointed to the governorship of Syria, an
honour which he owed, seemingly, to the good offices of
Narcissus, the athlete who strangled Commodus.[2] In this post
he succeeded his own future adherent in the war, Asellius
Aemilianus.[3] It was as Syrian legate some eighteen months
later that Niger heard of the death of Pertinax, and on the
receipt of that news immediately raised the standard of revolt.

The character of Niger as transmitted to us by the pens of
ancient historians forms a strange medley of conflicting statements, and at the risk of some tediousness the matter is worth
looking into, if only as a striking example of the raw material
on which the modern historian has to work. Dio[4] paints him
in neutral colours, finding in him cause neither for blame nor
praise. Herodian[5] gives him a good character, stating that he
had the reputation of being a skilful and a kindly man, and
mentioning his good rule and consequent popularity in Syria;

tore) co(n)s(ularis) Dac(ium) (trium).' The restoration seems to me
a very bold one.

There is, moreover, no reason for believing Niger's command in Gaul
(circ. 188) a consular one. On the other hand, we have Spartian's word
(Vit. Nig. iv. 6) that Severus and Niger were both consuls in the same
year, the latter being set above the former. This puts Niger's consulship
in 190. (The lower Moesian milestone—CIL. iii. 7607—bearing the
name Pescennius Niger belongs almost certainly to the time of
Gordian III. Prosopogr. iii. 19, no. 139.)

[1] Spart. Nig. iii. 3-4. Cf. vi. 7.

[2] Spart. Nig. i. 5; Dio Cass. lxxiii. 13. 5, lxxiv. 6. 1; Herod. ii. 7. 4
Συρίας ἡγεῖτο πάσης, i. e. Syria was not as yet divided; but this cannot be
taken to mean that he was also governor of Palestine. This was a
separate command : besides, we are expressly told by Dio (lxxiii. 14. 3)
that he had three legions under his command. Had he governed Palestine
he would have had five.

[3] Herod. iii. 2. 3; Prosopogr. i. 159, no. 998: see below, p. 80.

[4] lxxiv. 6. 1 οὔτε . . . ἐς τὸ κρεῖττον οὔτε ἐς τὸ χεῖρον ἐπίσημος, ὥστε τινὰ ἢ
πάνυ αὐτὸν ἐπαινεῖν ἢ πάνυ ψέγειν. He curiously realizes Pericles' or
Thucydides' ideal of womanhood; cf. Thuc. ii. 45. 2.

[5] ii. 7. 5.

nevertheless he informs us that Niger's delay in Antioch was due entirely to his insatiable pursuit of the pleasures of that city, and to his over-mastering interest in the shows and festivals wherewith he amused the flighty populace.[1] His conclusion is that Niger paid the penalty for his slackness and procrastination, two faults which marred a character otherwise irreproachable, were he judged as a general or as a private individual.[2] So far we are not involved in any startling contradiction : for them we must look to Spartian. Herodian has found fault with his slackness : Spartian calls him ' in re militari vehemens ', and gives many anecdotes illustrative of his firm and energetic generalship.[3] The other quality of Niger upon which Herodian commented was his ἐπιείκεια : yet Spartian assures us he was ' moribus ferox '.[4] Marcus Aurelius, we are told, gave him credit for gravity of life :[5] if Herodian correctly pictures his life in Antioch we can only marvel at the unseasonableness of Niger's departure from the paths of virtue. But it must not be supposed that Spartian differs in his judgement of Niger's character only from his brother historians : that he is at liberty to do. He unfortunately differs from himself. In spite of the justice with which he credits him,[6] he admits that he was at the same time ' vita fictus ' and ' moribus turpis '.[7] He was ' vini avidus ',[8] yet two anecdotes are told which intimate that he had but little sympathy with his soldiers' desire for liquor : true, these statements are not irreconcilable.[9] Lastly, the account (by his biographer) of his

---

[1] Herod. ii. 8. 9 ἐς τὸ ἀβροδίαιτον ἀνειμένος τοῖς 'Αντιοχεῦσι συνεφραίνετο.

[2] iii. 4. 7.

[3] Spart. Nig. iii. 5, iii. 8, 9 (so in the opinion of Septimius), iv. 1, ' Strenuum '.

[4] Spart. Nig. i. 4.

[5] Spart. Nig. iv. 1 ' vita gravem ': cf. also Chap. XI, where anecdotes of his austerity are given.

[6] Vit. iii. 6.

[7] v. 1. It must be confessed that this is given as Septimius' estimate of him. We can only say that that emperor must have been wofully deluded by Niger when both were in Gaul. Then no praise was high enough for him (iii. 5).

[8] vi. 6.   [9] vii. 7, 8.

attitude to the less reputable pleasures of life awakens suspicion in the most credulous reader.[1] Spartian's conclusion is that he would have made a good emperor; certainly a better one than Septimius.[2] Victor's verdict is short and to the point: 'hominem omnium turpitudinum.'[3]

Ad maiora redeamus. We have already noticed the fact that of the three competitors for empire Niger was the most popular at Rome. We have next to consider what material strength he possessed and what chances he stood in the struggle. Geographically he was at a disadvantage as compared either with Albinus or Severus: that is to say, given the fact that all three struck at one and the same moment,[4] Severus would reach Rome considerably sooner than either of the other two. As regards spheres of influence and popularity we may say roughly that western Europe was for Albinus, central and eastern Europe for Septimius, and Asia pro-Nigerian to a man. This meant that Albinus could count on his three British legions, on what troops could be raised in Gaul, and possibly on the legion in Spain,[5] that Septimius had sixteen or seventeen legions at his back,[6] and that Niger commanded the allegiance of the nine legions of the East.[7]

---

[1] Cf. i. 5 'libidinis effrenatae ad omne genus cupiditatum'; vi. 6 'rei venereae nisi ad creandos liberos prorsus ignarus'.

[2] xii. 3. Two points may be pleaded in defence of Spartian. First, that he is, on his own showing (v. 1), quoting from (? the Memoirs of) Septimius, whose later judgement, no matter what his earlier one was, must have been biased. Secondly, that his more reliable source, Marius Maximus, treated Niger very cursorily (cf. Vopisc. Firm. i. 1), so that Spartian was thrown back on his own very fertile imagination.

[3] Aur. Vict. Ep. xx.

[4] There seems little doubt that both Severus and Niger *intended* to bid for empire at the same time, viz. on the death of Pertinax. So Cap. Alb. i. 1. Spart. Nig. ii. 1 wrongly says that Niger only decided to move on the news of the death of Julianus.

[5] i.e. leg. VII gemina stationed at Leon. Höfner (p. 85) notes that no Gallic or Spanish troops are found on the side of Severus. Novius Rufus, leg. pro pr. Hispaniae Tarraconensis (*CIL.* 2. 4125), was certainly anti-Severian: cf. below, p. 111.

[6] See above, p. 62.

[7] It should be remarked that according to Spartian (Vit. Nig. vi. 6)

From non-Roman sources Niger got many promises and little
help. A 'king of Thebes' befriended him, but his goodwill
was expressed by nothing more useful than the gift of a statue.[1]
Vologeses V of Parthia was doubtless far too preoccupied with
the troubles that were so soon to prove destructive of his own
empire to do more than make a nominal peace with the revolted

Niger held Greece, Thrace, and Macedonia. Our historian, however,
traverses his own statement in his life of Severus (viii. 12), where he says
'miserat (Severus) legionem, quae Graeciam Thraciamque praeciperet,
ne eas Pescennius occuparet, sed iam Byzantium Niger tenebat'. For
Byzantium cf. Dio Cass. lxxiv. 6. 3. The legions loyal to Niger were as
follows:

(1) three in Syria. IV Scyth. at Orima. XVI Flav. at Samosata
(*CIL.* iii. 13609). III Gall. at Phaena (*CIL.* iii. 126).

(2) two in Cappadocia. XII fulm. ? at Melitene (Joseph. *Bell. Iud.*
vii, § 18, edit. Niese, 1894). XV Apol. ? at Valarsapa. It seems to
have been at V. in 185 (*CIL.* iii. 6052).

(3) two in Judaea. VI ferr. X fret. at Aila (= Elath on the Red
Sea). (So *Not. dig.* xxxiv. 30; also Euseb. *Onom.* Αἰλάμ, p. 22.)

(4) one in Arabia. III Cyren. at Bostra (*Not. dig.* xxxvii. 21).

(5) one in Egypt. II Trai. at Alexandria.

Leg. III Cyren. subsequently declared for Albinus (Spart. Sev. xii. 6).
One knows for certain of the pro-Nigerianism of the Egyptian legion
from money struck at Alexandria in honour of Niger (Eck. iv. 81). For
the partisanship of the province as a whole see below, p. 122. It is
highly probable that the African legion, III Aug., fought for Severus.
From now, at least, it has the title 'pia vindex', which title it bore until
the time of Maximinus (*CIL.* viii. 2550, 2552. Cf. 2975). The reference,
however may be merely the service in the subsequent Parthian war: but
see above, p. 62, note.

[1] Spart. Nig. xii. 4. The personality of this monarch is a matter of
much uncertainty. Thebes is, of course, the Egyptian city of that name,
and there is doubtless some connexion between this occurrence and the
fact that Niger's sphere of action as *praef. castr.* was the Thebaid
(Ptolemy, vi. 7. 5, mentions a Thebes in south-west Arabia: for its kings
cf. Dittenberger, *Or. Gr.* i, p. 293). This king may have been the chief
of some nomad barbarian tribe across the border (so Lumbroso, *L'Egitto
al tempo dei Greci e dei Romani,* p. 55, 2nd edit. 1895). Wiedermann
(*Revue égypt.* ii. 346) believes in an independent chief of the Thebaid.
More likely is Milne's view (*Egypt under Roman Rule,* p. 214) that he
was an ἄρχων Θηβῶν (cf. P. M. Meyer, *Heerwesen der Ptolemäer und Römer,*
90, 331), i. e. some sort of civic officer (Ptolemais, the chief city of the
Thebaid, had one, *CIG.* 5000).

Roman governor.[1] The king of Armenia answered Niger's appeals for help by the statement that he would join neither side: and indeed the only assistance that actually arrived was a small force of archers sent by Barsemius of Hatra—a piece of generosity which, as we shall see, cost that monarch dear.[2] The chief centre of Nigerianism was, as we might have expected, Antioch, and it was here that nearly all his coins were minted.[3]

There seems to me absolutely no reason to doubt the truth of Herodian's account of Niger's dilatoriness in Antioch; [4] indeed, we may see in this fact one of the most effective causes of his failure. Had that general begun his march on Rome when Septimius began his, he should have reached the borders of Italy some time during Septimius' thirty days in Rome. With the help of his friend Asellius Aemilianus, proconsul of Asia, he might have won for himself the support of eastern Europe, whose adherence to Severus was one of compulsion rather than of goodwill,[5] and a second Vespasian might have won a third battle of Betriacum with more than nine legions at his back.

This is mere conjecture: the actual first steps in the war were as follows. Convinced of the importance of securing some *pied-à-terre* in Europe, and perhaps with the intention of marching thence upon Italy by the Via Egnatia, Niger sent forward an army to secure Byzantium.[6]

Three things helped him in this move. He held the Taurus passes, and indeed, perhaps with some premonition of what was

---

[1] Herod. iii. 1. 2, ii. 8. 6. Vologeses V reigned from about 190-208. Longpérier, *Rois Parthes Arsacides*, p. 152, etc. There is some uncertainty about the numbering of these monarchs.

[2] Herod. iii. 1. 3.

[3] Eck. vii. 153; Cohen, 'De la numismatique de Pesc. Nig.', *Rev. Num.*, 1868, p. 432, etc.

[4] Höfner does, p. 79. 'Gegenüber den Angaben des Cassius Dio und Spartian brauchen wir kaum darauf aufmerksam zu machen, dass die Erzählung des Herodian bezüglich der Untätigkeit des P. N. keinen Glauben verdient.' Unfortunately he can produce no such 'Angaben' on the part of these writers. Joan. Antioch. *F. H. G.* iv. 586 supports Herodian.

[5] e. g. Vit. Sev. viii. 12.

[6] Herod. iii. 1. 6. Herodian gives as his reason the fact that he wished to prevent Severus crossing thence into Asia.

to come, closed them behind him to guard against pursuit in case
of a reverse.[1] Secondly, as has been mentioned, he could count
on the hearty co-operation of Asellius Aemilianus, the proconsul
of Asia.[2] Thirdly, we read of no attempt at resistance from
Byzantium, and conclude that a voluntary surrender took place,
doubtless thanks to the goodwill of Claudius Attalus, the
governor of Thrace.[3] Advantage of this fact was taken to
secure Perinthus also and the northern coast of the Propontis, and
so to prevent a landing of Septimius' troops.[4]

Meanwhile Septimius himself was not idle. His first care was
to find some counter-move to his rival's advance on Byzantium.
In this he was helped by three men: his brother, Publius
Septimius Geta, was left as governor of the three Daciae in
charge of the middle and lower Danube frontier.[5] Marius

---

[1] Herod. iii. 1. 4.

[2] Dio Cass. lxxiv. 6. 1; Herod. iii. 2. 3; *CIG.* 3211. Aemilianus had
been legatus of Syria by the appointment of Commodus. He seems to
have been an excellent general, but the heartiness of his support has
been doubted, I think unjustly, by many. Dio (lxxiv. 6. 2), while
crediting him with σύνεσις and ἐμπειρία πραγμάτων, depicts him as μεσεύων
καὶ ἐφεδρεύων τοῖς πράγμασιν. Herodian (iii. 2. 3) goes still farther: φασὶ
δέ τινες προδοθέντα τὰ τοῦ Νίγρου πράγματα ὑπὸ Αἰμιλιανοῦ. He suggests
two reasons: (1) jealousy of Niger; (2) the prayers and entreaties of his
children, hostages in Severus' hands in Rome. The mere fact that
Aemilianus was defeated and *killed* seems to me fairly conclusive proof
of his good faith—we should otherwise doubt his σύνεσις and ἐμπειρία.

[3] We learn from Dio (lxxix. 3. 5) that he was subsequently expelled
from the Senate by Severus for help given to Niger in the war. For the
conjecture cf. Schulte, *De imp. Sept. Sev.*, p. 47, note 5; Borghesi, *Œuvr.*
iii. 279. Doubtless Claudius Attalus had influence in Byzantium, though
he had no authority. Byzantium was a free city, and in any case was
technically in Bithynia, not Thrace. Plin. *Ep. ad Trai.* x. 43 (Hardy's
note, p. 145).

[4] Dio Cass. lxxiv. 6. 3; Vit. Sev. viii. 13 (mentions fighting there).
Dio suggests that the attack on Perinthus was a failure, but we know
from what subsequently happened to the town that it was pro-Nigerian.
We see doubtless in these facts the basis of the remark in the life of
Niger (v. 6) to the effect that that general held Greece, Thrace, and
Macedonia: cf. p. 78, note 7.

[5] *CIL.* iii. 905. It seems that this brother's loyalty was not above
suspicion (Vit. Sev. viii. 10; cf. x. 3). Yet all that Spartian's remarks
come to is that Geta was an ambitious man, whose hopes for power were

Maximus was set in command of the Moesian troops, and at their head marched straight on Byzantium from the west,[1] while L. Fabius Cilo supported the latter with a body of soldiers possibly from Galatia.[2] Cilo indeed it was who fought the first

naturally raised when his brother assumed the purple. The second passage suggests that in making Caracalla Caesar (in 196) Septimius had as his object the disillusioning of his brother.

[1] His full name was L. Marius Maximus Perpetuus Aurelianus. Neither Dio, Spartian, nor Herodian mentions his Byzantine campaign, and we know of the fact only from an inscription (*CIL.* vi. 1450) where he is mentioned as 'duci exerciti (*sic*) Mysiaci aput Byzantium'. We come across the name in three connotations : Marius Maximus, the general of Severus; Marius Maximus, the historian; and Marius Maximus, the city prefect under Macrinus (Dio Cass. lxxviii. 14. 2 ; cf. lxxix. 2. 1). Of these the historian is almost certainly not the same as the general. Otherwise, how account for the slovenly and ignorant account of Septimius' wars given by Spartian when we know that Marius was one of Spartian's main sources? It is possible, however, that the general and the city prefect are identical. His *cursus honorum*, as given in various inscriptions (*CIL.* vi. 1450-3, iii. 1178, x. 6567, 6764; *Bull. de Corr. Hell.* x, p. 417, etc.; Höfner, pp. 301, 302, cites six in full), was as follows :

    tribunus laticlavus of leg. III Italica
          ,,   ,,   ,, XXII prim.
    quaestor urbanus
    tribunus plebis candidatus
    (adlectus inter praetorios)
    curator viae Latinae
    legatus leg. I Ital.
    ? Cos. I
    legatus Germ. infer. (between 198-209)
    legatus Aug. pr. pr. Coele-Syriae.
    [? praefectus urbi]
    procos. Asiae
      ,, Africae.

He thus early in life saw service in Upper Germany (leg. XXII prim. was stationed at Mainz) and in Raetia (leg. III It. at Regensburg). Leg. I Ital. was stationed at Novae in Lower Moesia, and its legateship must have been held by Marius in the year 193. He was possibly consul for the first time in 197 (cf. Borghesi, *Œuvr.* v. 465). Ceuleneer (p. 66) says : 'Il dirigea si bien le siège de Byzance que Sévère le nomma consul en 197.' No proof of the truth of this categorical statement exists. His second consulship was in 223 (*CIL.* iii. 14565, vi. 32542, etc.).

[2] *CIL.* vi. 1408-10. There are other inscriptions which mention

action in the war, for, coming into contact with Aemilianus'
troops somewhere west of Byzantium, he suffered a defeat at
their hands.[1] The advance of Marius with the main body seems
to have checked any attempt on the part of Aemilianus towards
further westerly aggression. In fact Niger's general, leaving
a strong force to hold Byzantium, soon afterwards left that city
and crossed over into Asia. For the cause of this move we must
look to Septimius and the main army.

Before he could leave Rome for the East it was obvious that
the emperor must guard against any possible rear attack. Only
two such were at all likely. Niger might put Vespasian's plan
into execution and use Egypt—a country of whose loyalty he
was well assured [2]—as a base whence to starve Rome into
submission.[3] To safeguard himself against such a contingency
Septimius sent a force to hold that country.[4] The other source
of danger was D. Clodius Albinus, governor of Britain. Him
Severus seems to have won over by the offer of the title
'Caesar'; in other words, by making him heir-apparent. In spite
of the existence of Caracalla and Geta, Albinus seems to have

him, but these give his *cursus honorum* (1408, 1409 are both cited *in
extenso* by Höfner, pp. 304, 305, and Ceuleneer, p. 69). He was once
legate of the Syrian legion (XVI Flav. at Samosata), governor in turn
of Narbonensis, Galatia, Bithynia-Pontus, Moesia superior, and Pannonia
superior—this last certainly by 201, perhaps even as early as 198.
Liebenam (pp. 26, 27) notes one of his name who was consul in 193
(Lamp. Comm. xx. 1) and again in 204. We know from the inscriptions
that our Fabius Cilo was a consul at some time. Dio (lxxvii. 4. 2) calls
him the tutor of Caracalla. He was also city prefect (Dig. i. 15. 4, etc.).
It is probably he (Chiloni) to whom Severus and Caracalla wrote in
197 (Cod. Iust. ii. 50. 1). The provenance of Cilo on this occasion is
uncertain, as one cannot tell what post he held at the time. Had he
been legate of Bithynia-Pontus one would have thought he might have
prevented the surrender of Byzantium to Niger. Hence we may perhaps
conclude that he was legate of Galatia at this time. Stout (*Governors of
Moesia*, p. 37) makes him governor of Bithynia *after* this victory and of
Moesia in 195.

[1] Eck. vii. 155; Coh. Pesc. Nig. 23–6 VICTORIA. AVG. NIG.
[2] See below, p. 122.
[3] Tac. *Hist.* iii. 48.
[4] Vit. Sev. viii. 7; Spart. Nig. v. 4; Eck. vii. 171; see above, Chap. IV,
p. 62, note.

considered this in the light of a genuine offer : at least it kept him quiet for more than two years.[1]

Some time early in July, probably, Septimius left Rome at the head of those forces by whose help he had won his way into Italy.[2] That he went by land, and not by sea, we know from the fact that nine miles north of Rome, along the Via Flaminia at Rubra Saxa, a mutiny occurred among the troops.[3] Some of

---

[1] Of the exact position of Albinus we shall treat later; but two questions must be raised at this point : (1) Did Albinus only accept the Caesar title when Septimius offered it, or did he anticipate that offer? (2) When was the offer made?

1. According to Spart. Nig. ii. 1 and Cap. Alb. i. 1 Albinus rebelled contemporaneously with Severus and Niger. If this were so we cannot imagine that Septimius offered to make him Caesar, for he would already have arrogated to himself that title. At the same time there are many passages which tell us expressly that Septimius really did send this offer (Dio Cass. lxxii. 15. 2; Cap. Alb. x. 3; Herod. ii. 15. 3; cf. iii. 5. 2). Another small point seems to me to lend support to this view. In the life of Severus (x. 1) we read how Albinus 'post bellum civile Nigri (i. e. in 196) . . . rebellavit in Gallia'. Had he raised the standard of revolt in 193 we should have expected the imperfect here, not the perfect — i.e. 'was in a state of revolt.' We must conclude that Albinus was allowed by Septimius to call himself Caesar: Heraclitus was the messenger sent (Vit. Sev. vi. 10; Spart. Nig. v. 2 reading *Britanniam* for *Bithyniam*; so Hübner). Hence the coins of 194 (Eck. vii. 162) calling Albinus Caesar were of constitutional minting. It was only when the Caesar styled himself Augustus that he committed an illegality (so Herod. iii. 5. 2, βασιλικώτερον ἐντρυφῶντα τῷ τοῦ Καίσαρος ὀνόματι). Coins with 'Augustus' on date from 196 (Eck. vii. 162, 163; Coh. iii. Alb. nos. 40-6).

2. The only two definite statements as to the time of the sending of Heraclitus are Dio Cassius (lxxii. 15. 2), who puts the occurrence prior to Severus' leaving Pannonia, and Herodian (ii. 15. 3), who as clearly states it to have happened during the emperor's thirty days in Rome. We have already seen reason to date Albinus' rebellion as in 196: how then should Septimius know of any threatenings of a rebellion when in Pannonia in April 193? We should therefore conclude that Severus did not make the offer to Albinus until at least on the way to Rome, if not when actually in Rome.

[2] He seems to have been still in Rome on June 27: Cod. Iust. iii. 28. 1.

[3] Vit. Sev. viii. 9 (cf. Froehner, *Les médaillons de l'empire romain*, p. 154, who cites a medallion which represents Septimius haranguing the troops and bears the legend IMP. III. FIDEI MILIT.).

the emperor's forces, however, seem to have gone by sea from Brundisium to Dyrrhachium, whence they would proceed towards Perinthus and Byzantium by the Via Egnatia.[1] Whether these troops joined Marius Maximus outside Byzantium or waited for the main body under Septimius we do not know. The emperor himself knew better than to waste time in laying siege to so well-fortified a city as Byzantium;[2] he accordingly left Marius to carry on the investment and himself crossed over to Cyzicus. Meanwhile Aemilianus had left Byzantium on the somewhat late arrival of Niger, and had crossed over once more into Asia, possibly also to Cyzicus, though he must have arrived there some little time before Septimius.[3] We are not told whether any attempt was made by Aemilianus to prevent the landing of the Severan troops, though several skirmishes seem to have taken place,[4] in one of which Aemilianus lost his life.[5] The result of this defeat was instant flight on the part of the Nigerians,[6] and a *pied-à-terre* in Asia for Severus: also the adhesion to his side of several Asiatic cities, among whom the old Greek spirit of στάσις was by no means a dead letter.[7] The most important instances of this were Nicaea, which joined Niger, and Nicomedia, which espoused the cause of Severus. Another

---

[1] According to Herodian (ii. 15. 6, iii. 2. 1) the army went by land; on the other hand, he clearly states that all the triremes in Italy (i. e. the fleets of Ravenna and Misenum) were requisitioned to transport a body of legionaries.

[2] Herodian (iii. 1. 6) comments on its strength.

[3] We have no express statement that Aemilianus ever was in Byzantium, but from the fact that he defeated Cilo, as also from the remark of Herodian (iii. 2. 2) μαθὼν ἐπιόντα τὸν τοῦ Σεουήρου στρατὸν . . . καὶ αὐτὸς ἐτράπετο, he must have been at least on the European side of the Bosphorus.

[4] So Herodian (iii. 2. 2); Dio (lxxiv. 6. 4) mentions only the one battle.

[5] Dio Cass. lxxiv. 6. 4; Herod. iii. 3. 2. 2; Vit. Sev. viii. 16; Spart. Nig. v. 7. Some fairly important engagement must have taken place near the river Aesepus, for there exists a coin (*Mionn. supp.* 365, B. M. 247) figuring Septimius, a trophy, and the river god.

[6] Herod. iii. 2 6. Some fled over the Taurus passes.

[7] Zos. i. 8. 1 πόλεις διέστησαν: Herodian (iii. 2. 7, 8) moralizes on the point. He adds: Νικαεῖς δὲ τῷ πρὸς Νικομηδέας μίσει τἀναντία (i. e. Nigerianism) ἐφρόνουν. For the mutual hatred of these two cities and an attempt to reconcile them cf. Dio Chrys. *Or.* xxxvii.

and a still more important effect of the defeat of Aemilianus
was the retirement of Niger from Byzantium into Asia. After
his victory at Cyzicus, Severus moved eastwards through Mysia
into Bithynia. The meagreness of our sources, and the rather
cursory treatment of the war by the best of them, makes the
strategy difficult, if not impossible, to understand. Niger presumably crossed to Chalcedon and marched south, his objective
being Nicaea. To do this he must have passed Nicomedia, but
the Severan party seem to have made no attempt to bar his
progress. Meanwhile we may suppose Septimius' army to have
advanced through Miletopolis to Prusa. Thence it probably struck
due north for Cios. The two armies thus lay at Nicaea and Cios
respectively, and from those towns they advanced to meet one
another, the route lying along the shores of Lake Ascanius. It
is impossible to say with certainty whether the battle took place
on the north or the south side of the lake. Dio's account is as
follows : [1] the scene of the action was a plain.[2]　Severus' troops
were under the command of Tiberius Claudius Candidus,[3] the

---

[1] Dio (lxxiv. 6. 4–6) gives the fullest account of this battle. He
mentions the actual presence of Niger, in which he receives some slight
support from Spartian (Vit. Sev. viii. 17). Herodian does not mention
Niger in this connexion, and indeed treats this second battle of the war
rather as a piece of inter-urban στάσις (iii. 2. 10).

[2] The most obvious plain is that which surrounds the town itself and
stretches north-westward almost as far as the village of Bojalydscha.
From the opportune appearance of Niger we should suspect the battle
to have been fought at no great distance from Nicaea, and if we suppose
the neighbourhood of Tschakyrdscha to have been the exact spot this
requisite is fulfilled. Everything in this instance, however, is a matter
merely of conjecture, and to me it seems more probable that the battle
took place on the south side of the lake—possibly in the neighbourhood
of Islam Sölös. The only two reasons for this guess are : (1) the
fact that the road leading from Cios to Nicaea south of the lake is
shorter than that running north of it ; (2) that the Sary Mesche Dagh
would answer to the hill mentioned by Dio better than the smaller
slopes on the north.

[3] The most important inscription concerning Candidus is *CIL.* ii. 4114.
He was (omitting his earlier and less important offices) *legatus* of
Hispania citerior, where he was entrusted with the task of stamping out
the remnants of Albinus' revolt. He served also in the Parthian war,
and was *consul suffectus* some time during Septimius' reign.

emperor himself being presumably not present. They avoided the plain, taking up a position on the slopes of a hill. The Nigerians, forced to occupy the lower ground, sought to create a diversion by manning some boats, putting off from shore, and raining arrows upon the Severans as they advanced down the slope. The sudden appearance of Niger himself caused a reaction, and things would have gone ill with the Severan army had not Candidus succeeded in rallying his scattered forces and, eventually, in driving the Nigerians in rout from the field of battle. So ended the second important engagement of the war. The emperor had again been successful and took the title Imperator for the third time.[1] The defeat must have been a crushing one for Niger, for it caused him to fall back upon his last line of defence, the Taurus passes. Leaving a body of troops to hold the Cilician Gates which lead from Cappadocia into Cilicia, the defeated general himself retired to Antioch, where he found himself obliged to deal with enemies in his own province. As in Asia, so here, the spirit of στάσις had been at work : out of hatred of the people of Antioch those of Laodicea had espoused the cause of the Illyrian, while in Phoenicia a similar motive had thrown the inhabitants of Tyre and Berytus into the arms respectively of Septimius and Niger.[2] They were recalled by Niger to their allegiance in no lenient manner.

Meanwhile Septimius hastened after his fugitive rival. Passing through Dorylaeum, Pessinus, Abrostola, and Tyana the army arrived at the Cilician Gates,[3] a pass difficult enough to negotiate

---

[1] Ceuleneer, p. 71, thinks that this title was adopted after the Cyzicus victory. We have already seen (p. 32) that the second, third, and fourth imperial salutations belong to the war against Niger, and that the most probable supposition is that the three refer respectively to the victories of Cyzicus (ii), Nicaea (iii), and Issus (iv).

[2] Herod. iii. 3. 3. Sidon seems to have struck Nigerian coins : Eckhel, however (vii. 159), doubts their genuineness. There exist also Tyrian coins of Niger (De Boze, *Essai sur les médailles de P. N. et sur quelques singularités de sa vie.* Acad. des Inscript. Anc., coll. xxiv, p. 109).

[3] Herodian (iii. 3. 1) says he traversed Bithynia and Galatia and entered Cappadocia. Dio gives no indication of his route. Ceuleneer (p. 75) suggests an alternative route via Ancyra and Tavium. The arguments in support of such a view are : (1) a Severan coin of Tavium

even without the presence of a hostile force. The Nigerians were posted on the heights overlooking the pass, while others had constructed, and were now holding, some kind of earthwork fortification in the pass itself. The Severan army, under the command of Anullinus and Valerianus,[1] advanced to the attack. The Nigerians rained down stones upon them from their superior position, and succeeded in holding them at bay for some considerable time. At last, however, Valerianus, taking the cavalry with him, made a détour through some high wooded ground on one side of the pass and soon appeared in the rear of the Nigerians, Anullinus the while holding his ground in the northern entrance of the pass. This decided the affair. Those of Niger's army who could not cut their way through Valerianus' cavalry, or fly over the mountains, were easily surrounded and overcome. The pass was forced, and Cilicia and the road to Antioch lay open to the victor.[2]

---

of the year 193; (2) the fact that Herodian says that Severus went through Galatia. But (1) many cities, through which Severus certainly did not pass, minted such coins (cf. Coh. iv, p. 83, etc.); (2) Herodian's geography is notoriously unreliable. Besides, Pessinus is in Galatia. The anecdote related by Dio (lxxv. 15. 4, lxxvi. 4. 2) about Severus in Tyana does not seem to me to afford any proof of his having passed through that city on this occasion (cf. Ceuleneer, p. 75, note 1). It is told with reference to Plautianus, whom we have no reason to suppose was not at the time in Rome keeping a watch on Niger's family (Vit. Sev. vi. 10: see above, p. 66). If an alternative route may be suggested the most probable seems to me that of the Bagdad railway, viz. via Dorylaeum, Acroenus, Philomelium, Iconium, Cybistra. This, however, is slightly longer and does not touch Galatia.

[1] (1) P. Cornelius Anullinus, city prefect, consul, proconsul of Africa and Baetica, and legate of Syria (perhaps during Septimius' Parthian war). We do not know the year (it was prior to 193) in which he was *consul suffectus*, but his second (ordinary) consulship was in 199 (*CIL.* xiii. 6689). (2) Of Valerianus we know nothing. Capitolinus (Vit. Pert. xii. 7) mentions a friend of Pertinax who bore this name, but there is no reason for identifying him with Septimius' general.

[2] It may be well at this point to attempt to justify this account by an appeal to the sources. An account of the war is contained in:

    1. Spart. Vit. Nig. v. 7, 8.

    2. ,,   ,, Sev. viii. 15—ix. 1.

    3. Herod. iii. 2. 1—iii. 4. 9.

The news of the forcing of the Cilician Gates roused Niger from his punitive measures against the rebellious Syrians to a more effective strategy. Leaving Antioch he marched north with all haste, and met the victorious Severan army at Issus.

4. Dio Cass. lxxiv. 6. 1—lxxiv. 8. 3.

1. mentions only the defeat of Aemilianus ; an offer thereafter of safe exile from Septimius to Niger if the latter would lay down his arms ; a second defeat 'apud Cyzicum' where Niger flies 'circa paludem '— a clear reference to the battle of Nicaea and the lake of Ascanius—and the death of Niger.

2. gives us : the same offer (only made before the defeat of Aemilianus); ' Aemilianus victus apud Hellespontum '; a defeat of Niger by Severus' generals (i.e. Nicaea); a battle at Cyzicus in which Niger is killed.

Both these are obviously hopeless.

3. and 4. agree in main outline. There are three battles : Cyzicus, Nicaea, Issus. In their account of the first two there is practically no divergence. Herodian (as has been mentioned) speaks of μάχαι at Cyzicus ; Dio of only one conflict. Dio clearly intimates that Niger was present at Nicaea ; Herodian does not. In this latter point Dio gets some slight support, if he needs it, from Spartian (Vit. Sev. viii. 17 ' fusae sunt item copiae . . . Nigri '). From the arrival of Severus' army at the Cilician Gates, however, the two accounts are difficult to reconcile. Herodian gives : Niger's retirement to Antioch ; Septimius' army's advance into Cappadocia and siege of the ἔρυμα in the pass ; a violent rainstorm which washes away the ἔρυμα ; the army's consequent forcing of the pass ; the hasty arrival of Niger ; and his defeat in the plain of Issus.

Dio has : a battle ἐν Ἰσσῷ πρὸς ταῖς καλουμέναις πύλαις at which Niger is present in person ; the holding of the gates ; the détour of Valerianus ; sudden thunder, lightning, and tempest in the face of Niger's army which hinders and demoralizes them ; their flight ; the attack delivered on the routed army by Valerianus, who has by then completed his détour, and the consequent victory of Severus' two generals. Now in this last account one thing at least is clear. It is geographically impossible to speak of a battle of Issus at the Cilician Gates, for the two places are eighty miles apart as the crow flies. Dio has therefore confused two engagements : one at the Cilician Gates, the other at Issus. These two Herodian keeps separate—rightly. The second question is : was the forcing of the pass due to (a) rain which washed away the fortification (Herodian) ; or to (b) rain + the turning movement of Valerianus ? Now (1) rain washing down fortifications is a tall story, (2) a flanking movement would in itself be decisive. (3) Rain in the face of an army fighting on the plain (i.e. Issus) is a natural phenomenon

There, where, more than five hundred years before, the forces of the West had met and defeated those of the East, the Syrian general underwent his final reverse. We know no details of the battle save the fact that a violent rainstorm which beat in the faces of the Nigerians was no small cause of their defeat. The slaughter was enormous, and the streams ran with blood,[1] while many were driven into the sea and perished in the waves. Those who escaped seem to have counted little on the possible lenience of the victor, and preferred to take refuge with the Adiabeni or the Parthians rather than to fall into his hands. Their presence in the East, if we can believe Herodian on the point,[2] gave Septimius considerably more trouble than he would otherwise have had with his subsequent Eastern campaigns, owing to the fact that they were able not only to reinforce, but (a much more important matter) to train these peoples in the usages of Roman warfare.

Niger himself realized that the end had come. Mounting a swift horse, he rode full speed for Antioch, where he found the citizens in a state of utter consternation, and the city full of lamentation, the women weeping for sons, brothers, or lovers killed in the last battle. Feeling no doubt unsafe in Antioch he fled farther East and succeeded in reaching the Euphrates; but he was not destined to cross that river. Septimius had entered Antioch and sent a party in pursuit of the fugitive. On the banks of the Euphrates they found him, beheaded him, and dispatched the head to Septimius, who in turn sent it on to Byzantium, to be at once a proof of the success that had

and often no small cause of defeat : one remembers the Lancastrians at Towton. Probably therefore Valerianus decided the engagement in the pass, while the weather was largely responsible for the result at Issus.

The Cilician Gates are the modern Gülek Boghas, the summit of the pass which the railway traverses at the height of nearly 1,200 metres. By this way had advanced Alexander the Great, and by this way were to march the soldiers of the First Crusade.

[1] Herod. iii. 4. 5 : Dio Cassius (lxxiv. 8. 1) puts the number of slain at 20,000 ; but ancient historians are notoriously inaccurate in such statements (cf. Delbrück, *Kriegskunst*, 2nd edit., vol. i, pp. 10 sqq.). Half this number would be a wild exaggeration when we remember that Niger's whole force could not have numbered more than 40,000 or 50,000 at the outside.

[2] Herod. iii. 4. 8.

crowned his arms, and an example of the fate in store for those
temerarious enough to defy his sovereignty.[1]

We have now reached the late autumn or early winter of the
year 194.[2] One of the emperor's rivals was dead, the other
scarcely as yet considered dangerous, but the empire was not
yet won, nor could there be any question of Septimius' immediate return to Rome. Not only did Byzantium still offer a
stubborn resistance : there remained also the Eastern supporters
of Niger to punish, besides possible wars of aggression or
frontier defence to be undertaken in the unsettled hinterland.
The emperor's vengeance fell upon two classes of people—those
at home who showed ill will to his cause, and those who had
actually opposed his arms in Asia. Those at home resolve
themselves into the Senate, and to this body he seems to have
shown an unusual leniency. No senator was killed, though
many suffered banishment and the loss of all their property.
By this method, as well as that of fining individuals and cities
to the tune of three times the sums of money they had lent
Niger, Septimius gained no small store of wealth.[3] Dio [4]
preserves for us an anecdote of one Cassius Clemens who boldly
pointed out to the emperor that for himself his one care had
been to be rid of the usurper Julianus, and that his being
found on Niger's side was a mere matter of chance, inasmuch
as he had no personal knowledge either of Niger or Septimius,

[1] It is Dio (lxxiv. 8. 3) who says that Niger was killed by the Euphrates.
Herodian (iii. 4. 6) and Ammianus Marcellinus (xxvi. 8. 15) tell us that
he perished in a suburb of Antioch. Spartian (Vit. Nig. vi. 1) says his
head was sent to Rome, not Antioch, but both Dio and Herodian are
against him. He is clearly confusing the somewhat similar ends of
Niger and Albinus. The head of the latter was sent to Rome.

[2] The second, third, and fourth imperial salutations all belong to this
year (Eck. vii. 170, etc.).

[3] Dio Cass. lxxiv. 8. 5. He it is who tells us that Septimius put no
senator to death, and as he himself was one of them we may trust him
for knowing the truth of the matter. Spartian contradicts himself on
this point. In his life of Severus (ix. 3) he says only one senator was
punished : three sections farther down he tells us that Severus punished
many besides the senatorial order, while in Vit. Nig. vi. 4 he assures us
that the emperor ' innumeros senatores interemit '.

[4] lxxiv. 9. 1–4.

nor yet of their qualifications for the governance of the empire. The emperor acknowledged and rewarded this temerity by the remission of one half of Clemens' property : the other half was duly confiscated.

In his treatment of the pro-Nigerian cities Severus does not seem to have shown excessive rancour. The first to suffer was Antioch, a city against which he had long nursed a spite on account of the jokes levelled by its inhabitants at him during his previous sojourn in Syria.[1] Not only was it taken and sacked : it was also deposed from its position as capital of Syria and made subservient to Laodicea, which now received the title of Metropolis.[2] The Samaritan city of Neapolis—the biblical Sichem—was another sufferer for its adhesion to Niger ; the hatred of the Samaritans for the Jews is reason enough for the former's support of the Eastern pretender, whose hatred of the latter race was notorious and ineradicable.[3] But besides punishing enemies Septimius was careful to reward friends. We have already seen how that Laodicea was honoured by its elevation to the rank of capital of Syria, and may add that it now received the *ius Italicum*.[4] A similar right was conferred on Tyre, and both cities assumed the title *Septimia*.[5] The evidence of coins and the *Digest* goes to show that many towns became ' Septimian ' colonies and received the *ius Italicum* or the right to style themselves metropolis about this time,[6] while

[1] Vit. Sev. ix. 4.

[2] Herod. iii. vi. 9 ; so too Joh. Mal., p. 293 ; cf. *CIG.* 4472. For coins of Niger struck by Antioch see Eck. iii. 290 ; Antioch as metropolis, Eck. iii. 279 ; Laodicea as metropolis, Eck. iii. 317, 318.

[3] Destruction of Sichem, Vit. Sev. ix. 5. Hatred of Niger for the Jews, Spart. Nig. vii. 9. In spite of this fact some cities in Palestine seem to have espoused the cause of Niger (Vit. Sev. xiv. 6—unless, as is quite probable, this is merely an echo of ix. 5, and itself refers to Sichem), and there exist Nigerian coins of Jerusalem (Eck. vii. 157) ; but see below, p. 206 note 6.

[4] *Dig.* l. 15. 1, 3 ; Eck. iii. 319.

[5] Eck. iii. 387 ; *Dig.* l. 15. 1. Tyre also styled itself Metropolis.

[6] e. g. Philippopolis in Thrace—metropolis (Eck. ii. 44) ; Heliopolis— ius Italicum (*Dig.* l. 15. 1, 2—per belli civilis occasionem) ; Eleutheropolis, Diospolis, and Sebaste— colonies (Eck. iii. 448, ibid. 432, ibid. 441 ; and *Dig.* l. 45. 1, 7).

others attested their joy by the celebration of games in the emperor's honour.[1]

Meanwhile Severus wasted no time. Early in the spring of the year 195 he left Syria and marched at the head of his troops to the Euphrates. Crossing this river, perhaps at Serrhae, he struck boldly into the Mesopontine desert. The weather was intensely hot, and the troops suffered terribly alike from it as from the want of water,[2] but at last his objective, Nisibis, was reached. During the war with Niger three Mesopotamian peoples had seized what they considered a favourable opportunity to enlarge their territories at the expense of Roman dependencies or vassals. These were the Adiabeni, the Osrhoeni, and the Scenite Arabs.[3] The first two peoples had laid siege to Nisibis, and had been repulsed by a force dispatched by Septimius in the course of the Civil War. On the news of Niger's death, they had sent an embassy, in which they explained that their action against Nisibis had been due entirely to a desire to punish a city which they knew to be favourably disposed towards Severus' rival. As, however, they showed no inclination to relinquish their recent acquisitions, and raised objections to the presence of a Roman force in their countries, the emperor had realized the hollowness of their professions and had declared war on them. Much the same had happened with regard to the Scenite Arabs : they too had sent an embassy making demands so preposterous that Septimius refused to hear them. A second deputation had proffered more

---

[1] e. g. ἐπινεικία, coin of Tarsus, doubtless in reference to the battle of Issus (Eck. iii. 79); Σεουηρεία, Caesarea in Cappadocia, Nicaea, and Nicomedia, Sardis, Perinthus, Ancyra, etc. (Eck. iv. 453).

[2] Dio Cass. lxxv. 2. 2.

[3] Dio Cass. lxxv. 1. 2 : Dio merely says Arabians; from a Syrian inscription (*CIL.* iii. 128) and from Zosimus (i. 8. 2) we learn that they were the Scenite Arabs—those called Arabs simply by Xenophon (*Anab.* i. 5. 1). Their land lay towards the east of Mesopotamia (cf. Strabo, 748; Plin. *H. N.* v. 21; Ptolem. vi. 7. 21), and they are probably the same people as are referred to as Shasu in Egyptian documents (so Maspero, *De Carchemis oppidi situ,* 28). Later they were not infrequently confused with the Saracens (e. g. by Ammianus, xxii. 15. 2; cf. xiv. 4. 3; Lactantius, *de Orig. Error.* ii. 13, even calls Palestine Arabian).

reasonable requests, but as the Arab chiefs had been above
visiting the emperor in person, the latter had been offended
and had seized upon that fact as sufficient excuse for the
declaration of war.[1] On his arrival in Nisibis, which city he
rewarded for its faithfulness by raising it to the dignity of
a colony and by putting it under the administrative care of
a Roman knight,[2] the war commenced. Severus himself took
no part in it, remaining all the time in Nisibis itself, and
entrusting the conduct of the campaign to Candidus, Lateranus,[3]
Laetus,[4] Anullinus, and Probus.[5] The war opened with the
dispatch of Candidus, Lateranus, and Laetus in charge of troops
whose sole object seems to have been the laying waste of the
country. They do not appear to have met with any great
success, and the threat of the Scythians [6] to join forces with
the enemy—a threat which only atmospheric phenomena of the
gravest import prevented that people from putting into execution—aroused the emperor to the realization of the necessity for
a more systematic strategy. Some time, therefore, in the late
summer of 195, Laetus, Anullinus, and Probus devastated the
enemy's country in three divisions, and finally captured the
chief town Arche.[7]

---

[1] This I take to be the meaning of the curt notice in Dio, lxxv. 1. 4.

[2] Col. Septimia, Eck. vii. 517 ; Dio Cass. lxxv. iii. 2.

[3] T. Sextius Lateranus: mentioned as a friend of Severus by Aur.
Vict. Epit. xx: he was consul in 197 (CIL. vi. 32526, xiii. 1754, 7427 a).

[4] This is probably the same Laetus of whose death we shall hear in the
following Parthian war (Dio Cass. lxxv. 10. 3; Vit. Sev. xiv. 6; Herod.
iii. 7. 4; Zon. xii. 9). He is probably not the same as the Laetus who
took part in the battle of Lyon (see below, pp. 108-9 and 175 note 2).

[5] This general is not mentioned elsewhere, but we may conclude with
comparative safety that he is identical with Septimius' son-in-law of the
same name (Vit. Sev. viii. 1).

[6] These 'Scythians' (Dio Cass. lxxv. 3. 1) may be the Alani whom we
know to have appeared on the Cappadocian frontier as early as 135 (Dio
Cass. lxix. 15. 1; Moses Chor. ii. 50). For the vague use of the term
'Scythian' for almost any Eastern people, see Minns, Scythians and
Greeks (Cambr., 1913), passim, and especially pp. 98-100. Cf. below,
p. 118.

[7] Dio Cass. lxxv. 3. 2. Nothing really is known about this town,
though some identifications have been hazarded, e. g. with Hatra. This,

This settled the campaign, and by the winter of the year Septimius was ready to return to Europe. In spite of the three more imperial salutations[1] we may doubt whether this war was really the success Septimius would have people believe. Dio[2] is loud in his denunciations of the emperor as involving Rome in a series of Eastern wars as unnecessary in origin as they were inconclusive in effect, and does not hesitate to attribute this campaign to his inordinate ambition and love of glory.[3] We must, I think, keep the two considerations separate. The return of Septimius to the East barely three years later certainly shows the unsatisfactory character of the conclusion arrived at by the war. At the same time Severus, as we shall see later, had a definite policy of Eastern expansion. He cannot fail to have known that the Parthian empire itself was tottering to its fall, and must have realized that now, if ever, was the time to establish a definite frontier such as the Tigris. Is it likely, too, that so level-headed a man would leave the most important city in Eastern Europe in revolt behind him, not to mention the clouds of rebellion visibly gathering on the Western horizon, had he been actuated merely by motives of personal aggrandizement?[4] Whatever may have been the real result of the war we find the emperor quite early in 195 assuming the title of conqueror, and on his coins we now for the first time read Parthicus Arabicus, Parthicus Adiabenicus,

at least, is unlikely when we consider the trouble Septimius afterwards had with that city. Might it possibly be the same as Asicha, on the Euphrates, not far from Zaitha?

[1] Imp. V, VI, and VII all seem to belong to the ,year 195, and may refer to the three peoples over whom he triumphed. Eck. vii. 172–4.

[2] lxxv. 3. 3.

[3] lxxv. 1. 1.

[4] We are indebted for our knowledge of this war almost entirely to Dio (lxxv. 1. 1–3. 3), whose meagre and unsatisfactory account I have reproduced. Herodian knows nothing of it. Spartian (Vit. Sev. ix. 7–11) mentions it and keeps it distinct from the subsequent Parthian war, though he calls the vanquished 'Parthi'. Georgos Syncellus (p. 671) knows of a 'Persian' war which took place *before* the war with Albinus. Otherwise all our secondary sources confuse this war with the later one, e. g. Eutropius (viii. 18), Orosius (vii. 17), Aur. Vict. (Caes. xx), etc. I take all references to Abgarus to refer to the later war.

a title familiar to all who have seen the Arch of Severus in the Forum at Rome.[1]

Whether or not Septimius would have returned to Rome by way of Byzantium is impossible to say. Had this been his intention, however, it must have been dissipated by the news he received shortly after leaving Nisibis some time about June of the year 196. Byzantium had fallen. For nearly three years, that is to say from about autumn 193 until the summer of 196, it had undergone the closest investment.[2] The beleaguered garrison had received no small help from fugitive Nigerians who had somehow forced an entrance,[3] and the defence seems to have been carried on in a most spirited fashion. Especially noteworthy seems to have been the skill and energy of the engineer Priscus,

---

[1] This title is first found with Imp. V coins—i. e. rather early in the year 195 (Eck. vii. 172). Some uncertainty attaches to this subject owing to the remark of Spartian to the effect that Septimius refused the title Parthicus to avoid offending the Parthians (Vit. Sev. ix. 11). Finding the above-quoted title on coins and inscriptions many have endeavoured to avoid what they imagine to be a contradiction. Bayer, for instance (*Historia Oshr.*, p. 165), considers that he took the title in consequence of his victory over Abgarus, king of the Oshroeni. As Abgarus was not the Parthian king (Aurelius Victor and Spartian call him ' Persarum rex '), I do not see how this solution helps matters. It is also more than probable that Abgarus does not figure at all until the second war. Eckhel (vii. 172) suggests that the Parthians sent help to the Arabians and Adiabeni. All such suppositions are quite unnecessary. Severus did *not* adopt the title Parthicus: what he called himself was in effect victor of the Arabs and Adiabeni who dwell on the borders of, or who are the vassals of, Parthia. The cases in which the title Parthicus is found alone fall into two classes. First, such coins and inscriptions as date from 198 or 199, and therefore belong to the second war—for Spartian's remark is, after all, only made of the first war (e. g. Eck. vii. 177. The more usual title is Parth. Max.). Second, such rare cases as have escaped the eye of authority (e. g. *CIL.* ix. 2444). As for the coin of 196 with the legend PART. MAX. we can only, with Schiller (ii. 712, note 5), suppose that it was minted before the refusal of the title was known of. Philatelists will recall several such occurrences in the case of stamp issues; see above, p. 33.

[2] Dio (lxxiv. 12. 1) says ἐπὶ ὅλον τριετῆ χρόνον, but we cannot set the commencement of the siege before (?) August, 193; see below, p. 103.

[3] Herod. iii. 6. 9.

to whom, indeed, the prolongation of the resistance was largely
due. On the subsequent fall of the city he received the pardon,
and entered into the service, of the victorious Septimius, and we
shall meet him again doing as good service for that emperor
at the siege of Hatra as ever he had done against him from
the walls of Byzantium.[1] Of those in command, and of their
object in holding out now that they knew of Niger's death,
we are told nothing. Dio[2] gives a long and detailed account
of the siege. He dilates upon the strength of the city's walls, the
natural advantages of its site, the number and diverse character
of its ships, and does not omit those sensational incidents without
which any account of a siege would be incomplete. We have
the divers who cut the anchor ropes of the enemy vessels; the
patriotic females who sacrificed their hair for manufacture into
the cords of engines; the statues, stone or bronze, fragmentary
or entire, which, in lieu of more commonplace ammunition,
those engines hurled, and finally the efforts of the starving
citizens to obtain nourishment from the consumption of soaked
leather, and even of each other. It was indeed owing to famine
that the city fell.[3] The punishment meted out by the emperor
was severe in the extreme. The city lost all political rights,
was made subject to tribute, and placed in an inferior position
to its neighbour Perinthus, much as Antioch had been to
Laodicea. Its fortifications were destroyed, its public buildings
demolished, and its citizens deprived of all their property.[4] Dio
tells us that he saw the ruined city, and comments on the folly

[1] See below, p. 119.
[2] lxxiv. 10–14.
[3] We know from Tertullian (*ad Scap.* iii) that one Caecilius Capella
persecuted the Christians in Byzantium during the siege. He may have
been one of those in command. Having gone so far we may suspect
that the Byzantines realized the uselessness of surrender on the news of
Niger's death. Severus' position was even then by no means secure, and
a second Niger might at any moment arise. There was Albinus, too.
Schiller (ii. 713, note 5 of 712) rightly corrects Ceuleneer's statement
(p. 89) to the effect that Septimius took the title of Ponticus. The
PONT. in *CIL.* vi. 225 = *pontifex* (cf. *CIL.* iii. 3664). The only addition
to the emperor's titles in consequence of the fall of Byzantium is an
eighth imperial greeting (Eck. vii. 175).
[4] Herod. iii. 6. 9; Dio Cass. lxxiv. 14. 3–5.

of an emperor who, to indulge a personal spite, opened the way
for the ingress of barbarians into the empire. He omits to
notice that not long afterwards either Septimius or Caracalla
rebuilt the city.[1]

[1] No first-hand literary authority mentions this fact, but the weight of
second-hand authority is, I think, conclusive: Spart. Car. i. 7; Chron.
Pasc., p. 494; Joh. Mal., p. 291; Hesych. Mil. Müller, *F. H. G.* iv. 153;
Suidas, *Severus.* Hesychius' remark that it received the name Antoninia
is vouched for by numismatic evidence (Eck. ii. 32). Zosimus, too (ii.
30. 2), mentions buildings set up by Severus.

CHAPTER VI

THE WAR AGAINST ALBINUS

THE reason for the hasty return of Septimius from the East, and for the consequent unsatisfactory condition of affairs he left behind him, is to be seen in Decimus Clodius Ceionius Septimius[1] Albinus, propraetorian legate of the province of Britain. Born at Hadrumetum on the 25th of November in the year 143 or thereabouts,[2] he received the literary education usually accorded to the upper-class Roman, though his military ambitions even at that age prevented his caring to be a scholar.[3] One thing at least his 'classical' education gave him—a motto: 'Arma amens capio nec sat rationis in armis,'[4] a line of which, so his biographer tells us, he would often repeat to himself the first half.

Freed from the restraints of the schoolroom he entered upon

---

[1] There is no need to suppose, as some do—e.g. Mommsen, *St. R.* ii. 1141—that this name proves adoption by Septimius Severus. It was almost certainly a family name of Albinus (Eck. vii. 162, 165).

[2] The exact year is unknown: Aelius Bassianus was proconsul of Africa at this time (Cap. Alb. iv. 5).

[3] Cap. Alb. v. 1. His mother was Aurelia Messalina, his father Ceionius Postumus, so that the blood of the Ceionian and Postumian families ran in his veins (Cap. Alb. iv. 1, 3). It is perhaps strange that a man of 'noble' family should be born at Hadrumetum, but it would be rash to disbelieve the combined (and disinterested) statements of Dio (lxxv. 6. 2), Herodian (ii. 15. 1), and Capitolinus (Vit. Alb. vii. 5, i. 3) on this point. The correctness of the genealogy supplied by his biographer is more open to question. Dessau's view that it was forged to flatter a fourth-century family of Ceionii Albini can be as easily and as naturally held of the third-century Ceionii (see above, p. 13), and we thus get a possible motive for falsification. Notice further a confusion between Postumi and Postumii, and the turning of Albinus into a family name: Capitolinus himself remarks later on (Vit. Alb. iv. 4 and 6) that the name was given him by reason of the fairness of his complexion.

[4] Virg. *Aen.* ii. 314; Cap. Alb. v. 2.

a military career, in which he received no small support from
influential friends who introduced him to the notice of the
Emperor Marcus. The latter seems to have been pleased with
him, and to have entrusted him with the command of two
auxiliary cohorts, dispatching him with a letter of recommenda-
tion to his superior officers :[1] he was also at some time early in
his career tribune of a *cohors miliaria Dalmatarum*.[2] Excused the
quaestorship he only held the aedileship for a period of ten days,
when he was suddenly called away on active service.

This was, without much doubt, the Marcomannian war, which
broke out in the year 167, and the post held by Albinus during
this, or the early part of this, war, was that of commanding
officer of the fourth legion (Flavia).[3] From the command of
the fourth legion he seems to have succeeded to that of the first,
though whether of legio I adiutrix, stationed at Brigetio in

[1] vi. 1, x. 6.

[2] vi. 1. Capitolinus' words are 'egit tribunus equites Dalmatas '. This
is a pure anachronism. These 'equites Dalmatae' are not found until
the fourth century—they occur with great frequency in the Notitia.
Probably Capitolinus found in his source 'tribunus cohortis miliariae
Dalmatarum' (these double cohorts are rare, but some were, as a matter
of fact, raised about 166 by Marcus): not understanding this he translated
the title into the nearest corresponding title he knew. Failing this
explanation we must suppose the statement of the *Scriptor* a mere lie.

[3] Ceuleneer, p. 57, suggests that he preceded Severus in his legionary
legateship and that the legion was leg. IV Scyth., not Flav. I cannot
think this right, for the following reasons. Though Capitolinus does not
mention the legionary legateship in connexion with the curtailed aedileship (only ' quod ad exercitum festinanter mitteretur '), it seems obvious to
see in the former fact the reason of the latter (so Ceuleneer, p. 57).
There are two possible wars which might have necessitated his presence :
(1) the Eastern war of 162-4 (Lucius Verus set out in 162, Eck. vii. 89,
90); (2) the war against the Marcomanni of 167-75. In the first of these
two wars the IVth Scythian legion (stationed at Orima) would have
served; in the second the IVth Flavian (at Singidunum) (cf. *CIL.* viii.
2582, 2745). Supposing Albinus to have been born in 140, he would
have been but twenty-two when the Eastern war broke out—too young
to be entrusted with the command of a legion. In 167 (supposing him
to have served even in the first year of the war) he would have been
twenty-seven, and of age for a legateship. Hence I conclude he served
in the Marcomannian war and was legate of the IVth Flavian legion.

Upper Pannonia, or of I Italica at Novae in Lower Moesia, we are not told.[1]

Returning to Rome after the turning-point of the war in 172 he was appointed in 174 to the praetorship, and left the city in the year following to assume the duties of propraetorian legate of Bithynia. His holding of this office synchronized with the rebellion of Avidius Cassius in Syria, and his biographer notes the success with which he fortified the loyalty of the troops stationed in his province.[2]

The date of his first consulship we do not know for certain. It was clearly during Commodus' reign, and quite possibly at the beginning of it, if we may suppose that he held it before the series of military appointments which we go on to mention. The first of these was a command in the Dacian war of 182 or 183, where he had as one of his colleagues his future rival, Niger.[3]

He was next appointed legate of one of the German provinces,[4] where he seems to have done good service in repelling a transrhenane invasion. Meanwhile there had been trouble in the province of Britain. At least as early as 184 the governor, Ulpius Marcellus, had to face a Caledonian invasion, and the year following found a still more dangerous enemy in his own army, which seems to have shown symptoms of an inclination to bestow upon him an imperial title. In 186, as we have seen (p. 57), this piece of insubordination was put down by Pertinax, who himself ran some risk of a similar elevation—such was the eagerness of the Western Island for an emperor of its own nomination.[5] If we may believe his biographer, Capitolinus,

[1] Leg. I adi. also fought in the Marcomannian war (*CIL*. xiv. 3900).

[2] Vit. Alb. vi. 2. The date of his Bithynian command rests on the date of the Avidius Cassius revolt. We have already seen reason to attribute that to 176 (see above, p. 56).

[3] Dio Cass. lxxii. 8. 1 ; Vit. Comm. vi. 1, xiii. 5; Zon. xii. 4. This war preceded the British war of 184.

[4] Vit. Alb. v. 5. Ceuleneer (p. 57) says 'leg. pr. pr. of the Lower province', though without sufficient authority. Schiller also (ii. 665) says 'against the Frisians', and gives the date as 186: cf. Cap. Alb. vi. 3 'gentibus transrenanis', and *CIL*. xi. 6053.

[5] For Pertinax see Vit. Pert. iii. 5, 6; Dio Cass. lxxii. 9. 2. For Ulp.

Albinus was offered the title of Caesar by Commodus, and the vigorous speech in which he refused that dignity, and attempted to vindicate the position of the Senate as supreme arbiter of the Roman world, while winning him considerable popularity with that self-complacent body, nevertheless brought about his recall by the emperor, and the appointment of Junius Severus to take his office. The pro-senatorial Pertinax seems to have restored him to his position in Britain.[1] It was then as legatus of this province that Albinus in the year 193 heard of the death of that emperor, of the elevation of Julian, and later of the attempts of Septimius and Niger to seize the empire for themselves.

Whether in Albinus or Septimius is to be seen the prime mover and first instigator of the war is a question which has received no unanimous answer from either the ancient or the modern historian. It is possible to lay the blame entirely on Albinus' shoulders and to suppose that only on hearing of the assumption by the British legate of the imperial insignia was a generous emperor bound to vindicate his authority, and to make war upon one whom he would otherwise have continued in his honourable office, and later, perhaps, have raised to a still higher one. On the other hand, we may see in Albinus a harmless dupe who would have rested content with his province and his Caesarship had the emperor left him alone : one whose arrogation of the Augustan title was a last desperate step motived only by a desire to be hung for a sheep rather than for a lamb. The truth, as so often, would seem to lie between these two extreme suppositions. We cannot believe that so sound a soldier as Septimius imagined for one moment that he had done more than shelve the Eastern question, or that he failed to realize the temporary nature of the peace of 196. Given no Albinus the Parthian war would probably have followed the Adiabenian

---

Marc. see Dio Cass. lxxii. 8; Vit. Alb. xiii. 4; *CIL.* vii. 504. The chronology is very confusing. Ceuleneer, perhaps wisely, attempts to fix no temporal relation between the activities of Pertinax and Albinus in Britain.

[1] Vit. Alb. xiii. 14. The story of the offer and refusal of Caesarship is of more than doubtful authenticity. The date of Albinus' original governorship it is impossible to determine exactly.

without a break.   At the same time the consciousness that he
did not intend to continue regarding Albinus as Caesar, now
that Niger was removed, together with vague reports indicative
of the fact that Albinus now realized the insecurity of his
position, was quite enough to justify his termination of the war
by means of a safe, if inglorious, armistice.[1]

Accordingly, some time towards the end of June Septimius
left Nisibis for Europe. He was not yet clear of Mesopotamia
when he received the welcome news of the fall of Byzantium,
and hastened to impart it to his troops.[2]

Returning, doubtless, the same way as he had come, the
emperor should have reached the newly captured city by the
beginning of September, and should have been in Viminacium
some time early in the following month. Here occurred an
event tantamount to a declaration of war on Albinus, supposing
that declaration not as yet formally made. Caracalla was raised
to the position of Caesar and *imperator designatus*. Thus Severus
deprived his brother Geta of any hopes of succession he may
have entertained, and at the same time stripped Albinus of
what shreds of constitutional authority he might still claim.[3]

---

[1] Spartian alone (Vit. Sev. x. 1) categorically attributes the first move
to Albinus.   Capitolinus (Vit. Alb. vii. 2–viii. 4) tells us only that
Septimius, after the defeat of Niger, sent messages to Albinus, (*a*) to
suggest joint empire, (*b*) to murder him. (*a*) is clearly a garbled version
of the fact that Severus made Albinus Caesar. (*b*) may or may not be
true.   Neither really throws any light on the problem.   Herodian
(iii. 5. 3) says that Septimius discovered treasonable correspondence
between Albinus and the Senate and therefore declared war πρὸς ἄνδρα
μηδεμίαν εὔλογον παρεσχημένον αἰτίαν. Dio (lxxv. 4. 1) merely remarks that
a civil war 'befell' Severus.

[2] Dio (lxxiv. 14. 1) says he got the news in Mesopotamia.   Byzantium
must have fallen about the end of June, as we learn from Dio that that
event took place about harvest time (lxxiv. 12. 5).   Herodian (iii. 6. 9) is,
as usual, vague.   Dio's ἐπὶ ὅλον τριετῆ χρόνον (lxxiv. 12. 1) is rather an
overstatement ; cf. above, p. 96.

[3] Vit. Sev. x. 3.   The two earliest rescripts in which Caracalla appears
as joint ruler with Severus are Cod. Iust. ix. 41. 1 (Jan. 1, 196) and
iv. 19. 1 (June 30, 196).   Clinton (*F. R.* i, p. 198) alters the former to
December 1, inasmuch as coins vouch for the fact that Caracalla was
not Caesar till 196 (Eck. vii. 199, 200).   If Dio's statements about the fall
of Byzantium are to be trusted, the necessity for considering both dates

Besides his new title Caracalla received also a new name, that of
Marcus Aurelius Antoninus ; for Septimius himself, probably out
of spite against the Senate, had proposed the deification of
Commodus, whom he was pleased to term ' his brother ', and had
thus adopted himself as a son of the Stoic emperor.[1]

The movements of Severus and his army after their departure
from Viminacium are not easy to follow. The emperor did not,
as Herodian would have us believe, march straight into Gaul,
but preferred to pay a flying visit to Rome on his way. The
partiality felt by a large section of the Senate for Albinus
may have had much to do with his decision : besides, as we
shall see, he wanted to take some (or some more) of the
praetorian guard with him. Yet, in spite of his apparent
haste,[2] he did not seemingly select the shortest route, which
would have led him from Viminacium through Singidunum,
Sirmium, Mursa, Aemona, and Aquileia to the capital. Instead
of this he marched through Pannonia into Noricum, in all probability following the course of the Danube.[3]

Why, we may ask, did Severus adopt so circuitous a route ?

fallacious will at once be recognized. It would of course be possible to
retain the second rescript if we disregarded Spartian's statement that
the occurrence took place at Viminacium.

[1] Vit. Sev. x. 6, xix. 3, xi. 3, 4, xii. 8 ; Spart. Get. ii. 2 ; Lamp. Comm.
xvii. 11 ; Dio Cass. lxxv. 7. 4 (cf. also CIL. viii. 5328, where Vibia
Aurelia, daughter of Marcus, is also called 'divi Severi soror'). Most of
these passages suggest that the 'adoption' took place after the defeat
of Albinus, but coins of 195 call the emperor Marcus' son (Eck. vii. 173).
A subsidiary reason is supplied by Spartian (Vit. Sev. x. 4), viz. that
Septimius had dreamt that an Antoninus was to succeed him. It is
scarcely necessary to call attention to the aetiological character of this
statement.

[2] Herod. iii. 6. 10.

[3] That he was in Pannonia we know from two sources : (1) Spartian
(Vit. Sev. x. 7) mentions his consultations of Pannonian seers—the
source for the statement is Marius Maximus (Cap. Alb. ix. 2). (2) An
inscription (CIL. viii. 7062) records that a certain Porcius Optatus was
sent by the Senate to Septimius ' in Germaniam ', and to Caracalla ' in
Pannoniam '. Caracalla is called ' imperator designatus ', so that the
inscription undoubtedly belongs to this period. We must suppose that
Septimius had crossed the border into Noricum while his son was still in
Pannonia.

Only one explanation seems possible. He must have intended marching straight into Gaul via Besançon and Châlon, and have been deterred from his purpose by some disquieting piece of news from Rome. The hostile attitude of many of the senators has already been noticed, and Porcius Optatus, who was sent by the loyalist party to meet the emperor, may have been the bearer of this warning message.[1]

The arrival of the embassy must be put some time early in November, after which time the objectives of Severus and his army cease to be the same. The emperor hurried off over the Julian Alps or by the Brenner to Rome, which he reached in the latter part of the month, while the main army, perhaps under the command of Fabius Cilo,[2] continued its march north of the Alps, reaching Vindonissa about a week after the arrival of Severus in Rome, i. e. about the beginning of December.[3]

How long the emperor stayed in the capital we do not know : he probably left about the turn of the year, and it is not impossible that he was a witness of a curious scene described so graphically by Dio. The occurrence is worth at least a passing notice. On the day of the last horse-race before the Saturnalia (December 17) an unusually large crowd was gathered together, Dio himself being of the number, for one of his friends was consul. In spite

---

[1] Herod. iii. 5. 2 ; Dio Cass. lxxv. 4. 2, for attitude of Senate.

[2] Not of Caracalla (Höfn., p. 191), who was only eight years old. *CIL.* iii. 4037 (= 10868) records the dedication by a tribune of the tenth praetorian cohort ' proficiscens ad opprimendam factionem Gallicam '. It is clear that Septimius was not with this section of the army between Viminacium and Poetovio—the provenance of the inscription.

[3] The army's rate of progress must have been exceedingly rapid. From the mention of the various defeats of the ' duces Severi ' (Vit. Sev. x. 7) we must suppose that it arrived in Gaul by December 1 at the latest, inasmuch as the final battle was on February 19. Suppose the start from Nisibis to have been July 1 and the arrival at Vindonissa December 1, this means about a dozen miles a day. Theodosius in 379, for instance, in marching from Scupi to Vicus Augusti, took from July 6 till August 2—thus averaging only about nine miles per diem. If we suppose Severus to have been at Cetium by November 6 we may suppose him in Rome by November 19 or 20, allowing him an average of thirty miles a day. This was, e. g., Julian's average when he advanced from Antioch to join his army at Hieropolis between March 5 and 9 in 363.

of the fact that six chariots in place of the normal four were running, the attention of the people was not centred on the race,
and, on its conclusion, there arose cries and shoutings—μέχρι πότε
τοιαῦτα πάσχομεν, καὶ μέχρι ποῦ πολεμοῦμεθα; Such a disturbance
cannot have had a purely fortuitous origin, and the organization
necessary for the production of such unanimity testifies alike to
the existence of a strong pro-Albinian party, as to the weariness
and impatience of the people at the prospect of yet further war.[1]

Whether or not the emperor was a spectator of this outburst of
popular sentiment, he at least showed himself sublimely indifferent
to it. After exacting from the Senate a motion declaring Albinus
a public enemy (a step which must have tickled his sardonic
humour), Septimius provided himself with a detachment of the
new praetorian guard and set out for Gaul.[2]

Meanwhile Albinus had not been idle. Some time during the
autumn, exactly when we do not know, he left Britain and crossed
over to the mainland. The forces at his disposal cannot have
been numerous. The Rhine armies seem, somewhat unexpectedly,
to have remained true to Severus, and in some instances at least
to have done him good service.[3]

---

[1] Dio Cass. lxxv. 4. 2–7. He further mentions the usual portents—
among them the appearance of the Aurora Borealis—a rare but by
no means unknown phenomenon even as far south as Rome. Wirth
(*Quaestiones Severianae*, Leipzig, 1888, p. 10) puts Severus' stay in Rome
as 'after December 10, i. e. after the beginning of his fifth "tribunicia
potestas"', and quotes Eckhel (vii. 175) in support of his statement. As
a matter of fact Eckhel classes the coin in question (PROFECT. AVG.)
under the 4th trib. pot. (i. e. before December 10). However, as all the
coins bearing on the question (ADVENT. AVG. and PROFECT. AVG.)
bear no trib. pot. mark, only the eighth imperial salutation, it is
impossible, apart from a consideration of probabilities, to confine them
within closer limits than June, 196 (fall of Byzantium = 8th IMP.) and
February 19, 197 (battle of Lyon = 9th IMP.). Cf. Cohen, iv, p. 5,
no. 5; ibid., p. 61, no. 578, etc. No. 579, PROFECTIO AVG. with
IMP. VIIII, must surely be an error.

[2] Cap. Alb. ix. 1; *CIL.* iii. 4037—the reference of this inscription to
this time is by no means certain.

[3] Cf. *CIL.* xiii. 6800, where the 'civitas Treverorum' erects at Mainz
a monument 'in honorem L. Sept. Sev. legioni XXII prim. . . . obsidione
ab ea defensa'. This must almost undoubtedly have reference to the
invasion of Albinus. It is certainly curious to find military operations

The kernel of his army consisted of the three British legions, the 2nd Augusta from Caerleon, the 6th Victrix from York, and the 20th Valeria Victrix from Chester, besides a good number of British auxiliaries. Spain and Noricum also appear to have favoured his cause, though the Norican legion (II Italica) appears on Severan coins.[1]

In order to lend some show of constitutional right to his actions, Albinus issued a set of coins stamped with the well-known senatorial marks SPQR and OB C.S. That these were Gallic-minted it seems impossible to doubt, though some have seen in them the work of a pro-Albinian senate in Rome.[2] To suppose, as others have done, that these coins attest the existence of a Gallic Senate seems to me both unnecessary and unlikely : such a body could have been nothing more than a drag on Albinus' movements, while the fictitious arrogation of senatorial support was the most obvious move for one whose ostensible policy was the restoration of the dyarchy.[3]

It seems likely that Albinus, counting on support in Rome, had it in mind to march straight down into Italy. If such was ever his intention it was frustrated by Septimius, who, on his march, dispatched a force to hold the Alpine passes leading out of Gaul,[4] as well as by the surprising action of one Numerianus. Numerianus was a Roman grammarian, who, relinquishing the

so far west. The main body of Albinus' British army must have advanced across Gaul by the main south road, i. e. via Rheims, Auxerre, Autun, and Châlon-sur-Saône. The force which besieged Trèves would be a mere detachment. And yet why split up an army already not over-large ? The siege looks like a strategic blunder.

[1] Cohen, vol. iv, p. 31, no. 261. Schiller, *Gesch. d. r. K.* ii, p. 714, note 8, is wrong on this point. On the other hand, there is no instance of any pro-Severus coins of the Spanish legion (VII gem. at Leon). It quite probably fought for Albinus. That he received active support from Spain and Noricum is made certain by *CIL.* ii. 4114. Novius Rufus, governor of Hispania citerior, paid for his support of Albinus with his life (Vit. Sev. xiii. 7).

[2] Ceuleneer, p. 107, note 5, however, takes this view.

[3] Eck. vii. 164 ; Cohen, vol. iii, Alb., no. 47. Eckhel himself and Schulte (p. 79) hold the 'Gallic senate' view. The parallel cases of Pompey in Greece and Scipio in Africa may be quoted.

[4] Herod. iii. 6. 10.

profession of a schoolmaster for that of a soldier, left Rome for
Gaul, where, assuming a senatorial title, he gathered together no
inconsiderable force and prepared to support the Severan cause,
though holding no commission from the emperor himself. Not
content with routing some of Albinus' cavalry in an engagement,
he succeeded in amassing and sending to Septimius a sum of over
seventeen million drachmae, and, stranger still, was content on
the conclusion of the war to settle down on a farm, receiving but
a moderate pension from the emperor he had served so loyally.
The strange figure of the warrior pedagogue has its significance
as well as its interest, for it is indicative of the existence of
a strong party in Gaul for whom the institution of a Gallico-
British empire offered no attractions, and from whom it could
call forth no enthusiasm or support.[1]

Notwithstanding the energies of Numerianus the fortune of
war, as we have seen, was initially on Albinus' side. Lupus
seems to have suffered a crushing defeat at his hands, and the
fact was advertised by a new issue of coins.[2]

The arrival of Severus changed the face of affairs. His route
out of Italy is uncertain, nor is the question an important one.
Whether he marched via the Greater or the Little S. Bernard, or
by the Simplon, he must have passed through Vienne and have
advanced upon Lugdunum from the south.

The head-quarters of the main Severan army was in all
probability at Trinurtium, the modern Trevoux, and the emperor
must have made a détour round Lugdunum in order to join it.
That Albinus made no attempt, as it appears, to stop this junction
bears out Dio's statement that though Albinus was the completer
gentleman, Septimius was the better general.[3]

The final battle, then, fought on February 19, 197, took place
somewhere in the plain to the north of Lyon, between the Rhone
and the Saône. The numbers of the opposing armies seem to

---

[1] Dio Cass. lxxv. 5. 1-3. Zonaras follows him, xii. 9. *CIL.* xiii. 1673
also shows 'defection' in Albinus' own friendly Gallic province. It
shows the adhesion of T. Flavius Secundus Philippianus, governor of
Gallia Lugdunensis, to Severus.

[2] Dio Cass. lxxv. 6. 2; Eck. vii. 165; Cohen, vol. iii, Alb., nos. 42-4, etc.

[3] Dio Cass. lxxv. 6. 2 ὁ μὲν Ἀλβῖνος καὶ τῷ γένει καὶ τῇ παιδείᾳ προήκων,
ἅτερος δὲ τὰ πολέμια κρείττων καὶ δεινὸς στρατηγῆσαι.

have been about the same—Dio puts it at 150,000 each[1]—nor
was the bravery of Albinus' British troops inferior to that of
Septimius' Illyrians. Of the tactics of the battle we are not
well informed : the best and fullest account is that of Dio. The
Albinians must have faced north or north-east, the Severans
south or south-west: the left wing of the former was driven
back by its opponents, while the right wing secured a temporary
triumph by the device (practised so frequently in after-times) of
digging concealed trenches and pits into which the pursuing
Severan left wing fell on the simulated flight of the Albinians.
Severus, seeing his left wing in danger, dispatched the praetorians to its assistance, but with such spirit did its success
inspire the enemy's right, that he went near to losing these
troops as well, and only a personal appeal succeeded in rallying
his flying forces. The deciding blow was delivered by Laetus
and his cavalry, and, whether or not his previous inactivity is to
be attributed to the treacherous intention of throwing his weight
into the scale of the prevailing side, to him certainly must be
allowed the credit of securing the victory for Septimius and so of
ending the war in his favour.[2]

[1] With the usual exaggeration of numbers common to ancient historians.
50,000 would be nearer the mark.
[2] Dio Cass. lxxv. 6. 3-7. 2 ; Herod. iii. 7. 2-4 ; Vit. Sev. xi. 1, 2, 7.
The topography is very uncertain. Dio, Herodian, Aurel. Victor (Caes.
xx : also the Epitome), Eusebius (*Chron.*, p. 176—under the year 203)
all say 'at Lugdunum '. Spartian alone has ' apud Tinurtium ' or ' apud
Trinurtium '—the reading is uncertain. The mere fact that the hazy
Spartian should even have heard of such a place is strong evidence in
favour of the supposition that the battle took place there, and that we
here have traces of a contemporary source. Even then we have to choose
between Trinurtium-Trévoux, some twelve miles north of Lyon, and
Tinurtium-Tournus, distant a good sixty miles up the river. According
to Ceuleneer we cannot suppose the battle to have been fought so far
from Lyon as even Trévoux, since ' Dion nous apprend que le sang coula
dans les deux fleuves ' (i. e. the Rhone and the Saône), and therefore we
must believe that the site lay nearer the confluence. As a matter of
fact all that Dio says is ὥστε καὶ ἐς τοὺς ποτάμους ἐσπεσεῖν (lxxv. 7. 2).
There is no need to take this as a reference to the *two* rivers. Dio's
words are actually quoted by him on p. 103, note 3. The passage from
Tertullian (*Ad Nat.* i. 17) 'Adhuc Galliae Rhodano suo non lavant'
should, if he be right, read 'neque Rhodano suo neque Arari '. The

Though the battle of Lyon was the decisive engagement in the
war against Albinus it is not to be supposed that all opposition
to Septimius melted immediately away. Albinus himself was
removed from the scene by suicide, but he left behind him some,
at least, willing to avenge his defeat.[1]

The thirteenth urban cohort, stationed at Lyon, seems to have
continued to offer some resistance, but that resistance was short-
lived. The town was taken and sacked, nor, as in the case of
Byzantium, did a subsequent repentance on the part of the
emperor avail to check the city's consequent decline.[2] Of the
protracted resistance of Spain and Germany and of its extinction
we shall speak later.

The next on whom the vengeance of the conqueror was to fall
were the wife and children of the pretender. These, if we may

simplest solution seems to be to see in Spartian the embodiment of
a 'Severan' source—possibly the emperor's own speech mentioned in
xi. 4—whence the mention of Severus' head-quarters; and in Dio and
Herodian an anti-Severan account, whence the mention of Lugdunum,
the head-quarters of Albinus. Incidentally both these writers show that
their respective sources were pro-Albinian—λέγω γὰρ οὐχ ὅσα ὁ Σεουῆρος
ἔγραψεν ἀλλὰ . . . ἀληθῶς (Dio Cass. lxxv. 7. 3); οὐ πρὸς χάριν ἀλλὰ πρὸς
ἀλήθειαν (Herod. iii. 7. 3). John Malalas (p. 291) puts the battle in
Thrace. This, at least, is wrong. Was this the nearest he could get to
the 'Trinurtium' of his source?

[1] Suicide is Dio's account (lxxv. 7 3). Herodian (iii. 7. 7) says he
was taken and killed by Severus' soldiery. Capitolinus (Alb. ix. 3)
admits that the usual verdict is suicide, though some hold him to have
been killed by one of his slaves. That he was brought half dead into
Severus' presence and there executed (so in Capitolinus, loc. cit., and
Spartian, Vit. Sev. xi. 6) looks like an aetiological account made to
square with the prediction of the Pannonian seers that Albinus would
fall into Septimius' hands neither dead nor alive. Or, this may be the
truth, and the prediction may have been forged to suit the fact.
Ceuleneer (p. 104) quotes De Montfaucon, L'antiquité expliquée, suppl. iv,
p. 41, plate 19, where is figured on a gem a legionary surrounded by
a crowd of soldiers and carrying on his shoulders the 'dead body of
Albinus'. Severus, before whom the corpse is brought, is depicted as
commanding decapitation by a gesture.

[2] Schiller, p. 716, gives no authority for his statement that Septimius
on his arrival in Gaul found Coh. urb. XIII loyal, nor do I know of the
existence of any such evidence.

believe the Augustan History, Severus had killed and cast into
the Rhone together with the body of Albinus : his head the
emperor dispatched to Rome as a foretaste to the Senate and
people of what those might expect who had offended him.[1]
Septimius remained in Gaul some three or four months more,
engaged in exterminating any hostile feeling still existent by
a systematic persecution of prominent pro-Albinians and the
confiscation of their property. To this period too is attributed by
Herodian [2] the division of the province of Britain into an upper
and a lower section.

Of the extinguishing of the last flickers of war we know but
little. Candidus was entrusted with the pacification of Spain,
where the Albinians still held out under Novius Rufus;[3] C. Vallius
Maximianus performed a similar duty in Baetica and Tingitana;[4]
while Marius Maximus apparently assisted the emperor in the
subjugation of Gaul.[5] About this time also we hear of the
revolt of the Arabian legion (III Cyrenaica), prepared to uphold
the claims of an imperial candidate, news of whose fate had
seemingly not yet reached it. The attempt had no practical
consequences, and is only of interest as indicating the unpopularity of Severus; for we cannot believe that these Eastern
troops felt any personal interest in Albinus, or were in any way
in sympathy with the aims and objects of the legions of the
West.[6]

Some time towards the end of May Septimius left Gaul for
Rome, which city he entered in triumph on June 2.[7]   He was

[1] Vit. Sev. xi. 9; Cap. Alb. ix. 5.

[2] Vit. Sev. xii. 1; Herod. iii. 8. 2; Tert. *Ap.* 35 'Post vindemiam . . .
racematio': see below, p. 189.

[3] *CIL.* ii. 4114, 4125.

[4] *CIL.* ii. 1120, 2015, viii. 2786—if indeed these inscriptions refer to
this period (Schiller, p. 716, and Wilmanns, in his comment on the
African inscription) and not to the reign of Marcus (as Hübner on
ii. 1120).

[5] *CIL.* vi. 1450; Borghesi, *Œuvr.* v. 457.

[6] Vit. Sev. xii. 6.

[7] A *taurobolium* was performed in his honour at Lugdunum on May 4 ;
CIL. xiii. 1754. Cf. Herod. iii. 8. 3. *CIL.* xiii. 1753 records a *taurobolium* performed in 194 for Severus and Albinus—the latter's name is
erased.

met by the populace with every mark of honour, and awaited by
the Senate with ill-concealed alarm. To the former the emperor
showed his generosity by the bestowal of a *congiarium* and the
celebration of magnificent games; against the latter he wreaked
his vengeance in such a manner that we know not whether to
wonder rather at the pettiness of his spite or the virulence of his
cruelty. We have already noted his adoption of himself into the
Antonine family, and this adoption was now further emphasized
and confirmed by the formal deification of the dead Commodus.[1]

The emperor's motive for such an action is certainly difficult
to see. The unpopularity of Commodus in his lifetime precludes
the supposition that the apotheosis was, like that of Nero by
Otho, a bid for popular favour; and, indeed, the only hypothesis
which fits the case seems to be that Septimius was animated
solely by the desire to annoy and abase the Senate, whose
hatred of Commodus was still more intense than was that of
the people.

But the emperor was by no means contented with annoying
the Senate. On his entry into Rome his first action, after a
sacrifice of thanksgiving to Jupiter, had been to address to
that august body a speech bristling with invective, wherein he
deprecated the clemency of Pompey and Caesar, extolling the
cruelties of Marius and Sulla, offered an *apologia* for the deified
Commodus, contrasting his morals favourably with those of some
of the assembled fathers, and cast in their teeth the sympathy
they had felt and expressed for Niger or Albinus.[2] This speech
he followed up by setting on foot a series of processes against
those whom the private correspondence of the British legate, of
which he had possessed himself, proved to have been traitorously

---

[1] Vit. Sev. xii. 8, 9; Dio Cass. lxxv. 7. 4; cf. p. 104. For the existence
of a *sodalis Commodianus* cf. *CIL.* vi. 1577. The fact that Severus
became by this adoption the brother of Commodus is attested by many
inscriptions. Ceuleneer (p. 109) notes the especial frequence of dedication to the *divus Commodus* in Spain, Syria, and, above all, Africa, and
the comparative rareness of the same elsewhere.

The execution of the murderer of Commodus (Vit. Sev. xiv. 1) is
a natural corollary. Further, Commodus' birthday became a festival
(Lampr. Comm. xvii. 12).

[2] Dio Cass. lxxv. 8. 1-3; Herod. iii. 3. 8. 6-7.

disposed towards him. Of the sixty-four cases which came up for trial thirty-five ended in acquittal, a fact which shows that even if the principles of justice were not strictly observed in all cases, the emperor was not beyond the desire of seeming to act in accordance with them.[1]

The extorting from the Senate of a ratification of Caracalla's Caesarship, together with the bestowal on that prince of imperial insignia, was a final insult which the fathers must have been too stunned properly to appreciate.[2]

[1] Dio Cass. lxxv. 8. 3, 4. Dio being himself a senator is likely to be correct in his figures. Spartian (Vit. Sev. xiii) gives a list of some forty-one senators whom Severus is said to have had killed ' sine causae dictione'. We may either suppose, with Höfner (p. 204), that Dio's twenty-nine refer to immediate executions, whereas Spartian's forty-one contain not only Albinian senators who perished at some other time, but also pro-Nigerians, or—I think with greater probability—that the forty-one are all those out of the sixty-four whose names Spartian (i. e. Marius Maximus) was able to collect.

[2] Vit. Sev. xiv. 3 ; Herod. iii. 9. 1 ; Eph. ep. 5. 902.

CHAPTER VII

SEVERUS IN THE EAST

AFTER a short stay in Rome Severus received once more the call to arms. Taking advantage of the emperor's absence in Gaul, the Parthians had crossed the Tigris and invaded Mesopotamia. Nisibis, the importance of which as a Roman stronghold we noticed in the first Eastern war, felt the brunt of their attack, and would have fallen but for the sturdy defence offered by its garrison under Laetus.[1]

Leaving Brundisium some time in the late summer or early autumn of 197 Septimius reached Antioch, accompanied by the generals Statilius Barbarus, Lollianus Gentianus, L. Fabius Cilo, and C. Fulvius Plautianus, his praetorian prefect, together with a detachment of praetorians. Here he was probably joined by the major portion of the African legion, III Augusta. It is very doubtful whether the Western legions were requisitioned for this war, or were likely to be, considering the still unsettled state of such provinces as Gaul and Spain, in the latter of which Candidus seems yet to have had the last remnants of the revolt of Albinus on his hands.[2] On hearing of the arrival of Septimius in

---

[1] Dio Cass. lxxv. 9. 1. Dio's story of the war (chaps. 9–12), though far from perfect, is the only moderately intelligible one. Spartian's account (Vit. Sev. xv. 1–xvi. 6) is fragmentary and inaccurate; Herodian's is so nebulous as scarcely to merit so incisive an epithet as incorrect, while the later writers as a rule recognize no division between the two Eastern wars, mentioning but one Parthian war as occurring before (e. g. Eutrop. viii. 18) or after (Zosimus, i. 8) that against Albinus.

[2] For Statilius cf. CIL. vi. 1522; Gentianus, CIL. ii. 4121; CIG. 3180; Fabius Cilo, CIL. vi. 1408; Plautianus, Vit. Sev. xv. 4; CIL. vi. 227. For the praetorians cf. CIL. vi. 235; Leg. III Aug., CIL. viii. 2975. The presence of the Illyrian legion Adiutrix depends on the reading of CIL. viii. 217. The 'item Parthica' of the Candidus inscription (CIL. ii. 4114), coming as it does before the 'expeditio Gallica', must refer to the first, not the second Eastern war. Höfner (p. 250) supposes an

Syria the Parthian king (Vologeses V) hastily raised the siege of Nisibis and recrossed the Tigris.[1] The emperor wasted no time. Leaving Antioch he marched probably to Edessa, where he received the submission of Abgarus, king of Osrhoene, whose wavering loyalty he secured by a recognition of that monarch's autonomy, together with the bestowal on him of the title ' king of kings '. This being the appellation arrogated to themselves by the Parthian emperors, its transference to the Osrhoenian king was indicative of the fact that in Roman eyes the hegemony of the East was taken from the Parthians and given to another.[2] The grateful monarch adopted the name Septimius, and subsequently visited Rome on the invitation of his patron.[3] In pursuance of this policy of securing the country in his rear by means of concessions to native princes, Severus bestowed the *ius coloniae* upon the state of Palmyra, then in the hands of the influential Odaenathi family.[4] Among other advantages derived from this politic generosity were guides with a thorough knowledge of the country, and a sprinkling of native troops.[5]

Leaving Edessa Septimius advanced to Nisibis, only to find that the enemy had flown. He accordingly marched south,

inversion, and holds that Candidus served in the second war. Of auxiliary troops in the war we have evidence of a *cohors Britannica civium Romanorum* from Dacia and a *vexillatio Dacorum* (*CIL.* iii. 1193).

[1] Dio Cass. lxxv. 9. 3. Spartian (Vit. Sev. xv. 2, 3) makes Severus advance, ' remove ' (*summovit*) the Parthians, and retire again into Syria to prepare for a second campaign. However, as Dio expressly says that the Parthians did not wait for the Roman attack, we may safely believe him. The retreat of the Parthians, which must have occurred about November, 197, is commemorated by the tenth imperial salutation (Eck. vii. 176 ; Coh., vol. iv, Sept. Sev., no. 582). Imp. X is found on coins of 197 and 198, and must, I think, refer to this retirement rather than to the capture of Babylon and Seleucia, which events belong to 198.

[2] Longpérier, *Mém. sur la chron. des rois parthes Arsacides*, p. 85. The inscriptions βασιλεὺς ῎Αβγαρος and Αὐτόκρα Σεύηρος Σεβ. also occur on Osrhoenian coins (Eck. iii. 514 ; Mionnet, v. 617, etc., nos. 123-51).

[3] Dio Cass. lxxix. 16. 2. Caracalla afterwards imprisoned him (Dio Cass. lxxvii. 12. 1).

[4] *CIG.* 4485.

[5] 'Αγνωσία τῶν χωρίων (Dio Cass. lxxix. 9. 4) was naturally a common difficulty. Abgarus sent archers (Herod. iii. 9. 2).

probably following the course of the Mygdonius as far as its confluence with the Euphrates near the ancient (Biblical) Carchemish. Here, following the example of his predecessor Trajan,[1] he caused a fleet to be constructed on the river and continued his advance southward, attended by the newly built vessels, and under the guidance of a certain Tiridates and a cynic philosopher Antiochus, the latter of whom was useful, not only by reason of his knowledge of the country, but also in that he offered an example of endurance to the dispirited troops by rolling himself about in the snow, for which service he received so much money at the emperor's hands that he soon deserted with his gains to the Parthians.[2]

On reaching the Euphrates end of the royal canal connecting that river with the Tigris[3] it seems probable that Septimius divided his forces, sending or leading some farther south to capture Babylon, which city the enemy did not seek to defend, whilst the rest went by boat down the royal canal and disembarked at the Tigris end near to Seleucia, which city they proceeded to take, deserted as it also was by the Parthians. The next objective of the reunited army was the town of Ctesiphon, some few miles farther down stream.[4] Here some slight resistance was met with and a feeble attempt made by the Parthians to defend the city, though the disintegration of the waning Arsacid empire, of which the presence of Vologeses' brother in Septimius' camp was typical, was too far advanced to allow of any effectively concerted action being taken against the invader. The fall of Ctesiphon occurred in or about

---

[1] Dio Cass. lxviii. 26. 1.   [2] Dio Cass. lxxvii. 19. 1, 2.

[3] This is the canal referred to as Ναρμάλχας, or Ναρμάλχης (Isid. Char. 1; Plin. *H. N.* vi. 120; Zos. iii. 24; Amm. Marc. xxiv. 6. 1). *Nahar malkâ* in Aramaic. It is also known in the Greek translation as ὁ βασίλειος ποταμός (Strab. xvi. 10; Ptolemy, v. 18. 8) or ἡ βασιλικὴ διῶρυξ (Polyb. v. 51. 6). It branched off from the Euphrates at Sippar-Aganê and reached the Tigris near Seleucia (Theophyl. v. 6. 6). Just as Trajan had preceded Severus, so Julian was to follow him.

[4] Dio merely mentions the 'rapid' capture of Seleucia, Babylon, and then Ctesiphon. Geographical reasons certainly cause us to view such an order with suspicion (so Schulz, *Beiträge*, p. 54), and the above account is at least possible.

November, 198, and the emperor advertised the fact by a new (eleventh) imperial salutation.[1]

The city was given to the soldiery to sack, and we may judge of its size when we read in Dio that in spite of indiscriminate slaughter some 100,000 prisoners were taken.

No attempt was made on Severus' part to pursue Vologeses, who had succeeded in making good his escape from his fallen capital. Why this was so we are not informed with much certitude. By supposing synchronous Dio's two statements that no further advance was made τὸ μὲν ἀγνωσίᾳ τῶν χωρίων τὸ δ' ἀπορίᾳ τῶν ἐπιτηδείων (lxxv. 9. 4), and that his guides forsook him (lxxvii. 19. 2) some time during the war, we get a reason, but a more likely one is to be seen in the fact—known to us from other sources—that the army suffered severely from dysentery during this and other campaigns.[2]

The strategy of the war up to the fall of Ctesiphon in the winter of 198 is easily comprehended; after that event both the motives and the actions of the emperor become wrapped

---

[1] IMP. XI accompanies PART. MAX. on coins (Eck. vii. 176-8; Coh., vol. iv, Sept. Sev., 243, 251, etc.; *CIL.* iii. 205, 208). A parallel is afforded by Trajan, who assumed the title Parthicus and received another imperial salutation when he took Ctesiphon (Dio Cass. lxviii. 28. 2). We know from Spartian (xvi. 1), whom there is in this instance no particular reason to doubt, that the city fell in the winter—'hiemali prope tempore'. Ceuleneer (p. 118) and Höfner (p. 244) put the capture of Ctesiphon in the early spring of 198, relying on an inscription (*CIL.* viii. 4583) which records a dedication made on May 15, 198, in honour of a victory over the Parthians. If this victory = the taking of Ctesiphon, we must date that occurrence not later than early in March, which leaves only about six months (September, 197–February, 198) for the advance from Antioch to Nisibis, from thence to Babylon (nearly 500 miles), and on to Seleucia and Ctesiphon itself. I prefer to follow Duruy in attributing the inscription to some previous success of Severus' generals or to some small early victory of his own, and to accept November, 198 (as does Wirth, p. 11), as the date of the fall of Ctesiphon. That the inscription calls Septimius PARTH. MAX. does not seem of importance. There is no need either to see in the thank-offering for victory dedicated in Rome on Oct. 15, 198 (*CIL.* vi. 1052), a reference to the fall of Ctesiphon.

[2] Herod. iii. 9. 6; Vit. Sev. xvi. 2. The suggestion is Rawlinson's (*The Sixth Great Oriental Monarchy*, p. 341).

in some obscurity. It seems to have been Severus' intention
to return, as he had come, along the Euphrates bank, but to
such an extent had the army denuded the country through
which it had marched that a different return route was rendered
imperative. Accordingly fleet and army moved northwards
along the Tigris, though whether the objective was Hatra,
Armenia, or merely Syria it is impossible to say. Armenia,
however, we know to have shown herself friendly to Rome,[1]
while an invasion of the Khazars[2] must have checked any
possible desire on her part to embroil herself with a Western
enemy.

The next occurrence of which we read is the siege of Hatra,
which we may reasonably suppose to have taken place some time
in the summer and autumn of 199. Once more we are at a loss
to understand the emperor's motives or his anxiety to capture the
town, unless indeed it be on the supposition that his intention
was to punish all who had in any way assisted his rival Niger.[3]

---

[1] Herod. iii. 9. 2. The whole question as to the position of Armenia
in this war is a vexed one. Herodian makes Armenia Severus' first
objective, and accounts for its non-invasion by the anticipatory submission of its king. Not only is this contradictory to Dio's account, it is
also of itself unlikely. Armenia had refused Niger help (Herod. iii. 1. 2),
and therefore Severus could have had no *immediate* cause for invading it.

The story occurring in Dio Cass. lxxv. 9. 6 of how on the march
Severus encountered one Vologeses, son of Sanatruces, to whom, as the
price of peace, he ceded a portion of [Roman] Armenia, has been con-
clusively shown by Boissevain (*Hermes*, xxv, pp. 329–38) to refer to
Trajan's campaign of 116 and to correspond to the statements of
Malalas, i. 351, 352, and 357, 358. This king is referred to in Spart.
Hadr. 21. 10. The Severus mentioned in the fragment of Dio must be
taken, of course, as a general of Trajan.

[2] Zonaras, xi. 24; S. Martin (*Mém. sur l'Arm.* i. 301), following Moses
Chorenazi (ii. 65, etc.). The Khazars = the Alans : Moses apologizes for
his indiscriminate use of the two words, explaining that no boundaries
separate the two tribes. Indeed Kha-sar (cf. Sar in Sarmatae) seems to
mean no more than the 'great nomads' (cf. Massagetae = Getae maiores).
For Alan pressure on Armenia in Hadrian's reign cf. Dio Cass. lxix. 15 ;
Moses Chor. ii. 50. Severus is said to have strengthened the Armenian
frontier against them. Also to have pacified Colchis (George Syncell.
670).

[3] Herodian (iii. 9. 1) gives δόξα as Septimius' motive in this war and

Hatra, the modern el-Ḥaḏr, lies about midway between the Euphrates and the Tigris in the middle of the desert of Sendjâh. It was a fairly populous city and one of some importance as an avenue for trade, besides being blessed with an excellent water-supply: the wealth it had accumulated was very considerable.[1] Like Trajan before him,[2] however, Septimius was unable to make any impression upon the sturdy city, whose double circuit of walls was probably an asset less valuable in its defence than the sun-scorched sand which surrounded it on all sides, making life in a beleaguering camp unhealthy if not impossible.[3] The ingenuity of the besieged, too, seems to have been not inconsiderable: burning naphtha was thrown from the walls upon the Roman siege-engines, of which all but those of the famous engineer Priscus[4] were destroyed; while—still more ingenious—venomous winged insects were collected in pots, and showered down upon the heads of the besiegers, whose eyes and the uncovered parts of whose bodies they so stung as to force them to retire.[5] The siege was finally raised owing to dysentery attacking the Roman camp.

His ill success does not seem to have improved the emperor's temper, for we read of two apparently reasonless executions during the siege. One was that of the general Laetus, the gallant defender of Nisibis,[6] whose sole offence seems to have

the pro-Nigerianism of Barsemias of Hatra as its πρόφασις. Barsemias certainly had helped Niger (Herod. iii. 1. 2).

[1] There is an excellent monograph on Hatra by Andrae, published among the *Wissenschaftliche Veröffentlichungen der Deutschen Orient-Gesellschaft*, no. 9, 1907. The town is circular in shape and has a diameter of about 1,700 metres.

[2] Dio Cass. lxviii. 31. 1, 2.

[3] Dio Cass., *loc. cit.*; Amm. Marc. xxv. 8. 5.

[4] Dio Cass. lxxv. 11. 1. Priscus, it will be remembered, was the engineer whose skill had done so much to prolong the siege of Byzantium, and whom Severus, on the fall of that city, took into his service. See p. 96.

[5] Herod. iii. 9. 5. The methods of defence suggested by Aeneas Tacticus pale before this.

[6] There were certainly two Laeti at least: (1) the leader of the decisive charge at the battle of Lyon; (2) the defender of Nisibis. That they could not be one and the same person seems clear from the

been his popularity with the soldiery. The other victim of
the emperor's rancour was one Julius Crispus, a tribune of the
praetorian guard, whom a felicitous quotation brought to so
unhappy an end. His accuser Valerius, who succeeded to his
office, charged him with citing the words of Drances in the
eleventh *Aeneid* :[1]

> Scilicet ut Turno contingat regia coniunx,
> nos, animae viles, inhumata infletaque turba,
> sternamur campis;

and in spite of the disloyalty implied in the parable, one cannot
but recognize a considerable amount of justification for it.

The first attempt on Hatra had failed, but the emperor was
not the man to acknowledge defeat. In the winter of 199 or
the early spring of 200 he returned from Nisibis, whither he
had presumably retired, and renewed his attack on the town.
An investment was obviously impossible, thanks to the barren
nature of the surrounding country, and accordingly for some
twenty days the city was made to feel the full force of the
Roman siege-engines. Once more, however, the strenuousness
of the defence defied the attacks of the besiegers, the more distant
being struck down by catapult shots, the nearer overwhelmed
by the ignited naphtha. At one point, indeed, the Romans
succeeded in effecting a breach in the outer wall, and things
might have gone ill for the besieged but for the strange action
of Severus himself. Knowing that a vast quantity of treasure
lay stored up in the temple of Bel and elsewhere in the city, the

---

considerations: (*a*) that a suspected traitor (cf. p. 109) would not be
entrusted with the defence of Nisibis; (*b*) that the Laetus in Nisibis was
already in the East at the end of the Albinus war. Höfner (p. 299)
believes that there were two Laeti in this Eastern war; one the hero
of Lyon, the other of Nisibis, of whom the former was executed. It
seems to me more likely that Severus' jealousy would rest on the
defender of Nisibis. For the fact of the execution we have the combined
testimony of Dio (lxxv. 10. 3), Herodian (iii. 7. 4 — who takes the reference
as being to the Lyon Laetus), and Spartian (Vit. Sev. xv. 6). Laetus,
the praetorian prefect of 205, is probably a third of that name, though
he may be the same as the Lyon Laetus; cf. below, p. 175.

[1] Virg. *Aen.* xi. 371-3.

emperor hoped for a capitulation whereby the money would fall into his hands and not into those of his soldiers. No sooner, therefore, did he see the breach made, than he gave orders for the signal of retreat to be sounded, expecting from the inhabitants an offer of surrender at discretion. Instead of this the besieged employed the ensuing night in repairing their shattered wall and prepared to face the Romans again the next day. Once more the order for advance was sounded, but the European troops of Severus' army refused to attack. Determining that rebellion on the part of the troops should not frustrate his plans, the emperor hurled his Syrians at the wall, only to witness their ignominious repulse. ' Whence shall I get so many soldiers?' was his sarcastic reply to the offer of a member of his staff who engaged to capture the town, should he be entrusted with but an odd 500 European troops.[1]

This time Septimius admitted himself beaten, and withdrew to Nisibis, whence, after a short stay, he betook himself to Antioch. We may suppose him back in Syria by October, 200.[2] From Antioch the emperor journeyed south with the intention of visiting Egypt. To do this it was necessary for him to cross Palestine, which country he found in a state of some unrest, though we are ignorant alike of the causes of this disquietude and of the means adopted by Severus for allaying it. The Jews had always been a seditious people, and a somewhat oppressive taxation of which they had complained before,[3] or a feeling of sympathy with their co-religionists among the Parthians, was sufficient to rouse some small revolt which the presence of the tenth legion (Fretensis) at Elath was enough to check. Any outbreak of importance would not have been passed over by the ancient historians—at least not by Dio,—while the mere mention by Eusebius[4] of a 'bellum Iudaicum et Samariticum' and of

---

[1] Dio Cass. lxxv. 12. 5. The exact number requisitioned was 550: its significance will be commented on later.

[2] Spartian (Vit. Sev. xv. 3) may be thinking of this step when he mentions the emperor's return in the middle of the war.

[3] Spart. Nig. vii. 9.

[4] Chron., p. 177. His date (195) is certainly incorrect.

a 'triumphus Iudaicus' as celebrated by Caracalla[1] need not
lead us to suppose more than a slight commotion.[2]

Some time probably about March, 201, Septimius left Palestine
and entered Egypt. That, as Dio[3] said of him, he could leave
nothing uninvestigated, whether human or divine, may give us
one reason for his visit, but it was probably not, as that
historian suggests, the only, nor indeed the chief, one. Egypt
undoubtedly required the presence of Septimius to secure its
loyalty, for its previous partisanship of Niger had been unanimous and wholehearted. In the province of his earlier years
of office the Syrian legate was definitely regarded as emperor,
not usurper, and deeds are extant dated in the first and even
the second year of his reign.[4]

Naturally Alexandria was the first city he visited, and of his
entry into it we possess a strange story, interesting as indicative
of the complete acceptance of Niger's brief principate there. Τοῦ
Κυρίου Νίγρου ἡ πόλις was the inscription which the emperor observed upon the gate. Justifiably angry, he asked for the explanation of so disloyal a welcome, nor were the witty Alexandrians
unprepared with their answer. Οἴδαμεν, they said, εἰρήκαμεν τοῦ
Κυρίου Νίγρου ἡ πόλις· σὺ γὰρ εἶ ὁ κύριος τοῦ Νίγρου. Septimius,
we learn, accepted their explanation.[5]

Of Severus' actions in the Egyptian capital we hear of but
two. One was the closing of the tomb of Alexander in the quarter
of the city known as Neapolis. The superstitious emperor wished
to be the last to view the embalmed body of the Macedonian
conqueror and to pry into the sacred books kept in the precincts

---

[1] Spart. Vit. Sev. xvi. 7. To me Spartian's sentence reads like
nonsense: 'Cui (Caracallae) senatus Iudaicum triumphum, idcirco quod
et in Syria res bene gestae fuerant a Severo.' We may perhaps safely
disregard it. Incidentally Caracalla was only twelve years old at the
time.

[2] See below, p. 206, note 6.

[3] lxxv. 13. 2. His interest in the religion of the country is a point
which will receive further comment later.

[4] P. Grenf. ii. 60 Ἔτους β Γαίου Πεσκεννίου Νίγερος Ἰούστου Σεβαστοῦ.
BU. 454 is another papyrus dated during Niger's usurpation, but in his
first year.

[5] The story occurs both in Malalas, p. 293, and in Suidas, ii. 2. 700.

of the tomb.[1] The other is of more importance. Unlike the
other larger cities of the empire, Alexandria had never been
granted a municipal autonomy; it had no town council, but
obeyed implicitly the word of the imperially appointed *iuridicus*.
To this state of things Septimius put an end by the bestowal of
the ' ius buleutarum ', the right, that is to say, of being governed
by a local βουλή.[2]

Leaving Alexandria Septimius sailed down the Nile in his
tour of investigation. He visited Memphis and Thebes, at which
latter place he displayed no small interest in the famous statue
of Memnon which he heard ' sing ' at dawn. Such was his
enthusiasm that he caused the neck and head to be restored,
after which, unfortunately, the statue ' sang ' no more.[3] Advancing still farther south, possibly with the intention of exploring
the upper waters of the Nile, and of discovering its source,
Severus was checked on the borders of Ethiopia by an attack
of small-pox, on recovery from which he turned northward again.[4]
Either on his return or perhaps before he started south Septimius
paid funeral honours to Pompey, who lay buried in a humble tomb
near to Pelusium, where he had met his death. ' Templis auroque

---

[1] Dio Cass. lxxv. 13. 2.

[2] Vit. Sev. xvii. 2. Ceuleneer (p. 251) would restrict the reference to
the Greeks in Alexandria. It is impossible to extract this restricted
meaning from the Latin, nor does there seem any *a priori* reason for
postulating it. Moreover, if we attribute any importance to Schulz's
contention (*op. cit.*, pp. 114 and 212) that the ' sachlicher Verfasser ' was
himself an Egyptian and hence especially interested in things Egyptian,
one would expect him to have been more explicit in the present passage,
if he had meant to convey what Ceuleneer supposes. See also below,
p. 197.

[3] Vit. Sev. xvii. 4.; Letronne, *Rech. pour servir à l'hist. de l'Égypte
pendant la domination des Grecs et des Romains*, p. 263, and ' La statue
vocale de Memnon ' in the *Mém. de l'Acad. des Inscript.*, 1833, ix, p. 282.
The last of the ' Audi Memnonem ' graffiti (dated) is one of February 24,
196 (*CIL.* iii. 51).

[4] Dio Cass. lxxv. 13. 2. Dio enters at this point into a digression on
the sources of the Nile—which he puts in the Atlas mountains—though
he never makes the statement that they formed Septimius' objective.
The λοιμώδη νόσον is probably small-pox: mention has already been
made (p. 45) of the recrudescence about this time of the world-wide
Antonine epidemic of 166.

sepultus Vilior umbra fores' had been Lucan's comment, but we do not know the nature of Severus' ἐναγισμός.[1]

Some time towards the end of the year 201 the emperor left Egypt for Rome. He reached Antioch, probably by sea, before the close of December, and it was in that city that he entered upon his third consulship on the first day of the new year. His colleague was his son Caracalla, who was now to hold the office for the first time.[2] It may here be added that in the year 198, possibly in commemoration of the fall of Ctesiphon on the occasion of his own eleventh imperial acclamation, Septimius caused his troops to salute his elder son as imperator and Augustus. Geta also seems to have accompanied his father on this expedition, and it is probable that he received the title Caesar at the same time as his brother received that of Augustus.[3]

From Antioch the Augusti journeyed to Thrace, though whether they adopted the land or sea route we do not really know. By the middle of March they had reached Sirmium, having passed through Moesia, in which province, as well as in

---

[1] Dio Cass. lxxv. 13. 1 (τῷ Πομπηίῳ ἐνήγισεν); Lucan, *Phars.* viii. 859, 860.

[2] Vit. Sev. xvi. 8. For the return by sea to Antioch cf. *CIG.* 5889, 5973.

[3] The question of the titles of Caracalla and Geta is unimportant and confused. We have already seen that Caracalla became Caesar in 196. Spartian's statement (Vit. Sev. x. 3) we have seen supported by numismatic evidence and may believe. We have also remarked on his receiving of the name Antoninus. That this occurred in 196, not (as Lamprid. *Diadum.* vi. 8) in 198, on his becoming Augustus, is also proved by coins (Eck. vii. 199). Caracalla dated his trib. pot. from 198, and first in that year do coins (e. g. Eck. vii. 176, 200) and inscriptions (e. g. *CIL.* vi. 1052, October 15) call him Augustus. Spartian (Car. i. 1 ; Sev. xix. 2, xvi. 3 ; Get. i. 3, ii. 2, v. 3) thinks that on the occasion of Caracalla's acquisition of tribunician power Geta became Antoninus and Caesar : statements which Wirth (pp. 11 and 31, 32) accepts as true, citing *CIG.* 353 as further evidence for Caracalla's Augustan title in 198. The Scriptor admits, however (Vit. Sev. xvi. 4), that it is 'ut plerique in litteras tradunt', while Lampridius (*Diadum.* vi. 9) expressly states that 'multi Antoninum negant dictum'. However, no inscription or coin exists in which Geta is called Antoninus. Caesar first occurs in coins of (?) 200 (Coh., vol. iv, p. 283), but there is one inscription of 198 (*CIL.* iii. 218).

that of Pannonia, Severus inspected the various camps.[1] From
Sirmium it seems probable that the emperor passed through
Siscia and Aquileia, finally reaching Rome either by taking ship
from Aquileia to Ancona and so on to the capital, or else by
the more usual land route. He probably entered Rome about
May.[2]

The return of the victorious emperor was celebrated with the
utmost magnificence. Sacrifices, shows, and games were held,
and as much as fifty million drachmae distributed as largess,
each praetorian receiving ten gold pieces in commemoration of
Septimius' ten years of reign. The celebration of the Decennalia (June 2–8) indeed may have taken the place of the more
usual triumph, which, if we may believe his biographer, the
emperor refused on account of a bad attack of gout[3] which
rendered him unable to stand up in the triumphal car. One
witness to his triumph at least stands yet for all the world to
see—the huge Arch of Severus erected in the following year in
the north-east corner of the Roman forum. Here may still be
seen reliefs depicting the defeat and submission of the Parthians,
and the triumph of Septimius and his two sons, while an inscription with a nicer regard for persons than for accuracy records
the 'rem publicam restitutam imperiumque populi Romani
propagatum insignibus virtutibus eorum (Augustorum) domi
forisque'.[4]

In criticizing the Parthian war and its results we must of
course bear in mind the fact that our knowledge of its details is,
when all is said and done, very meagre. Yet, so far as a judge-

[1] Herod. iii. 10. 1.

[2] Eck. vii. 202, 180, etc.; Zon. xii. 9. For the question of his possibly
crossing the Adriatic see appendix at end of this chapter.

[3] Vit. Sev. xvi. 6. That he allowed Caracalla the triumph (§ 7) seems
most improbable. For the Decennalia, etc., cf. Herod. iii. 10. 1; Dio
Cass. lxxvi. 1. 1; Eck. vii. 182, LAETITIA TEMPORUM, ship and wild
beast hunt in the circus. Also the legends LIB. AVG. III and VOT.
SVSC. DEC.

[4] CIL. vi. 1033. Cf. ARCVS AVGG. S. C. on coins of 204 (Eck. vii.
185). The name of Geta has been replaced in l. 4 by the words 'optimis
fortissimisque principibus'. This is not the first instance of Caracalla's
jealousy that we have noted.

ment is possible, it is hard to pass a favourable one. In a sense, the main object of the war was effected before it was begun, if it be true (and we have no reason for doubting the fact) that the Parthians raised the siege of Nisibis and evacuated Mesopotamia on the mere news of Severus' approach. Doubtless a punitive expedition was necessary, but why no effort was made to capture Vologeses,[1] in spite of dysentery or lack of guides, is all the more surprising in that Septimius had before him the example of Alexander, who spared no pain and trouble in the pursuit of Darius. Further, the siege of Hatra seems to have been pointless; even Septimius recognized that, given the fact that Vologeses was not to be pursued, the war was over by 199, for a good number of troops were sent home that year.[2] No new territory was acquired,[3] and the fact that the Parthians remained quiet during the remainder of Septimius' reign seems due not so much to the campaigns of the emperor, nor yet to his possession of the young Chosroes as hostage,[4] as to the fact that, what with sedition at home and Persian pressure abroad, the Arsacid empire was tottering to its fall.

[1] Vologeses V had succeeded his brother Vologeses IV in 190 or 191. Coins of his exist dating from 192 to 208 (504–520 in the Seleucid era) (Eck. iii. 540; Mionnet, *Descr. de méd. ant.*, v. 677, suppl. viii, 454). Herodian (iii. 9. 10) calls him Artabanus, and both he (iv. 10. 1, of the year 216, and vi. 2. 1, of 229) and Dio (lxxviii. 1. 1, lxxx. 3. 2) mention an Artabanus as king of Parthia, though the coins of another Vologeses (VI) were minted until the Persian overthrow of 227. Evidently on the death of Vologeses V in 208 the succession was disputed between (?) two sons—Vologeses and Artabanus. It is doubtless of the latter that the inaccurate Herodian is thinking. Cf. also Longpérier, *op. cit.*, p. 154.

[2] *CIL.* vi. 225 a (a dedication by some troops 'genio turmae' on the occasion of their return from the Parthian war). The story of the Europeans and Syrians at the second siege of Hatra (Dio Cass. lxxv. 12. 3–5) seems to me to point to a dearth of European troops.

[3] Herodian's mention of the subjugation of Arabia Felix (iii. 9. 3) is of course absurd. He is confusing it with the Scenite or nomad Arabs who infested Mesopotamia. Incidentally he seems to think Arabia Felix next door to Adiabene.

[4] The inscription *CIG.* 4821 may refer to him.

NOTE ON CHRONOLOGY.

The chronology of the period is confused and uncertain. We have the following facts : Severus returned to Syria, traversed Palestine, visited Egypt (Dio and Spartian), and returned to Rome via Pannonia and Moesia (Herod. iii. 10. 1). Our only chronological data are: (1) the fact that the city of Abila issued coins in honour of Severus dated 201 (De Saulcy, *Num. de la Terre-Sainte*, p. 311); (2) the statement that Septimius and Caracalla entered upon their joint consulship (January 1, 202) in Syria (Spart. Vit. Sev. xvi. 8); (3) a rescript dated March 18 from Sirmium (*Cod. Iust.* ii. 32. 1); (4) Septimius' almost certain presence in Rome at the Decennalia (Dio Cass. lxxvi. 1. 3 ; Eck. vii. 183, viii. 482), June 2-8.

Thence (tentatively) conclude :

Nisibis	*circ.*	July, 200.
Antioch	,,	October, 200.
Palestine	,,	January–February, 201.
Egypt	,,	March–December, 201.
Antioch	January 1, 202.	
Sirmium	March 18, 202.	
Rome	before June.	

Of course both Herodian and a rescript are but feeble evidence, yet their united testimony is striking. Nor does there seem any valid reason for doubting a return by land. The coin (Eck. vii. 202) with the legend ADVENT. AVGG. and the figure of a trireme does not, as Eckhel believed, disprove Herodian's statement, as the reference in the ship may well be to a crossing of the Adriatic. The emperor might have crossed from the port of Aquileia to Ancona, though it must be confessed that this would be a strange route.[1]

It is, of course, necessary (and, one would have thought, obvious) to see the Augusti at Antioch on January 1, 202, *on their return*. To suppose Egypt visited and Sirmium reached between

---

[1] There are two types of these ADVENT. AVGG. coins, one bearing a trireme, the other the emperor on horseback. The latter is the commoner (cf. *Num. Chron.*, 4th series, viii (1908), p. 92). Were the former minted in anticipation of a complete return by sea which never occurred?

January 1 and March 18 is manifestly absurd; nor is there any
need arbitrarily to alter the date of the rescript as does Clinton
(*F. R.* i. 208), while to set Severus' return to Rome in 203 (as does
Tillemont, *Hist. des emp.* iii. 460, note 24) is opposed to numismatic evidence. Mommsen also (*St-R.*, ii. 778. 1) is in favour
of a return in 203, partly influenced by an inscription of that
year (*CIL.* vi. 1033), in which Septimius is referred to as proconsul,
and partly by an examination of the coins of 202, which, he considers, point not to an actual but to an anticipated return.

The chronology I have adopted seems to me to allow ample time,
even without Herodian's assurance that Severus marched quickly
(iii. 10. 1), and there can be no need to suppose with Höfner
(p. 247) the end of the war in 198, and the return to Antioch
with the visit to Egypt in 199. His only evidence for so doing is
(1) an inscription (*CIL.* iii. 14) and (2) a coin (Eck. vii. 178). The
inscription, of which the date is 199, records some monument
set up in Egypt in Septimius' honour by the decuriones 'alae
veteranae Gallicae et I Thracum Mauretanae'. But there is no
need to suppose the emperor in Egypt at the time of its erection.
The coin is certainly curious; it is not dated (but this is not unusual
in coins of 199), and bears on its obverse the words SEVERUS AVG.
PART. MAX and on its reverse PROFECT. AVGG. FEL. The
obvious solution is that the profectio mentioned is that of 208 for
Britain. Against the supposition is the fact that as a rule PIVS
takes the place of PART. MAX. after 201. Eckhel indeed denies
the existence of PART. MAX. on coins after 201, but he is disproved certainly by a coin in Cohen (iv. no. 100) which is of 202
and yet bears these words.

CHAPTER VIII

THE LAST PHASE

OF the six years which elapsed between the completion of the Eastern and the outbreak of the British war we possess singularly meagre records. The emperor himself, essentially a man of war, drops very much into the background, and his place is taken by the far less agreeable figures of his wife, his sons, and his praetorian prefect. Of Julia Domna and her study circle we shall have occasion to speak later at greater length : suffice it here to say that an empress who added the political caprice of a Catherine de' Medici to the intellectualism of a Christina of Sweden and the vices of a Messalina was not likely to conduce to the harmony of any government. At the same time it is as well to remember that history, ever chivalrous, has tended to exaggerate her importance in the political world even as surely as, with less delicacy of taste, it has over-coloured the delinquencies of her private life. The statement that she was the cause of the wars against Niger and Albinus is as little likely to be true as the accusation of incest with a son whom she heartily detested.[1]

As far as one can see, however, Julia Domna never deliberately set her will against that of her imperial husband, and Spartian's statement that she conspired against him deserves even less attention than most of that historian's remarks.' It was not from his wife but from his sons that Septimius learnt the lesson that a man's foes are only too often those of his household.

It has been the habit among ancient historians—and to a certain extent among the moderns also—to paint Caracalla black

---

[1] Cap. Alb. iii. 5 'illos utrosque bello oppressisse, maxime precibus uxoris adductum '. Incest mentioned by Spart. Car. x. 1 ; Eutr. viii. 11 ; Aur. Vict. Caes. xx, etc. Coins inscribed ' PVDICITIA' (Coh., vol. iv, p. 119, Jul., nos. 168 sqq.) suggest an overstatement on the other side.

and Geta white, and there may be some truth in the distinction thus made. Be this as it may, one thing at least is certain, and that is that the dissension between the brothers waxed so hot that they could not endure the sight of each other, and that, as a consequence, the declining years of the emperor were made a burden to him, so that, if report speak true, he was driven to war as a solace to himself, and a possible means of healing that long-protracted fraternal strife.

But more surprising than the indiscretions of his wife or the quarrels of his sons was the career of Gaius Fulvius Plautianus, the prefect of the praetorian guard. Little or nothing is known of the antecedents or early career of this remarkable man. Like Severus himself, Plautian was of African birth, and was apparently exiled from his native country by Pertinax, the then proconsul, on a charge of sedition and rebellion.[1] Where or when he first formed the acquaintance of the emperor is uncertain, as is also the exact relationship obtaining between the two. That ties of blood besides those of marriage united the pair seems to me an entirely unwarrantable assumption, while Herodian's insinuation with regard to the cause and nature of their friendship may or may not be a piece of idle gossip.[2] Whatever the reason, the fact is indisputable. Never, perhaps, since the days of Seianus did favourite exercise more complete control of a master, and contemporary historians never tire of descanting on his power, his cupidity, and his riches. There is Dio's story of the 'tiger-like horses' from the East, dedicated to the Sun, which the sacrilegious hands of centurions bore away at the orders of the greedy prefect.[3] The story, too, of how, when Plautian lay sick at Tyana and the emperor came to visit him, the prefect's bodyguard would not suffer Severus to enter with his suite; and of how, on another occasion, the official ' a cognitionibus ' refused

---

[1] Herod. iii. 10. 6 τινὲς αὐτὸν καὶ πεφυγαδεῦσθαι ἔλεγον ἁλόντα ἐπὶ στάσεσιν.

[2] The adfinis of various inscriptions, e. g. CIL. iii. 6075, v. 2821, probably means no more than it usually does, viz. relation by marriage. For Herodian's suggestion that Plautian was the παιδικά of Septimius cf. iii. 10. 6.

[3] Dio Cass. lxxv. 14. 3.

to call a case that the emperor wished to judge, 'for', said he, ' I dare not do so without the orders of Plautianus.'[1]

Naturally enough this influence over Septimius was much resented by Julia Domna, between whom and the prefect there seems to have been constant bickering, breaking out at times into open enmity; as, for instance, when Plautian dared to bring certain specific charges against the empress, during the examination of which several Roman ladies suffered torture at the emperor's orders.[2] Still, Septimius' indulgence had its limits. Buildings and statues erected in honour of Plautian in the provinces, and even in Rome, were outnumbering those inscribed to the emperor himself, but when the prefect caused his own image to be placed among those of the imperial family he found himself sharply reprimanded,[3] and orders given for the demolition of his statues wheresoever set up. His disgrace, however, was short-lived, and an evil fate attended those who, in his hour of abasement, had presumed to scorn the favourite, for banishment was decreed to all such as had called him a public enemy. Among others so to suffer was Racius Constans, governor of Sardinia.[4]

Reinstated in imperial favour, the power and arrogance of Plautian assumed still larger proportions. By the murder of his colleague Aemilius Saturninus he had succeeded in grasping all the power of both the praetorian prefects in his own hands, and such designations as *vir clarissimus, nobilissimus, Augustorum necessarius* attest the extent of his dignity, as does the existence after his downfall of a *procurator ad bona Plautiani* that of his opulence.[5] The year 202 marks his zenith, when was solemnized the marriage between his daughter Fulvia Plautilla and the heir-apparent Caracalla;[6] and in the year following he became

---

[1] Tyana story, Dio Cass. lxxv. 15. 4; court story, ibid. lxxv. 15. 5.

[2] Suidas, i. 2, p. 1013.

[3] Vit. Sev. xiv; Dio Cass. lxxv. 16. 2, 15. 6.   [4] Dio Cass. lxxv. 16. 2.

[5] Cf. *CIA*. iii. 633; *CIL*. vi. 1074, 224–7, 643, 1035, iii. 6075 for these titles. *CIL*. iii. 1464 mentions the procurator. The future emperor, Macrinus, held the post (Dio Cass. lxxviii. 11. 2). The procurator was appointed to wind up his vast estate.

[6] Vit. Sev. xiv. 8; Dio Cass. lxxv. 15. 2, lxxvi. 1. 2; Herod. iii. 10. 7;

consul for the second time with the emperor's brother Geta. Great indignation was caused by this last assumption of office, partly because the sword of the praetorian prefect and the broad stripe of the senator were unconstitutionally vested in the same man,[1] partly also because the prefect's first consulship had been no more than the gift by Septimius of consular insignia, and the office of 203 should therefore have counted as the first and not the second.[2]

But Plautian's position contained the seeds of its own undoing. Whether or not we can credit the then current rumour that the prefect was destined by Severus as his successor, it is at least certain that he was not long in gaining the cordial hatred of Caracalla. The year 204 passed without mishap, but early in 205 the storm broke. Weary of the arrogance, or, as Spartian suggests,[3] of the cruelties, of his father-in-law, Caracalla devised the following plot for his destruction. He suborned a certain centurion, by name Saturninus, to warn the emperor of a conspiracy against his life of which he, Saturninus, together with nine other centurions, were to be the instruments, the praetorian prefect being the moving spirit. Septimius, believing the fabrication, sent for Plautian, who, suspecting nothing, repaired to the palace with such haste that the mule he was riding fell under him in the court-yard—an evil omen of which Dio recognizes the full significance. The emperor received the supposed culprit leniently enough, merely reproaching him for his ingratitude and asking the reason for his wish to kill him, and Plautian might even have got off had it not been for the action of Caracalla. The latter, foreseeing the possibility of his prey's escaping, rushed forward and struck him, and was with difficulty restrained by his father from delivering the *coup de grâce* with his own sword. The emperor's hand had been forced, and a soldier was

Zon. xii. 10; Eck. vii. 181, 202 PLAVTILLAE AVGVSTAE. PROPAGO IMPERI, etc.

[1] Dio Cass. lxxv. 15. 2; Herod. iii. 11. 2. Instances of this combination of dignities had been known before, e. g. Arretinus Clemens under Domitian (Tac. *Hist.* iv. 68). Alexander Severus first legalized the position of a senatorial prefect (Lamp. Alex. Sev. xxi. 3).

[2] Dio (xlvi. 26. 4) comments on this fact. Cf. Hirsch, p. 216.

[3] Spart. Car. i. 7.

bidden kill the fallen favourite.   So on the 22nd of January in
the year 205 ended the career of Plautianus.[1]

On the day which followed Plautian's death Septimius made
a speech before the Senate, in which he abstained from all
recrimination, lamenting merely the fact that mortals could not
bear more than a certain measure of success, and blaming himself
for his excessive affection for, and indulgence towards, the dead
favourite. Plautilla and her brother Plautius, whom Caracalla in
his rage would have had murdered, Severus banished to Lipari,[2]
nor were they the only ones involved in the prefect's fall. Dio
devotes some pages to the punishment by banishment or death
of Caecilius Agricola, Coeranus, and others, besides that of many
in no way connected with the conspiracy, such as Quintillus
Plautianus, Pedo Apronianus, Baebius Marcellinus, and Pollenius
Sebennus.[3]

For the rest of the year and during the two following the

---

[1] The story of the plot and its ending is given in some detail both by
Dio (lxxvi. 2. 5-4. 5) and by Herodian (iii. 11. 4-12. 12). Zonaras (xii. 10)
mentions it, and Ammianus (xxvi. 6. 8, xxix. 1. 15) confirms the name
Saturninus. Dio and Herodian differ a little in small and generally
unimportant points: e. g. Herodian calls Saturninus a χιλίαρχος. The
only important point of difference is that Herodian believes in the
genuineness of Saturninus' plot, while Dio (whom I have followed) takes
it for a fabrication on the part of Caracalla. I cannot see that
Caracalla's subsequent killing of Saturninus (Dio Cass. lxxvi. 6. 1) has
any bearing on the matter as Höfner suggests (p. 287), but the
probabilities of the case, as well as the general superiority in truthful-
ness of Dio to Herodian, lead me, as they lead him, to credit Dio's
version. There has been some slight difficulty too in connexion with
the date. The *Chronicon Pascale* (i, p. 496) fixes the day of the month
as January 22; Dio (lxxvi. 3. 3) also mentions the season as that of the
Palatine games — i. e. January 22-4 (Dio Cass. lvi. 46. 5). As to the year,
204 (so Ceul., p. 196) is impossible, as there exists a Plautian inscription
of that year (*CIL.* vi. 1035). Besides, we know (1) that those banished
under Severus were recalled by Caracalla in 212 (Dio Cass. lxxvii. 3. 3);
(2) that Coeranus was banished in connexion with this affair and
remained in exile seven years (Dio Cass. lxxvi. 5. 5), i.e. he was banished
in 205. Discussed at length by Prof. Bormann, *Bullettino*, 1867, p. 218.

[2] Dio Cass. lxxvi. 5. 1, 2, 6. 3; Herod. iii. 13. 3. Caracalla had his way
later. (Dio Cass. lxxvii. 1. 1).

[3] lxxvi. 5. 6, 5. 3, 7. 3, 8. 1, 8. 6, 9. 2.

emperor lived in retirement, chiefly, if we may believe Herodian, in the neighbourhood of the capital and on the Campanian coast, endeavouring, so far as in him lay, to distract his pleasure-loving sons from the snares of Roman life. Political and judicial affairs occupied most of his time.[1]

But events were happening in one of the outlying provinces which did not give the aged emperor much leisure for such pursuits of peace. For some time, in fact since the Albinian war, the state of Britain had been one of constant uneasiness. Albinus' successor, the legate Virius Lupus, had been obliged to buy peace from the Maeatae, which northern tribe had taken advantage of the absence of the British legions in Gaul to push their way farther south.[2] Eight years later we again get a glimpse of the unsettled state of affairs in that province, when the then legate, Alfenius Senecio, fought with success against the Britons.[3] Add to these disturbances the fact, if it be one, that Septimius looked forward to a war as the best, perhaps the one, means of healing the strife between his two sons,[4] and one sees cause enough for the expedition (destined to be his last) which the old emperor undertook in the spring of the year 208.

[1] Herod. iii. 13. 1. Two scraps of evidence suggest the possibility that the emperor travelled during this period. One is an inscription (*CIL.* viii. 2702) mentioning a 'familia rationis castrensis' at Lambaesis, the other a rescript dated from Antioch on July 22, 205. In any case the date of the inscription is 203, but the existence of the coin of that same year recording the INDVLGENTIA AVGG IN CARTH(*aginem*) (Eck. vii. 183, quoted above, p. 29), together with the passages in Ulpian and Spartian, do make it seem at least possible that Septimius visited Africa then. As to the rescript, another dated from Rome on July 1 of the same year rather shakes our faith in it; see above, p. 21.

[2] Dio Cass. lxxv. 5. 4: for Virius Lupus, *CIL.* vii. 210, 273 (both of 197); cf. Hübner, *Rhein. Mus.* xii. 66.

[3] Dio Cass. lxxvi. 10. 6. The date of this reference is 205, for the following reasons: Dio mentions the disturbance as contemporaneous with that caused by one Bulla Felix in Italy. Now Bulla was caught and brought before Papinian, who succeeded Plautian as praetorian prefect, i. e. in 205 (cf. *CIL.* vi. 228, which mentions Papinianus as praet. praef. on May 28, 205). *CIL.* vii. 200 (Doncaster, year 205), 269, 513. *CIL.* iii. 4364, Ceuleneer (p. 138) rightly attributes to some Danubian victory and not, as Höfner (p. 319), to a British war. Its date is 207.

[4] So Herod. iii. 14. 2.

It is possible that Severus, who was attended by his family
and relations as well as by the new praetorian prefect, Papinian,[1]
did not hurry on his way to Britain, though we have no records
of his journey save for the vague remark of Herodian that he
crossed the ocean, and for the still vaguer rumour that on his
passing through Lyon he ordered a persecution of the Christians
there.[2]

The autumn and winter of the year seem to have been spent
by the emperor in making preparations for the campaign, which
preparations appear to have consisted chiefly in the filling up of
marshes and the bridging of rivers. There is, in fact, a coin
of 208 which pictures a bridge, and another of 209 bearing the
legend TRAIECTVS.[3] It may also have been during this first
winter spent in Britain that the Caledonians (the other tribe
besides the Maeatae concerned in the war) sent a deputation to
Septimius seeking to obtain terms of truce. To this the emperor
lent an apparently willing ear, but meanwhile continued his
preparations for war.[4] The first campaign was fought in 209.
The natural difficulties of the country seem to have caused the
Romans more trouble than did the enemy, whose methods of
warfare, as barbarous as their existence in peace, of which both
Dio and Herodian give so thrilling a picture, consisted mainly in
night attacks on the Roman convoys or ambushes laid for them
while on the march.[5] It would be nothing more than waste
labour to attempt to describe this campaign, or indeed the whole

---

[1] Dio Cass. lxxvi. 11. 1; Herod. iii. 14. 1; Zon. xii. 10. For the date
(208) cf. Eck. vii. 206. PROF. AVGG: Coh., vol. iv, Sept. Sev., nos. 573,
574; Dio Cass. lxxvi. 14. 5.

[2] Irenaeus, bishop of Lyon, certainly suffered martyrdom, but for the
general massacre we only have the feeble authority of Bede and Gregory
of Tours.

[3] Bridge coins: Eck. vii. 187; Coh., vol. iv, Sept. Sev., no. 522.
TRAIECTVS, Eck. vii. 206 (of Caracalla); Coh., vol. iv, Car., no. 603.

[4] Herod. iii. 14. 4.

[5] The account of the war is to be found in Dio lxxvi. 11-15 and
Herodian iii. 14. Both pay more attention to the habits of the people
than to the strategy of the war, which indeed neither attempts to portray.
Dio's remark that the Britons can 'endure sitting many days in water
with only their heads sticking out' is not untypical.

war, in any detail. We are entirely ignorant even of the route
by which Severus marched north, or of the farthest point he
reached. Dio mentions his arrival at the extreme north of
Scotland, where he seems to have verified Ptolemy's calculations
as to the solar parallax,[1] but it is doubtful whether he really
ever crossed the Forth. The bridges mentioned by our two
authorities may possibly refer to this estuary, or they may
possibly have spanned the Solway Firth ; while Herodian's
mention of χώματα suggests at once the turf walls of ' Hadrian '
and Antoninus Pius.[2]

Whether Septimius retired south for the winter of 209–10 or
remained in Scotland is another point on which we must be
content to remain in ignorance. He seems to have spent two
summers in the field, carried about from place to place in a litter,
for the gout, to which he eventually succumbed, had long claimed
him as a victim. Geta he left in England to attend to the
government of the province, while he himself, together with
Caracalla, engaged in the actual fighting. On several occasions,
according at least to Dio, Caracalla attempted his father's murder,
but was as often pardoned by an emperor who was, in the words
of the same historian, φιλότεκνος μᾶλλον ἢ φιλόπολις.

In the autumn of 210 some sort of a peace seems to have been
arranged, in which considerable concessions were made by the
Roman to the Briton.[3]   Indeed, no marked success had crowned
the Roman arms and, if we can believe Dio, no fewer than
50,000 had succumbed to the hardihood of the natives or the
rigours of the climate.[4]   In consequence, however, of this peace
Septimius assumed the title of Britannicus Maximus and Cara-

---

[1] Dio Cass. lxxvi. 13. 3 ; Ptol. viii. 2.

[2] For an able discussion of the point see Oman, *England before the
Norman Conquest*, pp. 132–5. He discredits the notion that the bridge-
building concerns the Solway Firth on the ground that a road already
existed leading north to Birrens. Still, the reference may well be to the
repairing of this road. ὑπερβάντος τοῦ στρατοῦ . . . χώματα, Herod. iii.
14. 10. It is really quite unsafe to credit the historian with any conception so definite as that of the walls.

[3] Dio Cass. lxxvi. 13. 4.

[4] Dio Cass. lxxvi. 13. 2.   There is a rescript (*Cod. Iust.* iii. 32. 1) dated
from York on May 5, 210.

calla that of Britannicus.[1] Geta seems to have been raised to the
dignity of an Augustus some two years previously : [2] he also now
bears the title Britannicus.[3] But this triumph was short-lived.
The Caledonians had probably little further object in making
peace than the wish to gain time for more hostile preparations,
and no sooner were the terms settled than they were broken.
Once more the enemy poured south into Roman territory, and
once more the old emperor roused himself from a bed of sickness
to repel them. He was not, however, destined to fight a third
campaign.

Broken in body by the weight of years and by illness, as in
soul by the unfilial conduct of his eldest son, Septimius died at
York on the 4th of February, 211.[4]

His last words were addressed to his sons—ὁμονοεῖτε· τοὺς στρα-
τιώτας πλουτίζετε, τῶν ἄλλων πάντων καταφρονεῖτε : and nothing
perhaps is more remarkable than the soundness of the advice
unless it be the thoroughness with which it was disregarded.
No attempt was made on the part of Caracalla or Geta to
continue the war. After celebrating their father's obsequies in
York they returned with his ashes to Rome, where divine honours
and a flamen were accorded to him. Septimius was sixty-five
years old at the time of his death.[5]

---

[1] Vit. Sev. xviii. 2 ; Eck. vii. 188, 207; also various inscriptions where
BRIT. MAX. is often applied to Caracalla as well as to Septimius,
e. g. CIL. iii. 5324, vii. 222, 226.

[2] The earliest notice of this occurs in an Athenian inscription (CIA.
iii. 10; CIG. 353) of the month Ποσειδεών = end of December and
beginning of January. This puts the probable granting of the title
about October or November. Inasmuch as 209 is the year of his first
tribunicia potestas (Eck. vii. 230) the assumption of the Augustan title
must be put in the late autumn of 208. Cf. Wirth, Quaest. Sev., p. 13.

[3] Eck. vii. 230.

[4] Dio Cass. lxxvi. 15. 2 ; Vit. Sev. xix. 1 ; Herod. iii. 15. 3. Why does
Lombroso, Genie und Irrsinn (German (Reclam) edition, p. 16), attribute
his death to drink ? His only justification—a poor one—is to be found
in Spartian's remark ' vini aliquando cupidus '.

[5] The emperor was not buried in York, though a mount near Acomb
still bears the name Severus Hill (locally pronounced 'Sevĕrus '), and
tradition makes this his grave. The best authorities now hold this hill
to be glacial.

Excursus on the North Wall.

The literary evidence bearing on the question of military wall building in England and Scotland is as follows:

(1) Cap. Ant. Pii v. 4 'alio muro caespiticio ducto'. (i. e. clearly the Scotch wall.)

(2) Spart. Hadr. xi. 2 'murum per octoginta milia passuum primus duxit'.

(3) Spart. Sev. xviii. 2 'muro per transversam insulam ducto utrimque ad finem Oceani munivit'. (Cf. xxii. 4.)

(4) Dio Cass. lxxii. 8. 2 τὸ τεῖχος τὸ διορίζον αὐτούς τε καὶ τὰ Ῥωμαίων στρατόπεδα. (Of the year 184.)

(5) Ibid. lxxvi. 12. 1 οἰκοῦσι δὲ οἱ Μαιᾶται πρὸς αὐτῷ τῷ διατειχίσματι ὃ τὴν νῆσον διχῇ τέμνει. (Again probably the Antonine wall.)

(6) Herod. iii. 14. 10 speaks of χώματα.

(7) Aur. Vict. Caes. xx. 18. '(S.) muro munivit (Brittaniam) per transversam insulam ducto utrimque ad finem oceani.'

(8) (Aur. Vict.) Epit. '(S.) in Brittania vallum per triginta duo passuum milia a mari ad mare deduxit.'

(9) Eutr. viii. 19. '(S.) Vallum per cxxxii milia passuum a mari ad mare deduxit.'

(10) Euseb., p. 177. '(S.) . . . Vallum per cxxxii passuum milia a mari ad mare duxit.'

(11) Oros. vii. 17. '(S.) magnam fossam firmissimumque vallum per centum triginta et duo milia passuum a mari ad mare duxit.'

(12) Cassiod. (Migne 69, p. 1235). '(S.) vallum per cxxxii passuum milia a mari ad mare deduxit.' (He gives the consular date 207.)

It will be seen that, so far as the Severan building of a wall is concerned, almost all these passages are but repetitions of some common source. Whether the passage from Capitolinus means 'another turf wall' or 'another wall this time of turf' is a question which cannot possibly be answered by an appeal to the Latin.

We are not here concerned with the northern (Antonine) wall, nor yet with the Vallum, but with the wall which stretches from the mouth of the Tyne to the Solway Firth.

Relying ultimately on this literary evidence—and certainly consonantly with it—the generally accepted view[1] has been that

---

[1] e. g. Haverfield, Mommsen's *Provinces* (Eng. trans. 1909), vol. ii, p. 351; also in *Camb. Med. Hist.*, vol. i, p. 369, etc.; Stuart Jones, *Companion to Rom. Hist.*, p. 249; Oman, *England before the Norman Conquest*, p. 113.

Hadrian built a turf wall which Severus, some time during the British war, replaced by a stone one. Recent excavations, however, have rendered this view as it stands untenable.[1] That the stone wall superseded the turf one is a likely enough supposition ; indeed the former occupies the line taken by the latter along all its length except for about a mile (west of Birdoswald), where the stone wall keeps north of the turf one, so that here both exist side by side. Now the turrets and mile castles along the rest of the stone (once turf) wall show, as regards the pottery found in them, various fairly distinct strata, the lowest of all containing late first and early second century remains, often referred to as the Flavian-Trajanic level. This in no way vitiates the old theory, as its upholders admit the early (i. e. Hadrianic) construction of the forts, supposing these same stone forts to have been scattered along the turf Hadrianic wall. This is a tenable hypothesis where stone and turf walls coincide : where, however, they do not, as on the site of Mr. Simpson's excavations, we should naturally expect that the pottery found in the forts on this stone (and never previously turf) wall would not go back farther than about 180. Mr. Simpson's excavations, however, have produced conclusive evidence of the same Flavian-Trajanic level here as is to be found along the rest of the wall. It is clear, therefore, that the forts along this mile of wall date back at least until Hadrian's time. That the wall connecting them is equally early does not follow, but two further considerations should lead us to believe that this is the case.

(1) Neither here nor anywhere else along the wall does an examination of the masonry lead one to imagine that the wall was built after the forts. In fact, at one point where the wall makes an angle, the mile castle there situated makes the same angle, clearly because of the turn of the wall, for one cannot imagine the building of a non-rectangular fort for no reason whatsoever.

(2) Is it likely that although elsewhere the forts were joined to the wall yet for this one mile some four of them were built at a distance of anything from 100 to 300 yards from it ?

[1] Of particular importance are the excavations of Mr. F. G. Simpson at and about High House. For the statement of the new view cf. P. Newbold in *Excavations on the Line of the Roman Wall in Cumberland* (Kendall, 1913), pp. 339 sqq. ; also 'Excavations on the Roman Wall at Limestone Bank ' (*Arch. Ael.*, 3rd series, vol. ix, 1913), etc.

It is early yet to draw definite positive conclusions from this evidence, but it is quite enough to justify us in saying that Septimius did not build the stone wall as we now have it, though we are not precluded from supposing that he did some repairing work there—indeed literary and archaeological evidence warrant this presumption. Whether Hadrian built the turf wall which an Antonine hand converted into a stone one, or whether Hadrian himself wrought this conversion on a pre-existent turf wall, are questions to which it would be both impertinent and unsafe here and now to hazard an answer. The latter, at any rate, seems improbable, inasmuch as limes-construction before Hadrian is almost unknown, besides which the only man to whom it could obviously be attributed is Agricola. Now Agricola is unlikely to have built a limes, as he contemplated the reduction of the entire province. Further, if he built a wall why does not Tacitus mention it?

If, then, we do not accept the Antonine building of the stone wall, we can only suppose that there never was a turf one running across the island, and that the piece west of Birdoswald was a temporary erection, hastily finished off, maybe, at the end of one autumn, and superseded next spring by the completion of the stone wall along another line, which maturer consideration had decided to be more suitable.

CHAPTER IX

PHILOSOPHY AND RELIGION

To the student of what, for want of a better term, may be called *Sittengeschichte* there is ever present the temptation to regard the period under consideration as a time of intellectual flux—of transition—between two periods of comparative intellectual stagnation; the truth being that it is only a more careful examination that discloses motion in the mental or psychic life of a people. Nevertheless there may be some truth in the view that the century and a half which elapsed between the death of Marcus Aurelius and the founding of Constantinople does form such a period of transition.

The years which saw the death of the republic and the birth of the empire saw also the superseding of religion, in the form of the Olympian gods, by philosophy, and the further introduction of those Eastern or mystic cults by means of which the less intellectual sought to express their higher aspirations.

'From the time of Cicero to that of Marcus Aurelius Roman society advanced from unbelief to belief,' says Boissier.

Scepticism both in the region of morality and that of religion and metaphysics was steadily declining during the first century and a half of the Christian Era, nor is the superficial Voltairianism of Lucian typical of an age which realized with growing clearness the moral superiority of the barbarians who were knocking at the door not necessarily of a degenerate but certainly of an intellectually disintegrated empire.[1] The Stoic emperor may be said to mark the zenith of that philosophic religion of which Cleanthes had sowed the first seeds in Rome, and not only was he the last Stoic—he was the last emperor

---

[1] This feeling of admiration appears as early as in the *Germania* of Tacitus. Cf. also the story of Julia Domna and the Caledonian woman (Dio Cass. lxxvi. 16. 5). Also Phil. Vit. Ap. vii. 19.

before Constantine resolutely to accept a creed in its entirety, and with that intolerance of other creeds and fear of the contamination of his own without which a man or a nation so often passes through broad-mindedness into scepticism. After Marcus Aurelius we come upon a period of eclecticism and syncretism, moral, philosophic, and religious—a state of flux in fact out of which may be said to have crystallized but two religions, Mithraism and Christianity.

In matters purely religious syncretism was indeed inevitable. The actual number of deities worshipped in the Roman empire must have been something stupendous; 'nostra ubique regio tam praesentibus plena est numinibus ut facilius possis deum quam hominem invenire', grumbles Quartilla,[1] and the growing frequency of feast-days shows that this tendency was on the increase.[2] Not without reason did mortals legislate against the introduction of new divinities, or the gods themselves determine upon an Alien Act in Olympus.[3]

It is only natural that this unwieldy concourse of gods should lead to that identification of the divinities of one nationality with those of another until there dawned upon the minds of men the conception of one God of whom all these objects of worship were but the forms. The change, in fact, is clearly seen in the different outlook of Cicero and Plutarch : ' sua cuique civitati religio, Laeli, est ; nostra nobis,' cries the former ; θεοὺς ... οὐχ ἑτέρους παρ' ἑτέροις οὐδὲ βαρβάρους καὶ ῞Ελληνας οὐδὲ νοτίους καὶ βορείους, says Plutarch.[4]

As a preliminary step, therefore, towards the unification of the conception of God we get this period of syncretism. There is no need to multiply instances. The identification of Cybele with Bona Dea and Ops, and her later connexion with Bellona,

---

[1] Petron. *Sat.* xvii.   Cf. Plin. *H. N.* ii. 16 ' maior coelitum populus etiam quam hominum intelligi potest'.

[2] In the reign of Marcus Aurelius there were 135 as against 66 at the end of the Republic (Cap. M. A. x. 10), and in 354 there were as many as 165 (*CIL.* i, p. 378, Philocalus).

[3] Luc. *Deor. Conc.* 14–18; Paul. *Sent.* v. 21, § 2 'qui novas et . . . incognitas religiones inducunt ex quibus animi hominum moveantur, honestiores deportantur, humiliores capite puniuntur'.

[4] Cic. *pro Flacc.* 28 ; Plut. *Is. et Os.* 67.

with whom was identified the Carthaginian goddess Mâ; [1] the confusion of Mithras with Sabazios ; the various forms and activities of Serapis, who appears now as the god of healing, and as such represents Aesculapius or Apollo Salutaris, now as the god of the under-world, the Egyptian Pluto, and now as the sun-god, in which capacity he melts on the one hand into Mithras, and on the other into Jupiter.[2] The Emperor Tacitus marks a still more advanced stage, for with a most laudable economy of space and money he erected a ' templum deorum ',[3] and even in Christian times an emperor would not disdain the office of *pontifex maximus*, nor would a pope hesitate to convert a pagan festival into a feast of the church.[4]

The reign of Septimius, then, marks the beginning of this period of progressive religious syncretism : its typical philosophy is neo-pythagoreanism, and perhaps its most typical figure that of the Empress Julia Domna.[5] Although history, as has been suggested above, has tended to over-emphasize the importance of Julia in the sphere of politics, it would be hard to make a similar mistake with regard to her in the domain of philosophy and religion ; nor must we forget that the superposition of

[1] Cf. Strabo, xii. 2. 3.

[2] e.g. *CIL*. iii. 4560 ' I. O. M. Sarapidi '. For a joint-priest of Isis and Julia Domna as *mater deorum* cf. *CIL*. ix. 1153. Cf. also for Isis, Apul. *Met*. xi. 5. Good ' composite-god ' inscriptions are to be seen in *CIL*. ii. 2407 (containing some twenty gods and goddesses) and viii. 4578 (year 283).

[3] Vop. Tac. ix. 5.

[4] e.g. Gratian was the last Pont. Max. in 382. In 494 the Pope Gelasius turned the Lupercalia into the Purification of the Blessed Virgin. In Greece nowadays many a shrine of St. Dionysius is but an old τέμενος of Dionysus.

[5] It seems probable that the name Domna is not—as has generally been supposed—a shortened form of Domina. In the dialect of Cyzicus Domna is another name for Proserpine, and the frequent identification of Julia with Demeter makes her connexion with Proserpine obvious. A variation of spelling occurs in an African inscription (*CIL*. viii. 2670), where the empress appears as 'Dome'. So Réville, *Die Religion der römischen Gesellschaft im Zeitalter des Synkretismus*, p. 190. References to this book (to which I am deeply indebted) will always be to this German translation. In the original French the book is out of print.

Western culture upon a character essentially Eastern won for the empress such a world-wide popularity as would ensure everywhere the publication and acceptance of her opinions. Greece worshipped her as Demeter or Hera, and under the former name was built to her a temple at Aphrodisias in Caria,[1] while the town of Plotinopolis in Thrace seems at this period to have adopted the name Domnopolis.[2] After her deification by Heliogabalus she possessed a priestess at Naples.[3] In private life she must have been a woman of strong and imperious character, deeply imbued with that rather credulous mysticism so typical of the East, yet not without the ballast of calm reasoning which a philosophical training gave her : ἡ φιλόσοφος ᾿Ιουλία is probably no idle or unmerited compliment.[4]

Not less interesting than the empress herself was the circle of *savants* which she gathered round her. Of its members may be mentioned her sister Julia Moesa, and her nieces Julia Soemias and Mammea : another woman associate was that Arria to whom Diogenes Laertius thought of dedicating his book on the lives of the philosophers, and who seems to have inspired such affection and admiration in the breast of the doctor Galen.[5] Diogenes and Galen themselves belonged to the circle, as also did another doctor, Serenus Sammonicus, the naturalists Aelian and Oppian, the lawyers Papinian, Ulpian, and Paul, and Antipater of Hierapolis, to whom Julia entrusted the education of her sons and who compiled a history of Severus himself.[6] Besides these

---

[1] *CIG.* 2815 ; cf. 3642, 3956. Lampsacus also worshipped her as Hestia (Coh., iv, p. 124, Vesta) and Demeter, *CIG.* 3642. Lacina knew her as νέα ῞Ηρα ῾Ρωμαία, *CIG.* 3956 b.

[2] Eck. ii. 46.

[3] *CIL.* ix. 1153. The more mundane appellations of the empress may here be mentioned. They were *mater castrorum, mater senatus* (e.g. both in *CIL.* iii. 13655: also in lost Silchester Inscrip. *CIL.* vii. 7), *mater patriae* (e.g. *CIL.* ix. 4637 ; Eck. vii. 196).

[4] Phil. Vit. Soph. ii, p. 121 (ed. Kayser). For a general sketch of J. D. see Michael Field's book, Ballantyne Press, 1903.

[5] So Menagius, *Histor. mulier. philosopharum*, c. 47 ; Gal. *de ther.* i. 3 τὴν δὲ πάντα μοι φιλτάτην ᾿Αρρίαν.

[6] Phil. Vit. Soph. ii, p. 109 (ed. Kayser). Antipater was a consul and a governor of Bithynia. We are not surprised to hear that the tutor of Caracalla was deprived of this post for cruelty.

it is at least possible that the learned author of the *Deipno-sophistae* was a member, and we may suppose that such famous rhetoricians as Apollonius of Athens, Heraclides, and Hermocrates would not be unwelcome guests on their visits to Rome.[1] Alexander of Aphrodisias was also a contemporary. He seems indeed to have owed his position as head of the Aristotelian school at Athens to the patronage of Septimius and Caracalla. To them at least he dedicates one of his works in gratitude for his appointment.[2] Last, and perhaps most important, must be mentioned Philostratus.

The characteristics of this assembly are clearly marked. To begin with we notice the excess of erudition over purely literary gifts. If we discount the medical verses of Serenus, Oppian is its only poet, nor can the prose style of any of its members be said to struggle above the level of mediocrity. In the second place its productions are essentially artificial and ' precious '; and thirdly, the Latin element gives way very much to the Syrian. This last characteristic is of course particularly visible in the most important work to which the circle gave birth—the Life of Apollonius by Philostratus. In its nature the book is neither a novel nor yet a history : it is a gospel. Written at the instigation of the empress it sought to create a hero half human, half divine,[3] who should not be too philosophically minded to alienate the sympathies of the many, nor yet too mythological to offend the susceptibilities of the learned. There is no need to see in the publication any direct attack upon Christianity, except in so far as any such attempt to give society a religious ideal is of necessity a form of attack on all current religions and philosophies. Apollonius himself is an historical figure.[4] He was a Pythagorean thaumaturge who lived at

---

[1] Phil. Soph. ii, pp. 103, 102 etc., 109.

[2] Alex. Aphr. *de fato*, p. 163 ; cf. Suid., p. 182 A, also Euseb. *Praep.* vi. 9, p. 268 ; Zeller, iii. 1. 610 note (2nd edit.).

[3] It is worthy of notice that Apollonius claimed to be a ' son of man ' rather than a god (i. 6).

[4] Reference is made to Apollonius by Suidas, Porphyry (Vit. Pyth. ii— to the effect that he wrote a life of Pythagoras), Apuleius (*Apol.* 90), and Lucian (*Pseudom.* 5). For his pythagoreanism cf. i. 7, 13, 32, iii. 30, etc. He does not, however, lay much stress on metempsychosis or magic

Tyana in the second half of the first century of the Christian
era, and Philostratus' life contains references to all the emperors
from Nero to Nerva inclusive. The account given is founded
on the diary of Apollonius' disciple Damis, which purports to
have got into Julia Domna's hands and to have been handed on
by her to Philostratus for re-edition. It bears striking resem-
blances to the New Testament, except that the style is more
pretentious, and indeed better, the general tone infinitely more
erudite, and the matter still more miraculous. Everywhere one
comes upon echoes of classical authors,[1] and not infrequently are
to be found sentences of which Plato need not have been ashamed
and aphorisms which would not disgrace a Rochefoucauld.[2]
Most striking, however, are the constant likenesses, verbal or
material, to the New Testament story. Of such may be mentioned the theory of a virgin birth;[3] the story of an 'annun-
ciation';[4] the parable of the sower;[5] the healing of a demoniac
child;[6] the preaching of forbearance and broad-mindedness on
the occasion of a 'woman taken in adultery';[7] the metaphor of
a 'light under a bushel',[8] and that of the dogs and the 'food
which falleth from the master's table';[9] the appearance of Apollonius, as of Christ, before a judgement seat;[10] the refusal of the
disciple Damis, like that of Peter, to desert his master;[11] and,
most striking of all, a story like to that of Jairus' daughter in
almost all its details.[12]

numbers.   For an echo of the Stoic doctrine of the world-νοῦς cf.
iii. 34.

[1] Especially Plato, e. g. the 'republican', ship simile (iii. 35), the
digression on music (v. 21), and such remarks as οἱ ἄνθρωποι ἐν δεσμωτηρίῳ
ἐσμὲν τὸν χρόνον τοῦτον, ὃς δὴ ὠνόμασται βίος (vii. 26). Homer and Euripides
are quoted, and there are constant verbal reminders of Aeschylus (γαμψώ-
νυχος, ταυρηδόν) and Aristophanes (φροντιστήριον).

[2] e. g. τοὺς γὰρ σπουδαίους οἱ θεοὶ καὶ ἄνευ τῶν προξενούντων ἀσπάζονται
(i. 12). To a rich man : δοκεῖς μοι, οὐ σὺ τὴν οἰκίαν ἀλλὰ σὲ ἡ οἰκία κεκτῆσθαι
(v. 22) ; θεοῦ παίγνιον ἄνθρωπος (iv. 36).

[3] i. 4.   [4] i. 4.   [5] iv. 3.
[6] iii. 38. Cf. iv. 20.
[7] i. 37.   [8] vi. 18.   [9] i. 19.
[10] iv. 40, 44, viii. 5. On this latter occasion Apollonius, like Christ,
'passed from among their midst'.
[11] vii. 15.   [12] iv. 45.

Taking the book as a whole one cannot wonder that the religion of Apollonius of Tyana fell upon the ears of a heedless world. Failing by reason of its obvious artificiality in that simple directness which has won for the Gospel of Christ so many adherents, it yet lacks the logical cohesion of a philosophic system, and in fact, while aiming at giving birth at once to a religion and a philosophy, it succeeded in producing both still-born. Literature has preserved for us the mention only of three imperial devotees : Caracalla, who built for Apollonius a heroon ; Alexander Severus,[1] who, with a vagueness of sentiment typical of the man and of the age, found for the thaumaturge's image a place with those of Orpheus, Abraham, and Christ;[2] and Aurelian, who, warned by Apollonius' ghost, abstained from sacking the town of Tyana.[3]

In a city such as Rome, where, as Athenaeus said, one might see ' whole peoples dwelling together, Cappadocians, Scythians, and men from Pontus ',[4] it is not surprising to find adherents of every form of creed, nor can we be much astonished to discover that that with perhaps the fewest followers was the State, or Olympian, religion. And yet this was by no means defunct even at the turn of the second and third centuries. Especially do we notice a sort of old-fashioned revival of the specific Italian deities such as Silvanus and Minerva, to the latter of whom Septimius himself appears to have built a temple.[5] The semi-private worship of the Lares, Manes, and Penates seems also to have flourished with almost undiminished vigour,[6] while the religious guilds, such as the Salii, the Arval brothers (of which the emperor became a member in 195), and the Fetiales, continued at least until the fourth century.[7]

In connexion with these may also be mentioned the genii and

---

[1] Dio Cass. lxxvii. 18. 4.   [2] Lamp. Alex. Sev. xxix. 2.
[3] Vop. Aur. xxiv. 3.   [4] Athen. *deipn.* i. 36.

[5] Eck. vii. 187. He also built a temple in Rome after the Parthian war in honour of Heracles and Bacchus, the two gods whom he considered the patron deities of Leptis (Dio Cass. lxxvi. 16. 3 ; Eck. vii. 171). At Heliopolis he dedicated a temple to Jupiter.

[6] Certainly in Lucian's day. Cf. *Char.* 22 ; *de luctu*, 9.

[7] Severus as an Arval brother, cf. *CIL.* vi. 1026 ; Eck. viii. 422. Ammianus (xix. 2. 6) mentions the Fetiales in 359.

daemons, the μυσταγωγοὶ τοῦ βίου as Menander called them, who, attendant upon every man in his lifetime, were credited with some sort of nebulous existence after his death, and, after the manner of the old chthonic deities, required at times some mollifying or apotropaeic treatment.[1] The belief in the existence and power of these supernatural beings was very widespread, and that not only among the unenlightened. Even so excellent a philosopher as Plotinus imagined the space midway between heaven and earth as peopled by demons;[2] while the Christians, who were not above such intellectual weaknesses, repudiated genii and preferred to believe in evil spirits.[3]

But of the State religion, properly so called, Caesar worship still continued the most vital element. Not only was the reigning emperor adored, but all, right back to Augustus, received some meed of honour : the worshipper was free to exercise some discretion in his choice, and Capitolinus (whoever he was and whenever he wrote) testifies to the evergreen popularity of the image of Marcus Aurelius even in his day.[4] The binding nature of an oath taken on the genius of an emperor is made the subject of scornful comment by Tertullian.[5]

Of far more widely spread popularity, however, than either the national or the established religion were those Eastern cults, of which undoubtedly that of the Persian sun-god Mithras was the chief. This religion, as is well known, had been established

---

[1] Cf. Amm. Marc. xxi. 14; Max. Tyr. 14. Censorinus (de Die Nat. 2) recommends bloodless offerings every birthday.

[2] Plot. Enn. iii. 5. 6. His disciple Porphyrius has a tale of an Egyptian priest who summoned Plotinus' own daemon from the dead (Porph. Vit. Plot., p. 108, ed. Didot, 1878).

[3] Tert. Apol. 22.

[4] Cap. Mar. Ant. xviii. 6 'hodie in multis domibus Marci Antonini statuae consistunt inter deos penates'. CIL. vi. 575 gives a list of twenty divi worshipped by the Arval brothers in the time of Alexander Severus. Such colleges, too, as the Flaviales show the continuance of this form of worship. The Arvales had a Caesarium (CIL. vi. 561).

[5] Tert. Apol. 28 'citius . . . apud vos per omnes deos quam per unum genium Caesaris peieratur'. The amusement of the Senate when called upon to regard Commodus as a god (Lamp. Comm. viii. 9) and Caracalla's scornful 'sit (Geta) divus dum non sit vivus' (Spart. Get. ii. 9) show the other side of the picture.

in Rome since the earlier years of the first century of the Christian
Era,[1] but it was not until the closing decades of the second that
the cult can be said to have shown any marked predominance
over other Eastern creeds. In the reign of Severus Mithraic
inscriptions are of no uncommon occurrence, and a *sacrarium* of
the god seems to have been built in Rome to commemorate that
emperor's Eastern victories.[2] In some features Mithraism seems
closely to have resembled Christianity. It recognized a baptism,
a sacrament,[3] a mediation, and a regeneration wrought by the
cleansing blood of the god;[4] its chief feast-day was December 25,

---

[1] Common even earlier in the East; the Cilician robbers, whom Pompey
conquered in 70 B.C., recognized him as a god (Plut. *Pomp.* 24). For the
cult in Armenia about A.D. 66 cf. Dio Cass. lxiii. 5. 2. The inscription
(*CIL.* vi. 968*) of Tiberius' reign is a forgery: so Cumont, *Textes et
monuments figurés relatifs aux mystères de Mithra*, vol. ii, p. 477. The
poet Statius had obviously seen statues representing the slaying of the
bull—'seu Persei sub rupibus antri Indignata sequi torquentem cornua
Mithram' (Stat. *Theb.* i. 719, 720). Hadrian was a worshipper (Porph.
Abstin. ii. 56; Euseb. *Praep. Evang.* iv. 16. 7), and under Antoninus Pius
a temple was built him at Ostia (*CIL.* xiv. 58, 59). For its rites in
Commodus' reign see Lamp. *Comm.* ix. 6 (cf. *CIL.* vi. 725, 727, 740, 745).
Later the mother of Aurelian was a local priestess of Mithras (Vop. Aur.
iv. 2), and it was not until 377 that the city prefect Gracchus ordered the
demolition of his temple (Hier. *Ep. ad Laet.* 57).

[2] *CIL.* vi. 738. For a priest 'invicti Mithrae domus augustanae'
cf. Marini, *fr. Arv.*, p. 529. *L'Ann. ép.* 1911, no. 56, shows a *speleum*
erected by some praetorians returning from the Eastern war in the year
202 at Palaiopolis in Andros.

[3] 'Celebrat panis oblationem,' says Tertullian (*de Praescr.* 40), and
adds 'a diabolo scilicet'. Plutarch (*Is. et Os.* 46) speaks of Mithras as
μεσίτης, though in that passage he seems to use the word rather to
express the god's nature as midway between those of Ahuramazda and
Ahriman.

[4] *CIL.* vi. 510 'taurobolio ... in aeternum renatus'. Firmicus Maternus
recognized and commented on the similarity between the two religions
(xxvii. 8). A strange echo of Athanasius' *incomprehensibilis* is to be
found in the word *indeprehensibilis*, which is not infrequently applied
in inscriptions to Mithras (e.g. *CIL.* v. 805). It has recently been doubted
whether the *taurobolium* belongs to Mithraism and is not rather part of
the religion of the Magna Mater (so Domaszewski, 'Magna Mater in
Latin Inscriptions', *J. R. S.*, vol. i. 1, pp. 50–6). Certainly *CIL.* xii. 4321
and 4322 (Narbo) mention *taurobolia* in connexion with the latter divinity.

when the new birth of the sun was celebrated. Like Christianity it preached the doctrine of immortality, and again like that religion claimed sole validity for its doctrines. The initiated took upon themselves strange names, being known as lions, hyenas, Persians, warriors, and the like, and all devotees were divided into seven classes in a way which reminds one of the Freemasons, and which has also been not inaptly compared to the practices of the Salvation Army.[1]

Persia, however, was not the only country to supply Rome and its empire with a creed. The gods of Egypt[2] seem to have enjoyed, during the reign of Septimius, a popularity as great as, or greater than, they had ever done. Most important among them at this time was the goddess Isis, whose worship dates back well into the time of the republic.[3] Commodus had shown her especial honour,[4] and had seemingly forced the unwilling Niger to do the same, while Caracalla had built her a temple[5] and founded a festival in her honour.[6] In Severus' reign we find epigraphic evidence of prayer offered to Isis for the well-being of the royal family.[7] No deity offers a much better instance of syncretism, for she combines in herself the personalities and characteristics of Juno, Ceres, Proserpine, and Venus, added to which she seems to have been the especial patron of traders and sailors.[8] Closely connected, too, with her were Anubis and Harpocrates. Of the Egyptian pantheon, however, Serapis seems to have been the special favourite of Septimius, who showed considerable interest in his worship on his Egyptian tour,[9] nor

---

[1] Cf. Phythian-Adams, 'The Problem of the Mithraic Grades,' *J. R. S.*, vol. ii. 1, pp. 53–64; Réville, *op. cit.*, p. 95. To the orthodox Christians of the time it suggested a sort of heathen gnosticism (Orig. *c. Cels.* vi. 22).

[2] One recalls Minucius Felix's words (Oct. 22) 'haec . . . Aegyptia quondam, nunc et sacra Romana sunt '.

[3] Augustus tolerated it outside the pomerium (Dio Cass. liii. 2. 4). Expulsion under Tiberius (Tac. *Ann.* ii. 85; Joseph. *Ant.* xviii. 3, 4, 5).

[4] Lamp. Comm. ix. 4.

[5] Spart. Nig. vi. 8.

[6] Spart. Car. ix. 10.   [7] *CIL.* vi. 354.

[8] 'Isis marina' she is called in various inscriptions. Cf. Apul. *Met.* xi. 8.

[9] Vit. Sev. xvii. 4.

was this cult deserted by his successors Caracalla and Alexander.[1]
Gradually, in fact, his popularity seems to have eclipsed that of
Isis, and by Macrobius' time he too had merged into a sun-god
and become but one more aspect of the universal divinity.[2]

Another sun-god who appears to have had no small vogue at
this time was the Syrian Jupiter Dolichenus, inscriptions attesting whose worship come to us in considerable numbers from
provinces so wide apart as Britain, Dacia, and Numidia.[3] It is,
however, to be noted that the worship of this god was almost
entirely confined to military circles, and that the seeming popularity of his cult is due to the troops stationed in a province
rather than to the provincial civilians.[4] His temple also stood
on the Esquiline, and to him was attached a regular priesthood
by or through whom prayer and offerings were constantly made
for the health and prosperity of Severus and his family.[5] So
advanced by this time was the process of syncretism that it is
difficult clearly to distinguish one Syrian or Syro-phoenician god
from another. Septimius' temple to Jupiter of Damascus or
Heliopolis, erected in the latter city, has already been mentioned.
Half Roman Jove, half Phoenician Bal, he is not improbably to
be identified with the Malakbelus, of whose worship we now
begin to find traces in Rome.[6] The Syrian goddess on whom
Lucian wrote his brochure, and to whom alone the atheistic Nero
bowed the knee,[7] possessed under the Severi a temple in Rome,[8]
and was worshipped at Ostia as the goddess of prostitutes, where
she was identified indifferently as the Cyprian Venus or Majuma

---

[1] Dio Cass. lxxvii. 23. 2, 3; Lamp. Alex. Sev. xxvi. 8.

[2] Macrob. *Sat.* i. 20. 13.

[3] Réville, *op. cit.*, p. 45, numbers eleven in Dacia, eight in Britain,
three in Numidia, besides many others, including twenty-nine Italian
examples (twenty-one in Rome).

[4] So Toutain, *Les Cultes païens dans l'empire romain*, vol. ii, p. 259 sqq.

[5] Cf. *CIL.* vi. 406, 407. He had a second temple somewhere in
Rome.

[6] *CIL.* vi. 51, 701. As the god came from Emesa he may have entered
Rome with Heliogabalus.

[7] Suet. *Ner.* 56 'religionum usque quoque contemptor praeter unius
Deae Syriae'.

[8] *CIL.* vi. 115, 116, 399.

of Antioch.[1] Along with her may be mentioned the similar Carthaginian (i. e. also Phoenician) goddess, Juno Caelestis, a moon and star deity with whom Julia Domna was perhaps identified.[2]

Of the Phrygian deities it is scarcely necessary to do more than mention the Great Mother, to the worship of whom Herodian and Lampridius assure us that both Commodus and Alexander Severus were much addicted.[3] Attis is another instance of a budding sun-, or universal, god;[4] and it is a point perhaps worthy of passing notice that his priests, even the archigalli, were by this time not invariably Phrygians; they were sometimes Romans.[5]

Of the position and importance of Christianity at this time, as of the actual numbers that religion could claim as its own, we are neither fully nor trustworthily informed. It is certain that by the year 200 a considerable number of churches were in existence. There were the seven churches of Asia mentioned by St. John—Smyrna, Pergamum, Thyatira, Sardis, Philadelphia, Laodicea, and Antioch ; besides these the even then famous church of Alexandria, those of Jerusalem, Nisibis, Seleucia, Beroea, Apamea, Hierapolis, and Samosata.[6] Of all the provinces, however, that apparently most thickly peopled with Christians was Africa, in which, if we may believe Tertullian, every city could boast a numerical superiority of Christians to pagan inhabitants.[7] Carthage was possessed of a bishop as early as 197, and some eighteen years later was the seat of a synod.

---

[1] Clem. Alex. *Protrep.* ii. 14; Arnob. v. 19; Firm. Mat. *de err.* 10; Lact. i. 17.

[2] Eck. vii. 204. The goddess of course equals Astarte, who was as Tertullian said (*Apol.* 23) 'pluviarum pollicitatrix'. For her worship in Rome, Britain, and Dacia cf. *CIL.* vi. 77-80, vii. 759, iii. 993.

[3] Herod. i. 10. 5 (mentions her feast); Lamp. Alex. Sev. 37. 6 ditto.

[4] Macrob. *Sat.* i. 21. 7 ; Arnob. *adv. gent.* v. 42.

[5] Domaszewski (*J. R. S.*, vol. i. 1, p. 50) doubts this inasmuch as the archigalli were eunuchs.

[6] Ceuleneer, p. 210. He reckons 500,000 Christians all told. The Belgian savant in this chapter goes into more detail on the question of the various Christian sects than I have thought it necessary or desirable to emulate.

[7] Tert. *ad Scap.* 2 'pars paene maior civitatis cuiusque'. Ceuleneer, p. 211, reckons 100,000.

Persecutions, too, and martyrdoms were of no uncommon occurrence in this province. Among the proconsuls unfavourably disposed towards Christianity may be mentioned Vigellius Saturninus (198–200 or 201), the first,[1] according to Tertullian, to shed Christian blood in Africa, Apuleius Rufinus (203–204), and that Scapula to or against whom Tertullian wrote his treatise. The protomartyr of Africa was one Namphamo, who suffered death under the proconsulship of Saturninus on the 4th of July, 198. Some five years later Carthage was the scene of one of the most famous of the early martyrdoms, that of Perpetua.[2]

In general, however, persecutions seem to have been neither widespread nor systematic. The legal status of a Christian was a somewhat uncertain one. Up to the year 201 no edict or law upon the subject existed save for the famous rescript of Traian, which ordered the Christians not to be sought out or hunted down but merely punished if discovered.[3] This, of course, left the provincial governor full power to exercise his discretion and to deal with Christians leniently or severely as he chose. A change came with the end of the year 201, when, not improbably influenced by what he had seen in Palestine in the course of his visit there, Septimius issued an edict forbidding conversion either to Judaism or Christianity.[4]

As far as the Jews were concerned the edict seems to have been but little put into force. Judaism had always, as Tertullian observed, been a religion ' certe licita ',[5] and Eusebius comments on the fact that the conversion of one Domnius from Christianity to Judaism was provocative of no trouble whatsoever.[6] Naturally enough this partiality roused a still bitterer hatred for the Jews

---

[1] *ad Scap.* 3.   [2] Tert. *de Anima*, 55.
[3] Plin. *ep. ad Trai.* 97 ' conquirendi non sunt '.
[4] Euseb *Eccles. Hist.* vi. 1 ; Vit. Sev. xvii. 1. It may have been this edict which called forth Hippolytus' *De Antichristo*, written about this time. In it H. protests against the laws levelled against Christians, and identifies Rome with the fourth beast of the prophet Daniel; cf. Gwatkin, *Church History*, i, p. 118.
[5] Tert. *Apol.* 21. Severus indeed seems to have sanctioned legislation in favour of the Jews (*Dig.* l. 2. 3; cf. Friedländer (8th edit.), iv, p. 242) ; but see Graetz, iv. 255.
[6] Euseb. v. 22, vi. 12. 1.

in the hearts of the Christians, who complained that the corpses
of their friends were not infrequently destroyed by the former
sect as a pragmatic disproof of the doctrine of the resurrection of
the body.   Tertullian went so far as to speak of synagogues as
'fontes persecutionum '.[1] Of active persecution of the Christians
before the edict of Severus we hear little.   There seems to have
been some in Byzantium before the time of its capture, though
Caecilius Capella, the official who was responsible for it, is
represented by Tertullian as realizing like others elsewhere
that it was bound to fail in the end, and that the Christians
were in reality better off than their persecutors.[2] We hear
also of a fairly vigorous persecution in Alexandria at the
time of the emperor's visit in 201, which he did nothing to
check.[3] Yet, at least in his earlier years, Severus seems to have
looked upon the Christians with no unfavourable eye.   He gave
his son Caracalla a Christian nurse[4] and allowed him a Jewish
playmate,[5] while he himself is said to have been cured of some
disease by one Eutychius Proculus, a Christian, by whom he was
anointed with holy oil, and whom, in gratitude, he retained in
his service until his death.   There is some likelihood, too, that
the procurator Euodus, the same who was connected with the
plot for the overthrow of Plautian,[6] was no other than the
Christian tutor of Caracalla to whom Tertullian refers as
Torpaeion.[7] But whatever his early views there can be no doubt

---

[1] Tert. *Apol.* 7 ; *ad Nat.* i. 14.

[2] Tert. *ad Scap.* 3 "Caecilius Capella in illo exitu Byzantino,
"Christiani, gaudete" exclamavit '. See above, p. 97, note 3.

[3] Euseb. vi. 1. In his *Hist. Eccles.* (vi. 2. 2) Eusebius gives the date as
202—δέκατον τῆς βασιλείας ἔτος : the *Chronicon paschale* (i. 496) as 205.
The right date (201) is to be found in Abulfaragius (*Hist. Dyn.* 360).
201 must be correct, as all agree that Septimius was in Egypt at the time,
and we know that he had left that country before New Year's Day, 202.
The various Egyptian martyrdoms, such as those of Leonides, father of
Origen, and of Potamiena, are all subsequent to the edict (Euseb. vi. 5).
Clement mentions a persecution in the Stromata (ii. 414).

[4] Tert. *ad Scap.* 4 'lacte Christiano educatus '.

[5] Spart. Car. i. 6.

[6] Dio Cass. lxxvi. 3. 2 ; cf. lxxvii. 1. 1.

[7] Tert. *ad Scap.* 4. Torpaeion (? reading Torpacion) = τροφεύς.

that the emperor was opposed to Christianity as a religion [1] and to Christians as a class, nor can we be much surprised at the fact. Three causes of complaint were always brought forward against them. First, the well-worn charge of flagrant immorality supposed to take place at their *agapai*,[2] a charge not much more absurd than similar ones brought by orthodox Christians against the Gnostics ; [3] secondly, the flat and stubborn refusal to acquiesce or participate in any form of Caesar worship; and thirdly, that constant spirit of unrest—common to Christian and Jew alike— such as found expression in the Barchochebas' rising some sixty years before this,[4] and was still more agitating the hearts of the faithful about the year 202–3, at which exact time the end of the world was expected with some trepidation in accordance with the prophecy of Daniel.[5]

Of the various sects and heresies which troubled the peace of the Church at this time this is not the occasion to speak at length. The very freedom of Christendom from outside persecution only served to foster internal strife,[6] as Tertullian suggested. Mention has already been made of the Gnostics, with their fatalistic doctrine of morals, and their virtual denial of the doctrine of the Incarnation by the sharp division they sought to establish between the Logos or Christ and Jesus the man.

Two more sects worth a passing notice are those founded respectively by Artemon and Theodotes, the Byzantine. The latter was excommunicated in 189 by Pope Victor [7] and the heresy soon died out. Both Artemonism and Theodotism were

---

[1] So was Ulpian (Lactan. *Inst.* v. 11).

[2] Cf. Plin. *ep. ad Trai.* 96. 7, etc. Thyestean banquets and Οἰδιπόδειοι μίξεις were charges often brought against the early Christians.

[3] Just. *Apol.* i. 426 ; Iren. i. 26, 31, iii. 11 ; Clem. Alex. *Strom.* vii. 17 ; Euseb. iv. 7, vi. 14—especially remarks on the Cainites.

[4] In Hadrian's reign, *circ.* 135. See Schiller, ii, p. 613.

[5] Euseb. vi. 7 ; Daniel ix. 24–7.

[6] Tert. *de Cor. Mil.* 1 ' mussitant denique tam bonam et longam pacem periclitari '.

[7] Euseb. v. 28. This orthodox and energetic Christian also excommunicated the Quartodecimans in 197, in spite of the protests of Irenaeus (Euseb. v. 23, 24).

unitarian in character, and denied the divinity of Christ.
Another heresy to win the practically expressed disfavour of
the papal see was that of Montanus, against which Pope
Zephyrnius launched an edict in the year 205.[2]
To sum up. The reign of Septimius marks almost the
beginning of a period of considerable moral, intellectual, and
spiritual ferment. Scepticism was rare, and the generality of
mankind more inclined to believe in anything than in nothing.
Though in the majority of men religion can scarcely be said to
have risen above the level of credulity and superstition,[3] yet,
such as it was, it was genuine and, as a wealth of epigraphic
evidence attests, publicly expressed with as little reticence as
niggardliness. The renewed popularity of the oracles of Delphi
and other places is typical of the age.[4] In the domain of morals
there was growing up a distinct tendency towards the ideals of
purity and holiness, and though the age of asceticism had not as
yet descended upon the world, the few instances where it occurred
commanded instant and widespread respect.[5] Besides this we
begin to see during this period. traces of that connexion between
morals and religion so rare in the ancient, so common in the
modern, world—ἀνθρώπου μὲν εἶναι τὸ ἁμαρτάνειν, θεοῦ δ' ἢ ἀνδρὸς
ἰσοθέου τὰ πταισθέντα ἐπανορθοῦν.[6]
In conclusion, we cannot do better than cite the words of

---

[1] Euseb. v. 28; Epiph. adv. Haeres. liv. 1.

[2] Tert. de Pudic. 1. Tertullian himself, curiously enough, became a
Montanist. The turning-point of his belief is marked by the appearance
of his de Corona Militis in 202. In his earlier years he had been a bitter
and consistent adversary of all species of nonconformity—attacking
especially the sect of the Patripatientes.

[3] The philosopher Celsus had a lively faith in the Phoenix (Orig.
c. Cels. iv. 98).

[4] Cf. Spart. Nig. 8. For their silence the century before cf. Juv. vi.
555 'quoniam Delphis oracula cessant'; cf. Luc. v. 75.

[5] e. g. Phil. Vit. Ap. bks. 3 and 6. The comparatively new imperial
titles pius and sanctus cannot be quite without their meaning in
this connexion.

[6] Luc. Demonax. 7. Yet the parodies of the gods on the stage still
continued: cf. Tert. Apol. 17 'moechum Anubim'; Arnob. adv. Gent.
iv. 35.

Réville : ' The religious syncretism of the early third century is the religion of a cosmopolitan society without interest in patriotism or politics, under a military despotism, without literary or artistic inspiration, without fixed philosophical opinions, yet educated, over-refined, and thirsting after a moral ideal better than that which had been handed down to it.' [1]

---

[1] *Op. cit.*, p. 22.

CHAPTER X

DE RE MILITARI

As might be expected from the character of the emperor himself, the principate of Septimius Severus was one of unusual importance in Roman military history. The secret of empire, as Tacitus called it, had long been divulged—' posse principem alibi quam Romae fieri '—and as a corollary it had followed that the *Scheinkonstitutionalismus* of Augustus had given way to the open and recognized military despotism which reached perhaps its height during the third century, and of which the reign of Septimius is at once typical and initiative. As has been well said, the turn of the second and third centuries marks an epoch in the development of absolutism.[1]

For the proverbial tyrant two things are necessary—first, the Platonic body-guard; secondly, a policy of favouritism and concession towards the army in general; and under these two headings we may examine the military conditions of Severus' reign. That which engages our attention immediately is the question of his reorganization of the praetorians. We have already seen how, on his arrival in Rome, the emperor assembled that body in the Campus Martius and then and there dismissed them. The new guard[2] he formed from his own Illyrian troops. This was, in effect, to throw open to any legionary service in that most special *corps d'élite*, reserved hitherto for the inhabitants of Italy and the more Italianized provinces, Spain, Macedonia, and Noricum.[3] As might be expected, the lion's share fell to the Danubian ex-legionaries, and it is to these

---

[1] H. Stuart Jones, *Roman Empire*, p. 252.

[2] See above, p. 66.

[3] Tac. *Ann.* iv. 5; Dio Cass. lxxiv. 2. 4, 5; Zon. xii. 8. Of the fifty praetorians mentioned in *CIL*. vi. 2381 forty-nine are Italians and one Macedonian (date 153-6); cf. no. 2382.

troops [1] (and to those of the Rhine) that the emperor accorded
the honour of commemoration on his earlier coins. One result
of this was that the tie which united [2] the urban and praetorian
cohorts was loosed, if not broken, since the latter corps was
in earlier times often recruited from the former. From now on
the urban cohorts continue to keep their Italian character,
while the praetorian are cosmopolitanized.[3] Another corps not
only to retain, but even to increase, its social prestige was that
of the *vigiles*, which now ceases to be recruited, as was formerly
the case, from freedmen, and draws its men from the ranks of
free Roman citizens.[4] Whether or not Severus actually
increased the number of household troops, and, if he did so, by
how much, are questions to which, in default of any very definite
evidence, it is not easy to return any certain answer. Herodian,
with that fine disregard for detail which distinguishes him,
assures us that Septimius quadrupled the number of soldiers in
Rome,[5] but epigraphic evidence will neither allow us to believe

---

[1] Cf. *CIL.* vi. 2385. Most of the men mentioned come from Asia and
the Danube provinces: yet there are two Noricans, a Spaniard, one from
Celeia, one from Aelia Solva. *CIL.* vi. 2799 mentions a schola of nineteen
praetorians, all of whom came from Philippopolis (year 227).

[2] Eck. vii. 168; Coh., vol. iv, Sept., no. 149, etc. The return courtesy
of the legions' adoption of the title 'Severiana' or 'Septimiana' the
emperor seems to have deprecated. Not but what there occur instances,
e.g. *CIL.* vi. 3399, 3403, 3404, iii. 187 (leg. II Parth.)—also some of
leg. III Parth. and leg. III Aug. (III Aug., *CIL.* viii. 2624, 2904, etc.;
III Parth., viii. 2877). This custom became regular under Caracalla.

[3] Cf. *CIL.* vi. 2256, 2663; ix. 5839-40; x. 3733, etc. Domaszewski,
Rangordnung des röm. Heeres (Bonner Jahrb., 1908, Heft 117), p. 16 note;
cf. p. 75. To this work I hasten to acknowledge my indebtedness. The
exhaustive nature of the treatise must compel the admiration of all,
even of those who cannot entirely agree with the conclusions therein
arrived at.

[4] *CIL.* vi. 220, 1056-8. In the first of them Kellermann (*Vigiles,*
n. 12) finds twelve out of eighteen citizens and only five freedmen. So
Dio Cass. lv. 26. 5.

[5] Herod. iii. 13. 4 τῆς . . . ἐν 'Ρώμῃ δυνάμεως αὐτῆς τετραπλασιασθείσης.
Wirth (pp. 44-7) endeavours to vindicate the accuracy of Herodian's
statement by means of an examination of inscriptions recording the
years of service of various city troops. He concludes from this that
their numbers had been steadily on the decrease since Pius' reign, and

in forty praetorian cohorts nor yet in ten, each four thousand strong. At the same time we know of the erection in Rome of new barracks—the *castra Severiana* [1] certainly and perhaps also the *Peregrina*,[2] the former of which seems to have served as the camp of the *equites singulares*, that is to say of the cavalry attached to the praetorian guard. There is therefore at least the probability that the number of these *equites singulares* was increased. The *castra peregrina*, too, by whomsoever built, seems to have been full, and may have contained foreign troops of a similar order, as it certainly did later in the reign of Alexander Severus.[3] According to Domaszewski,[4] indeed, each praetorian cohort from the time of Septimius on numbered 1,500 instead of the usual 1,000 by reason of the addition of 500 *equites*: this gives us at once 5,000 more soldiers in Rome, a number which might easily account for the erection of new *castra*. Besides the probable, or at least possible, increase in the number of *equites singulares* and *frumentarii*, we may not unreasonably suppose that the praetorians themselves were kept up to full

---

that, taking also into consideration gaps caused in the ranks by the wars of Marcus and the subsequent plague, the urban and other cohorts were by the time of Septimius only a quarter of their former strength. Thus Herodian's statement merely points to his bringing them up to their establishment.

[1] On the Caelian in the second region (Amm. Marc. xvi. 12. 66). Mentioned in Diploma 51, *CIL.* iii, p. 893. It must be admitted that the name might refer to Alexander Severus as the builder. The camp πρὸ τῆς πόλεως mentioned by Herodian (*loc. cit.*) must refer to that at Albano.

[2] No reference to their camp exists earlier than the third century (e. g. *CIL.* vi. 354), and it is no improbable conjecture to suppose that Septimius built it—so Henzen (*Annali*, 1850, p. 33), Cagnat (Daremberg et Saglio, under Peregrini), and Schiller (p. 728, note 3). According, however, to Domaszewski this *castra* owes its origin to Hadrian (Domaszewski, *Rangordnung*, pp. 101, 104, note 1).

[3] Mauri and Osrhoeni; Domasz., *Rangordnung*, p. 167; *Rhein. Mus.* lviii. 542. Under Severus the *frumentarii* were stationed there (*CIL.* vi. 230, 231, 354). Possibly too it served as barracks for the *classiarii* in Rome, though there existed *castra Misenatium* and *Ravenatium* (*Not. Dig.* Preller, p. 31; Jordan, p. 573).

[4] *Rangordnung*, p. 20. He gives no evidence for his statement.

strength and never allowed to drop below their maximum total of 10,000.

Still more significant as a military innovation is the formation and establishment of the second Parthian legion. These new legions were raised for the Parthian war. On the conclusion of peace two of them, I and III, remained in the new province of Mesopotamia, the latter at Rhesaena:[1] the second, however, had its camp at Albano,[2] not twenty miles from Rome. It is scarcely necessary to point out the significance of this step. Not only was this the first legion stationed permanently on Italian soil, but its proximity to the capital must have roused inexpressible alarm and disgust in the hearts of the constitutionalists, already deeply scandalized by the ' barbarizing' of the praetorian guard. These new legions, incidentally, were under the command of *praefecti*; not, as usually was the case, of *legati*. This prefect was in origin the *praefectus castris legionis*, whose title was soon shortened into that of *praefectus legionis*, and who, as such, superseded the *legatus legionis* in this case.[3] The prefect was, of course, of equestrian rank, and not, as a *legatus* would have been, of senatorial. It is clear, therefore, that this new Italian regiment was meant to approximate in character to the praetorians rather than to form a true legion. This point becomes the more obvious when we observe that the praefect. leg. II Parth. was himself dependent on the praetorian prefect.[4]

[1] Cf. *Wiener Studien,* ix. 297 ; Dio Cass. lv. 24. 4; Eck. iii. 518; Mionnet, v. 630, etc.

[2] Dio Cass. (*loc. cit.*); *CIL.* vi. 3367–410. The troops were known as Ἀλβάνιοι, and as such referred to by Dio (e. g. lxxviii. 34. 5, lxxix. 2. 4, lxxviii. 13. 4) and Herodian.

[3] Praef. leg. II Parth., *CIL.* viii. 20996, vi. 3410; Praef. leg. I Parth., *CIL.* iii. 99 (Bostra)—a *ducenarius.* For the passage of *praef. Castr. leg.* to *praef. leg.* cf. Domasz., *Rangord.,* p. 120

[4] Dio Cass. (lii. 24, the pseudo-Maecenas speech) τῶν δὲ ἄλλων τῶν ἐν τῇ Ἰταλίᾳ στρατιωτῶν οἱ ἔπαρχοι ἐκεῖνοι (i. e. the praetorian *praefecti*) προστατείωσαν ὑπάρχους ἔχοντες. Here the ὑπάρχοι are such officers as the *praefecti classium, vigilum,* and leg. II Parth. For the close connexion between the two prefects and their troops cf. *CIL.* vi. 3408. Alexander Severus seems either to have started a regular (senatorial) *legatus* for the legion or to have intended doing so (*CIL.* viii. 20996, mentioning a *praef. leg. sec. Parth. vice legati*). This is natural in a Senate-loving emperor.

Another interesting observation tending to show the approxima-
tion of these new legions to the imperial guard has been made
by Mr. Stuart Jones. He points out[1] that on the standards
figured on the Arch of Severus are to be seen not only the usual
legionary *paterae*—as opposed to the *coronae*—but also the medal-
lions, which, together with the *coronae*, are the usual mark of the
praetorian standards. The troops there portrayed, he therefore
conjectures, are none other than certain of the new Parthian
legions, the standards partaking of the character both of those of
the guard and of those of the ordinary legion.

Important though the erection of the camp at Albano certainly was, its significance has often been not only exaggerated
but also perverted. To the general question whether Severus was,
in Gibbon's words,[2] 'the principal author of the decline of the
Roman Empire', we shall have to return later. Suffice it here
to say that the creation of the 'Αλβάνιοι need force no one to
entertain any such supposition, and that such statements as that
Septimius planted ' the despotism of the East in the soil of the
West ', or that ' it was his fault that the empire was handed over
to a pitiless soldiery who in self-devastating strife destroyed the
culture of the Mediterranean ', are little more than nonsense.[3]

Two natural tendencies are noticeable in this innovation :
first, there is that *Nivellisierungspolitik*—that levelling of Italy
with the provinces that started with Augustus and reached
a logical conclusion with the edict of Caracalla, by which
citizenship was granted to the whole empire. To station troops
in Italy is no more to barbarize it than was the garrisoning
of Raetia and Noricum under Marcus Aurelius to destroy the
culture of those provinces. In the second place, we see in
this increasing of the number of troops in Italy a significant
foreshadowing of the Diocletianic military reorganization. The
principate of Septimius forms in this way a sort of half-way
house between the definitely and entirely local army of the early
empire and the Diocletianic dual system of a centralized and
easily mobilized main army together with a carefully disposed
frontier force.

---

[1] *Companion*, p. 212.   [2] i, p. 125.
[3] Domasz., *Geschichte des röm. Reiches*, vol. ii, p. 262.

With regard to the legions already in existence no change of encampment (of a permanent nature) seems to have been made. We have already seen reason to believe that the legio V Macedonica had been moved from Troesmis in Lower Moesia to Potaïssa in Dacia some time before the advent of Septimius.[1] Of the auxiliary troops we may perhaps see in this emperor the founder of cohors I Septimia Belgarum, inscriptions of which have not been found before the third century.[2] From Septimius' reign also dates the disappearance of the *fabri* as a special corps and their drafting with the legions.[3] Another body of troops to disappear at this time is the 13th urban cohort stationed at Lugdunum. It had fought for Albinus in the war of 197, and was consequently disbanded by the victorious Septimius. Its place was taken by a *vexillatio* drawn from the four Rhine legions, it being found impossible to leave Gaul with no defending force whatsoever.[4]

But industriously though Septimius has been misinterpreted and censured for his strengthening of the forces stationed in Italy, or, as it is fairer to say, for his creation of the nucleus of a centralized field army, his detractors have made still larger capital out of the emperor's treatment of the individual soldier. Certainly we do find during this reign a marked increase in the material comfort of the troops, and a series of new privileges extended both to officers and men: concessions which the army was not slow to appreciate or backward in acknowledging.[5] The reign opens, as indeed did most, with a considerable donative,[6] and in its course the general pay for the army seems to have been

---

[1] See above, p. 71. Ceuleneer, p. 37, holds the other view.

[2] *CIRh.* 1030 (Mainz). Ceuleneer, p. 267, makes him the inaugurator of an 'ala IV Parthorum' stationed at Sidi Ali ben Yub. In the first place this is not ala IV, but ala I (*CIL.* viii. 9827, 9828), and in the second it is of much older standing. Cf., e.g., *Eph. Epigr.* vii. 798 in year 160; *CIL.* x. 3847 (time of Marcus).

[3] Marquardt, *L'Organis. milit.*, p. 251.

[4] Domasz., *Rangord.*, p. 64. He cites *CIL.* xiii. 1766, 1871, 1879, etc.

[5] Ceuleneer, p. 171 seq., notes the vast number of dedications in honour of the emperor and his family due to the goodwill of. the army.

[6] Dio Cass. xlvi. 46. 7; Vit. Sev. v. 2.

raised.[1] New honours, too, were now accorded to the soldiers :
the old-fashioned *phalerae* disappear, and their place is taken by
medals of silver or silver set in gold;[2] and the civic crown,
which since Claudius' time, with a few exceptions, had been
withheld from the military, was given back to them.[3] The gold
ring, which hitherto had adorned none but equestrian hands,
was now granted the common legionary to wear,[4] but the
emperor was careful to add that with this mark of distinction
went no further equestrian privilege—' honor eius auctus est non
conditio mutata '. We do note, however, a very definite ' eques-
trianizing ' of the army, if the phrase may be allowed. Centurions, for example, regularly became knights, and those of the
city troops are presented with the *equus publicus*.[5] The sons,
too, of centurions seem to attain to equestrian rank much as,
from this reign on, those of primipili did to the senatorial.[6]

   This fact is used by Domaszewski with great effect as a proof
of the barbarizing of the army by Septimius, inasmuch as he
believes that during this reign the Italian-born centurion gave
way entirely to the foreign one. ' The price which Severus
offered the provincial legionary for the crown was the extermina-
tion of the centurion of Italian-Roman origin.' His thesis,
however, is not strengthened by the admission (on the same

----

[1] Her. iii. 8. 5. According to Domaszewski the legionary's pay was
now 500 dr. a year, the praetorian's 1700 dr. (*Neue Heidelb. Jahrb.*, x.
231, 236).

[2] Marquardt, *L'Organ. milit.*, p. 328. *Armillae* and *torques* also disappear from inscriptions after Severus' reign, yet they are mentioned in
the *Scriptores H. A.* with reference to a considerably later period : e. g.
Vop. Aurel. xiii. 3 ; Prob. v. 1 ; and even in Procop. *bell. Goth.* iii. 1 (where
Belisarius donates ψελιά τε καὶ στρεπτούς). The *phalerae* may be different :
we note an inscription of Severus' reign in which they alone seem to be
absent from the *dona militaria—armillae, torques, corona aurea civica*, and
hasta pura argentea all being there (*L'Ann. ép.*, 1900, 95).

[3] *L'Ann. ép.*, 1900, 95 ; Domasz., *Rangord.*, p. 69.

[4] Herod. iii. 8. 5.

[5] Domasz., *Rangord.*, p. 81.

[6] Domasz., *Gesch.* ii, p. 256 ; cf. *Rangord.*, p. 172—they became *tribuni
laticlavi, CIL.* xiii. 6819 ; *IGRR.* 472. [I employ this abbreviation for
that *corpus* of inscriptions known as ' Inscriptiones Graecae ad res
Romanas pertinentes '.]

page)[1] that 'after the Severi the " Heimatsangabe " disappears
from the inscriptions of centurions'. In all this Domaszewski
sees a deliberate attempt on the emperor's part to play off the
provincials against the true Roman.[2] Italians and Romans are,
according to him, excluded from service in the cavalry, and he
even[3] goes so far as to accuse Septimius of a definite policy of
killing off Italian *viri principales*.[4]

To answer an archaeologist who knows his *Corpus* as does
Domaszewski is no light task and may savour of impertinence.
This much, however, may be said in reply. Any epigraphic
evidence for the *disappearance* of, e.g., Italian centurions and
tribunes is, from its very nature, negative evidence, and as such
always open to suspicion and liable to positive disproof.

Indeed archaeological evidence goes to show that Italian-born
centurions *did* continue in and after the principate of Severus.[5]
No doubt as the provinces became more romanized so the proportion between Italian and provincial centurions would alter;
but this gradual alteration, which must have been going on
steadily from the first century, is not the same thing as a definite
attempt on the part of any emperor there and then to exclude
Italians from the centurionate.

In any case, as Domaszewski has admitted, it is by no means
always possible to tell the birthplace of any soldier mentioned in
an inscription, though of course outlandish names might reason-

---

[1] *Rangord.*, p. 90.

[2] *Gesch.* ii, p. 247; cf. 256: 'Kein Italiker, kein Weströmer durfte im
Heere oder im Staate zu den höheren Aemtern gelangen.' On the same
page he speaks of 'seinen Feinden, den Römern'.

[3] *Rangord.*, p. 133. The last Italian legionary tribune occurs under
Commodus (*CIL.* xi. 6053). He further notes that all the *tribuni legionis*
in Mainz under Septimius are Asiatics (*CIL.* xiii. 6819).

[4] So *Rangord.*, p. 134, though the passage is obscure, and I am at
a loss to understand how the accusation is helped or strengthened by the
citation of two inscriptions (*CIL.* ii. 1085, viii. 9360) proving the presence
in Baetica and Mauretania respectively of an official, 'a cognitionibus'.
Was every one of them a Judge Jeffreys?

[5] e.g. *CIL.* v. 8275. Domaszewski made a similar generalization
about the auxiliaries, but Mr. Cheeseman (*The Auxilia of the Roman
Imperial Army*, Oxford, 1914, pp. 94–100) has clearly shown that the
Italian auxiliary officer continued after Severus' reign.

ably be held to stamp a non-Italian. In the third place, as we
have pointed out above, we might admit the now almost exclusive
use of non-Italian centurions without in the least committing
ourselves to the theory that the army, and hence the empire, was
thereby being barbarized. Epigraphic evidence certainly goes to
show that the Illyrian, African, or Syrian was little if at all
behind, say, his Norican brother in civilization. Indeed the
general high level of culture throughout the empire during
the first half at least of the third century is even easier to
prove from archaeology than is the 'barbarity' of the army,
supposed by Domaszewski to have destroyed it. But to that
we shall have to return later.

Considerable shortening and simplification of the private's
career seems to date from the reign of Severus, who appears to
have rendered easier the passage from the *caliga* to the centurionate. Inscriptions inform us of the advance of a *speculator*
and a *beneficiarius consularis* to the rank of centurions without
the intermediate step of a *cornicularius.*[1]

There remain still a few privileges worth at least a passing
mention. Veterans were excused personal service in their native
towns on retirement into private life [2] in much the same way as
officers of the guard were freed from the duty of guardianship
over the children of their comrades.[3] The status of veterans indeed as a whole was considerably improved by the opening to
them of the doors of the Civil Service. Equestrian procurator-
ships were now held almost exclusively by such ex-soldiers, and the
staff of those in charge of mines, city corn, and other such offices,
was largely composed of veterans. Looked at from another
point of view such measures indicate the growth of a specifically *military* despotism.[4] On ceasing to hold the post of tribune
the soldier now receives a new title—that of *a militiis*: indeed,

---

[1] Dessau, 484; *CIL.* iii. 14479—*speculatores*. The latter inscription,
however, shows that the rank of *cornicularius* might still form a connecting link. *CIL.* iii. 3306, viii. 17626—*beneficiarii*. These *beneficiarii*
could also pass into the cavalry from Septimius' reign (*CIL.* iii. 16259).

[2] *Dig.* l. 5. 7 'a muneribus, quae non patrimoniis indicuntur, veterani
perpetuo excusantur'.

[3] *Dig.* xxvii. 1. 9.   [4] Hirsch., p. 423.

like the sham tribunate of Claudius, it seems sometimes to have
been granted where the recipient had held no active military
post at all.[1]

Of all concessions made by Septimius to his army none has
raised more comment and criticism from historians ancient and
modern than that by which the legionaries were allowed, in
Herodian's words, γυναιξὶ συνοικεῖν.[2] The whole question of
marriage in the army in its legal aspect is one of considerable
difficulty, and made none the easier by the fact that the conditions
seem to have varied not only from time to time but from place to
place.[3] The general rule, however, seems to have remained in
force and unaltered from the earliest years of the republic :
a married man entering military service had the option of either
living away from his wife[4] or, if he wished, of divorcing her.[5]
With the exception of the ubiquitous *meretrix* no female might
have access to the camp, though many might sigh with
Propertius' love-sick girl, ' Romanis utinam patuissent castra
puellis ! ' Possibly at some time or other marriage between the
auxiliaries and the foreign women may have been recognized by
law, and it is not impossible that in Septimius' reign a similar
legal recognition may have been accorded to the legionary's
marriage. He seems always to have been allowed marriage with
one *focaria,* as she was called, the children of such a marriage
taking the name of the mother, not the father, and specifying
the camp as the place of their birth.[6] Indeed the number of
children born *castris* shows that the legionary was accustomed to
form some sort of permanent, though not legal, connexion with

---

[1] Hirsch., p. 422. For Claudius' 'imaginariae militiae genus', held
'titulo tenus', cf. Suet. *Claud.* xxv. Hirschfeld well compares the
'tribuni militum a populo' of the end of the republic and the first years
of the empire.

[2] Herod. iii. 8. 5.

[3] Jung, *Die röm. Prov.*, p. 134, note 1.

[4] *Dig.* xxiv. 1. 32. 8, xlix. 17. 8.   [5] *Dig.* xxiv. 1. 60-2.

[6] So Marquardt, *L'Organ. milit.*, p. 308 ; *Cod. Iust.* v. 16. 2 (213), vi. 46.
3 (215). Cf. *CIL.* viii. 2565 a, b, 2567, 2568, 2618. The first-cited
inscription contains the names of eighteen soldiers, six of whom were
born in the camp—such belonged to the tribe Pollia (Momm., *Hermes,*
xix, p. 10).

a woman. Before Septimius' reign such a connexion was only
legalized on the legionary's discharge, as we see from the recently
discovered Egyptian inscription.[1] The reform now instituted may
mean that the recognition of such an alliance as *iustum connubium*
was coincident with its contraction.

It is only right to mention another explanation which has been
given, more especially as it is the one which has held the field for
some considerable time and which has coloured and given rise to
much of the nonsense that has been talked about Septimius as
the relaxer of military discipline. That is the view according
to which barrack life, properly so called, ceased in Severus' reign
as a consequence of this permission. It has been thought that
from now on the legionary lived, not in the camp at all, but
with his wife in some house or lodging in the town where his
regiment was stationed—as was possibly the case in the fourth
century.[2] The camp itself, therefore, was restricted in its use to
a sort of combination of drill-ground and club-rooms.[3] If this
were, as we believe it was not, the case, there would be some
point in the remarks made by nearly all historians including, and
subsequent to, Dio and Herodian, to the effect that the bonds of
military discipline were first loosed in the reign of Septimius.[4]

---

[1] *L'Ann. épigr.* 1910, 75. This is interesting and important as being
the only instance of a diploma granted to legionary soldiers as opposed
to auxiliaries or praetorians.

[2] Cf. the Gallic troops' complaint when in 360 Constantius wished to
dispatch them to the Eastern war that they would be 'separandique
liberis et coniugibus egentes' (Amm. Marc. xx. 8. 8). Wilmanns
advanced the view, and was followed by Cagnat (*Armée d'Afrique*,
p. 451; cf. *CIL.* viii, p. 284). The latter, however, has now retracted
his opinion (*Les Deux Camps de Lég. III Aug. à Lambèse*, p. 56).

[3] The absurdity of this view has recently been pointed out by
Mr. Stuart Jones (*Companion to Rom. Hist.*, p. 240). His belief that
the comparative smallness of the camp of leg. II Parth. at Albano is
due to the fact that only the unmarried legionaries would live there
seems to me very questionable (*op. cit.*, p. 234).

[4] Herod. iii. 8. 5 πρῶτός γε ἐκεῖνος τὸ πάνυ αὐτῶν ἐρρωμένον καὶ τὸ σκληρὸν
τῆς διαίτης τό τε εὐπειθὲς πρὸς τοὺς πόνους καὶ εὔτακτον μετ᾽ αἰδοῦς πρὸς
ἄρχοντας ἐπανέτρεψε, χρημάτων τε ἐπιθυμεῖν διδάξας καὶ μεταγαγὼν ἐς τὸ
ἁβροδίαιτον. Dio (lxxviii. 36. 2) puts a similar complaint into Macrinus'
mouth—διαφθορὰν τῆς ἀκριβοῦς στρατείας. Gibbon (vol. i, p. 122) was of

As it is, all we can say is that the principate of Severus marks an epoch in the civilizing and refining of the legionary's life. In his reign we find the start, and rapid development, of the *scholae* or clubs for which we have such ample evidence in the case of the African legion.[1] Besides forming a club in the modern sense of the word, these *scholae* seem to have performed the office of an insurance company, members contributing so much of their pay and receiving in exchange a lump sum in case of degradation, illness, or discharge. As such, each *schola* had its *arca* and a *quaestor* to manage its money matters.[2] A similar institution was started in the year 200 in the camp at Lambaesis in the form of a college of *armorum custodes*.[3] The small rooms round the central court of the praetorium may have served as store-rooms for the arms.[4]

Of the activity in military building in general during the reign of Septimius we are assured by plentiful epigraphic evidence. Most obvious, if not most important, are the new buildings of the above-mentioned camp of the 3rd Augustan legion at Lambaesis.[5] Other African instances are : the building

the same opinion ; he further advances the view that the 16th satire of Juvenal was written at this time, and that it illustrates the licence of the army of Septimius.

[1] So Cagnat, *Les Deux Camps*, p. 38 et seq.; *CIL*. viii. 2554, *schola* of *optiones*; viii. 2557, ditto of *cornicines*; cf. *CIL*. iii. 3524, where the *speculatores* of leg. I and II Adj. formed a *schola* at Aquincum. For a *schola tubicinum* in 229 cf. *Eph. epigr.* iv. 503. A Dacian instance is supplied by *CIL*. iii. 876 (at Potaïssa in 200).

[2] e. g. *CIL*. viii. 2554 mentions both: also the *anularium*, apparently the sum given a man on his discharge. The *scholae* often bore a religious character; cf. *CIL*. vi. 2799. For the *scholae Principalium* cf. *Neue Heidelb. Jahrb.* ix. 149 et seq. These *scholae* developed later into regimental divisions—unless the word was used in a new significance (Amm. Marc. xxvi. 1. 4, xxv. 10. 9, xxvi. 1. 5 ; *CIL*. v. 4369).

[3] *L'Ann. épigr.*, 1902, 10 (date 200). That this was the year of its commencement is proved by the existence of an altar at the other side of the court of the praetorium dedicated in 199 by one 'L. Caecilius Urbanus optio valetudinarii curator operi armamentarii' (*CIL*. viii. 2563). Cf. also Cagnat, *L'Armée romaine d'Afrique* (Paris, 1913), p. 172.

[4] Cagnat, *Les Deux Camps*, p. 42.

[5] Cf. Cagnat, *Les Deux Camps de Légion III Augusta à Lambèse. L'Ann. épigr.* 1902, 11, etc.

of a gateway to the fort at Leptis Magna,[1] the restoration of a tower at Azeffun,[2] and of another at Daouark,[3] and the erection of some work of fortification at Siaoun.[4]

In the far East less trouble seems to have been taken, though even here we come across such inscriptions as one near Damascus telling of the construction of a camp ' in securitatem publicam et Scaenitorum Arabum terrorem '.[5] The Northern and Western provinces are more fertile. It seems at least probable that a complete and consistent strengthening of the *limes* connecting the Rhine with the Danube was undertaken in Septimius' reign: that some time during the years 201, 202 the camp buildings at Strassburg were restored is certain.[6] The stone wall, too, running between Lorch and Hienheim, and continued to the Rhine by an earthen bank and ditch, thus situated just behind Hadrian's limes, is possibly Severan in date.[7] Waterworks were constructed at Ems,[8] and an armoury rebuilt at Roomburg.[9] At Lauriacum there are evidences of building or repairing in the praetorium,[10] while we learn that the 7th Claudian legion in Upper Moesia ' canabas refecerunt ',[11] and that a camp was transferred to a new site at Matrica in Pannonia.[12] In Dacia the energetic legate Octavius Iulianus set some of his auxiliaries to rebuild with stone a turf wall in the neighbourhood of Bumbesti,[13] while the wall in Lower Moesia, connecting the Danube with the Euxine between Rassowa and Constanza, probably underwent one of its many reconstructions or repairings during the reign of Septimius.[14] Our own country supplies us with at least two

---

[1] *CIL.* viii. 6.   [2] *CIL.* viii. 8991.

[3] *L'Ann. épigr.* 1911, 119.   [4] *L'Ann. épigr.* 1907, 104: date 197.

[5] *CIL.* iii. 128. It was built by Livius Calpurnius, governor of Coele-Syria. These Arabs are those mentioned by Herodian ; see above, pp. 2, note, 93, note.

[6] *CIL.* xiii. 5970.

[7] So Stuart Jones, *Roman Empire*, p. 245 ; Pelham, *Essays on Roman History*, p. 207.

[8] *CIL.* xiii. 7734.   [9] *CIL.* xiii. 8824.

[10] *L'Ann. épigr.* 1909, 248.   [11] *L'Ann. épigr.* 1901, 14.

[12] *CIL.* iii. 3387.

[13] *CIL.* iii. 14485 a, year 201. This Iulianus was the builder of the Potaïssa schola: he is also mentioned in *CIL.* iii. 876, 1308, 1393.

[14] So Stuart Jones, *Companion*, p. 256; cf. Cagnat in Daremberg et

instances of military construction or reconstruction; a 'portam
cum muris' at Habitancum,[1] and a 'vallum cum bracchio
caementicium' at Bainbrig.[2] The vexed question of the North-
umbrian wall and the connexion Severus had or may have had
with it has already been examined.[3]

NOTE ON DIO LXXV. 12. 5.

Ὥστε τινὸς τῶν ἀμφ' αὐτὸν ὑποσχομένου αὐτῷ, ἐάν γε αὐτῷ δῷ πεντα-
κοσίους καὶ πεντήκοντα μόνους τῶν Εὐρωπαίων στρατιωτῶν . . . τὴν πόλιν
ἐξαιρήσειν.

Such was the offer of an officer at the siege of Hatra.

The question at once presents itself: why 550? It is clearly
not a vague round number—the '50' disproves that. To what
then can it refer? Possibly to the Vegetian cohort.

Vegetius (ii. 6), writing under Gratian, describes the old style
of legion ('antiqua ordinatione legionis') as follows: There are
ten cohorts in the legion. Of these the first contains 1,105
infantry, 132 cavalry (it is a double cohort, *miliaria*). The
other nine (*quinquenariae*) are composed of 555 infantry, 66
cavalry apiece. (The odd '5' are probably centurions.) This
gives us a total of 6,830 men—probably not including the
tribunes.

Now this figure is far too big for the legion of the first century,
which could not have numbered more than about 5,000: indeed
Hyginus tells us that eighty men to the century was the usual
thing. Also the number of cavalry here is far in advance of that
which was attached to the legion in the first century. Still less

---

Saglio (*Limes imperi*), p. 1258. Tocilescu believes it to be a construction
of Constantine the Great.

[1] *CIL.* vii. 1003 'iussu Alfeni Senecionis . . . curante Oclatinio Advento
proc. Aug.' and carried out by 'Coh. I Vangion. miliaria eq. cum
Aemilio Salviano tribuno suo'. Adventus was afterwards consul—in
218 (Dio Cass. lxxviii. 13. 2). Salvianus' name occurs also in *CIL.* vii.
986.

[2] *CIL.* vii. 269. By 'coh. VI Nerv.'

[3] It is not always easy to tell from an inscription the exact nature and
raison d'être of the building it once adorned. Instances cited above are
all of a definitely attested character, but it must not be supposed that the
list is, or is intended to be, exhaustive.

can Vegetius here refer to the Diocletianic legion, which we know could not have numbered above a thousand.   It looks, therefore, as though the reference were to some intermediate time between these two periods, i. e. to the end of the second and start of the third century; and this supposition becomes all the more probable if we can take this passage in Dio as alluding to this very cohort of 550 (subtracting the five centurions) mentioned by Vegetius.

CHAPTER XI

HOME ADMINISTRATION

THE so-called dyarchy, instituted by Augustus, has long been regarded as a highly successful attempt to give an appearance of constitutionalism to a virtually autocratic or tyrannous form of government. Its fictitious character became more and more obvious as the decades passed, and, by the beginning of the third century, even the most self-satisfied of senators must have recognized that he himself, and the body of which he was a member, were, to quote Velleius' words on the tribunate, 'nomina sine viribus'.[1]

The last stage in the long disease of the dyarchy is marked by the reign of Septimius, of whose policy the exaltation of the equestrian rank at the expense of the senatorial is so characteristic a feature. The equestrian *praefecti* of the new Parthian legions and the growing tendency to identify the military and equestrian classes generally (as typified by the emperor's treatment of centurions) have already received comment. Like the military, too, the *equites* at this time received new titles, which, if of little practical worth, were at least a sign and earnest of imperial favour. The 'egregiate' had been theirs since the Antonine period, when it had been bestowed perhaps as a set-off against the senatorial title *clarissimus*: from the reign of Septimius we find in inscriptions the further and loftier titles *vir perfectissimus* and *vir eminentissimus*.[2] Thus are formed two

---

[1] The monarchic character of even the Antonines' rule had not escaped notice or comment. App. *in prooem.* 6. Schiller notes (ii, p. 732, note 8) the increasingly bombastic titles of the emperor and his family, e. g. Septimius *invictus* (Eck. vii. 192); Caracalla 'super omnes retro principes invictissimus'.

[2] The origin of these titles is obscure. *CIL.* v. 532, col. 2. 28 (Pius' reign) supplies perhaps the first instance of a *vir egregius*, though the words may not here be used as a title. Even under Marcus the words

equestrian classes, the higher endowed with the title *perfectissimus* or *eminentissimus*, the lower with that of *egregius*.

Until the principate of Severus the *comites Augusti* had been drawn without exception from the ranks of the senators : now, for the first time, an emperor, himself of equestrian family, deigns to choose his retinue from equestrian circles.[1] It is possible, however, that a distinction was still made, and the title *amicus* preserved as a senatorial ornament. Senatorial governors sometimes bore that name.[2]

But the increased dignity of the knights was by no means merely titular. Their sphere of office was much enlarged in such a way that posts, hitherto reserved on the one side for senators and on the other for freedmen, were now thrown open to them. Among those usually senatorial may be mentioned that of the censitor or *legatus ad census accipiendos*, an office held only by those of senatorial rank until the reign of Hadrian, and but seldom by a knight until the dynasty of the Severi.[3]

---

are written out in full (e.g. *CIL*. viii. 20834). Perhaps the first shortened form is found in *CIL*. viii. 2276, year 175. For the other two titles: Dositheus (*Corp. glossar.* iii. 388. 5) attributes the eminentissimate to Hadrian ; the Codex Iustinianus (ix. 41. 11) to Marcus, also the perfectissimate. The earliest *perfectissimus* supplied by inscriptional evidence is one of the year 201 (*CIL*. vi. 1063 = xiv. 131) ; *vir eminentissimus* occurs in 211 (*Eph. epigr.* vii, no. 1207) when it is held by a *praefectus vigilum*. Almost certainly, too, the *e. v.* of *Eph. epigr.* vii, nos. 1204-6 should be completed as *eminentissimus vir*, though *em.* is the usual abbreviation. The *praefectus vigilum* was too important a person to be a mere 'egregius'.

[1] *CIL*. xii. 1856—one Iulius Pacatianus, procurator of the Cottian Alps. Hirschfeld (p. 449, note 3) suggests that he proved of service to Septimius on his way to Britain, and was for this reason chosen 'inter comite[s A]uggg.' For another third-century equestrian *comes* cf. *CIL*. v. 16809. There seems to me no justification for citing *CIL*. v. 5050 (= Dessau 206) as instancing an equestrian *comes* under Claudius, as does Seeck (Pauly-Wissowa, *Comites*, p. 627).

[2] *CIL*. iii. 781.

[3] The best-known inscription bearing on the point is *CIL*. xiii. 1680, referring to one Tib. Antistius Marcianus, and concluding with these words : 'integerrimo abstinentissimoque procur(atori) tres provinc(iae) Galliae primo umquam eq(uiti) R(omano) a censibus accipiendis ad aram Caesarum statuam equestrem ponendam censuerunt.' This inscription

More distinctive than any increase of dignity or of power accorded to the knights as a body is the enlarged sphere of activities which, from the reign of Septimius on, devolve upon its most influential member and representative—the praetorian prefect.[1] Except in the case of the prefecture of Plautian, Severus adhered to the customary number of two, and it is interesting to note that while one prefect was the well-known general, Maecius Laetus, the other was the far more famous jurist, Aemilius Papinianus.[2] The office, in fact, is now losing

has often been misinterpreted, and in particular by Ceuleneer (p. 244). The meaning is not that Marcianus was the first equestrian censitor *and* that he was accorded a statue, etc., but that he was the first equestrian censitor to whom this honour was granted. The run of the sentence shows that clearly. So, too, Dessau (*Inscr. sel.* n. 1390). Ceuleneer's hypothesis is disproved by inscriptional evidence : e. g. *CIL.* xi. 709, where is an equestrian censitor of lower Germany under Trajan (cf. diploma 31, *CIL.* iii, p. 1971). *CIL.* vi. 31863 mentions a 'proc. Aug. ad cens. Gallorum, proc. Aug. ad cens. Brit(t)', and *may* belong to the Claudian era.

[1] The senatorial rank of Plautianus is, as has been already pointed out, very exceptional. Only one other senatorial praetorian prefect of the third century is known—M. Aedinius Iulianus (*CIL.* xiii. 3162). He was probably appointed to the office under the pro-senatorial emperors, Pupienus and Balbinus (so Domasz., *Rhein. Mus.* lviii, p. 228).

[2] They were in office before May 28, 205 (*CIL.* vi. 228). Laetus, the praetorian prefect under Pertinax, was, as we have seen, killed at the orders of Didius Iulianus (Spart. Did. Iul. vi. 2 ; Dio Cass. lxxiii. 16. 5 ; see above, p. 64). The *Prosopographia* seems to confuse this Laetus with the similarly named defender of Nisibis. Inasmuch as the latter was killed by order of Septimius (see above, p. 119), this identification is absurd. The only question which remains is : Is Laetus the praetorian prefect the same as Laetus the hero of Lyon ? This problem does not seem to me to admit of a categorical answer either way. Against a natural supposition we have only the *a priori* argument that a man once suspected of treachery would not be advanced. The only other facts we possess are :

(1) that a Laetus was prefect of Egypt in 202 (Euseb. *Eccl. Hist.* vi. 2) ;

(2) that a Laetus was among those who persuaded Caracalla to murder Geta and that he was killed for his pains (so Spart. Car. iii. 4 ; Dio Cass. lxxvii. 5 gives a different version).

CIL. ix. 4972 '[Mae]cius [Laetus], cos. ord.' in 215 seems very slender evidence for anything.

It is scarcely necessary to comment on the man whom Cujas called

its military significance and acquiring fresh powers in the domain of law, and Papinian is but the first of a long series which could count among its numbers the lawyers Paul and Ulpian.[1] Among the most important functions of the legal praetorian prefect would of course be the presidency, in the emperor's absence, of the *consilium principis*. That he often assisted the emperor also we learn from a passage in Dio.[2] This *consilium principis* must not be confused with that founded by Augustus and active during the first century, though the second doubtless sprang from the first. Hadrian it probably was who so reconstituted the body that it lost its old political significance as the emperor's advisory board and acquired a new judicial one as his private court.[3] Besides helping the emperor in judicial matters[4] Papinian was himself invested with special legal duties and powers. To him came all appeals from provincial governors, just as those from city officials were made to the city prefect.[5] It is possible that the praetorian prefect may have been assisted in

---

'the greatest jurisconsult of all time'. Valentinian's rescript (Nov. 7, 426) to the effect that where a difference of legal opinion arose, Papinian's decision should be conclusive, is a clear indication of his merited prestige.

[1] Spart. Nig. vii. 4; Lamp. Alex. Sev. xxvi. 5. Before their respective elevations they held the posts of *ad memoriam* (Paul) and *ad libellos* (Ulpian).

[2] Dio Cass. lxv. 18, *re* Marcius Turbo under Hadrian.

[3] Hirschf., p. 339. In later times it was known not as the *consilium* but as the *consistorium*. However, the term does not occur in inscriptions until the middle of the fourth century (*CIL.* vi. 1739-42). The political *consilium* rose from its ashes under the senatorial Alexander (Herod. vi. 1. 2; cf. Hopkins, *Alex. Sev.*, p. 110).

[4] For Septimius' assiduity as a judge cf. Vit. viii. 4 'causas plurimas audivit'; Dio Cass. lxxvi. 17. 1.

[5] It is significant that in the time of Severus appeals *from* the authority of the praet. praef. were disallowed (Momm. *St.-R.* ii. 972, 974). As to the city prefect his duties were not seldom appropriated by the praet. praef. It is, for example, the praetorian prefect Perennis before whom was tried the Christian senator Apollonius (Euseb. *Eccl. Hist.* v. 21), in spite of the fact that the duty of dealing with *collegia illicita* (such as Christianity) was nominally vested in the city prefect's hands (*Dig.* i. 12, i. 14); cf. note on p. 181.

this capacity by a *vice praefecti.*[1] Another of his duties was the general supervision of criminal jurisdiction in Italy outside one hundred miles of Rome.[2] Besides matters legal, the prefect now acquired, apparently, the control over the corn supply, which up to this time had been in the hands of the *praefectus annonae.* At the end of the second century inscriptions pertaining to the staff of this *praefectus* disappear altogether, and it is no very bold conjecture to suppose that, while the *praefectus annonae* becomes a mere corn distributor under the control of the praetorian prefect, the under officials are now appointed from the *officium* of the latter. That at a later time the praetorian prefect saw to the importation into Italy of provincial corn is proved by literary evidence, and it is not improbable that the system was inaugurated by Septimius.[3] Doubtless, too, the distribution of oil, regular from the reign of Severus on, was in the hands of the praetorian prefect, or of an under-official responsible to him.[4] Nor was the *praefectus annonae* the only

---

[1] One such is mentioned in *Dig.* xxxii. 1. 4 ; Momm. *St.-R.* ii. 947.

[2] Momm. *St.-R.* ii. 930, 947 : Mommsen points out in the latter passage how that both civil and criminal cases could and did come before the *praefectus praetorio.* He compares *Dig.* xii. 1. 40, the case of a loan, and xxii. 1. 3. 3 (a *fideicommissum* case). I cannot find any justification for Schiller's statement concerning the *a cognitionibus* (p. 734): 'für die kaiserlichen Untersuchungen öffentliche Beamte (*a cognitionibus domini*) eingesetzt wurden.' Hirschfeld (p. 329), whom he cites, shows that the office goes back to Claudius' time (*CIL.* vi. 8634; Apocolocun. 15). Under Septimius we find such officers bearing the title *perfectissimus* (*CIL.* ii. 1085, etc.).

[3] Hirschf., p. 244, etc. For the later prosecution of this duty by the praetorian prefect cf. Cassiod. Var. vi. 18 'triticeas quidem copias praefectura praetoriana procurat'. Boethius attests to the lost prestige and importance of the *praefectus annonae (de Consol.* iii. 4)—' si quis quondam populi curasset annonam, magnus habebatur : nunc ea praefectura quid abiectius?' Such officials as *curatores annonae, frumenti, rei frumentariae,* and even a *praef(ectus) annon(ae) design(atus)* (*CIL.* xiii. 2949) must be local officials.

[4] Vit. Sev. xxiii. 2. A distributor under Marcus and Commodus is mentioned in *CIL.* vi. 34001. Such were almost certainly called 'adiutores praef. ann.': cf. *CIL.* ii. 1289, which mentions an ' adiutor . . . praef. annon. ad oleum Afrum et Hispanum recensendum ', but this man was doubtless stationed in Baetica, not in Rome. The equestrian *subprae-*

N

official whose duties were now so usurped. From this principate dates the disappearance of the *procurator annonae* at Ostia, and in his stead we find a *centurio annonae* under a *procurator portus*, who is, in his turn, answerable to the praetorian prefect.[1] Provincial corn, then, was shipped to Ostia under the direction of the praetorian prefect, received there by the *procurator portus*, and forwarded to Rome, where it was distributed in the old fashion, but, apparently, in a new place, viz. the Horrea which lie between the foot of the Aventine and the Tiber. The old seat of dispensation, the Porticus Minucia, seems now to have been converted into offices of the water-supply of the city.[2]

It would, in short, be difficult to over-estimate the power of the praetorian prefecture as reorganized by Severus. An office which combined within itself military, administrative, financial, and jurisdictional functions might with no small show of truth be said to fall not far short of kingly power, and to be greater than all other mortal authority.[3] A Misitheus

---

fectus is not a creation of Septimius as Ceuleneer (p. 147) maintains : one is known in Marcus' reign (*CIL.* v. 8659).

[1] The last *proc. annonae* mentioned in inscriptions occurs in *CIL.* viii. 1439 (year 211). The *proc. portus* comes to the fore in Caracalla's reign ; e. g. *CIL.* vi. 1020 ' proc. p(ortus) u(triusque) '—the reference is probably to the double harbour at Ostia (so Hirschfeld, p. 250), not to those of Ostia and Puteoli (as Mommsen, *CIL.* x, p. 183 ; cf. Dessau, *CIL.* xiv, p. 6, note 9). This new *centurio* is to be distinguished from such as were in former times employed in an extraordinary capacity in the corn supply ; e. g. *Dig.* xiii. 7. 43. 1 ' missus ex officio annonae centurio' (under Marcus). This centurion would not hold the title *centurio annonae* at all. I observe that Mr. Ashby doubts the Severan origin of the Emporium at Ostia, though its erection is usually assigned to the reign of that emperor (*J. R. S.* ii. 2, p. 159, ' Recent Discoveries at Ostia ').

[2] There exist no inscriptions mentioning the Minucian dispenser (*proc. Minuciae*) later than the end of the second century. Perhaps *CIL.* iii. 6753 = 249 is the latest. From that time we find ' curatores aquarum et Minuciae '. *CIL.* vi. 10211 (if Mommsen's restoration is correct) shows that there was a precedent for distributing corn in different places. See Hirschfeld, p. 239 ; de Rossi, ' Le *horrea* sotto l'Aventino e la *statio annonae urbis Romae* ', in *Annali dell' Instituto archeol.*, 1885, p. 223 sqq.

[3] Herod. v. 1. 2 οὐ πολύ τι ἐξουσίας καὶ δυνάμεως βασιλικῆς ἀποδεούσης. Phil. Vit. Ap. vii. 18 μείζων ἢ πάντα ὁμοῦ τὰ ἀνθρώπων.

under Gordian is more easily understood and explained than
a Seianus under Tiberius.

And what the Equites gained, the Senate, in a large measure,
lost. We have already seen the Pannonian legate receiving with
kindness the senatorial embassy at Interamna, and have heard him
a few days later take the customary oath to condemn no senator
to death without previous trial by his peers.[1] This, however,
did not prevent the emperor from getting rid of a good number
of pro-Nigerian and pro-Albanian senators, and from thereby
gathering together no small sum of money.[2] On his entry
into Rome he dispensed entirely with the usual senatorial confirmation of his election by the soldiery, and contented himself
with pointing out the bald fact of imperial inauguration to
the assembled fathers.[3] Indeed, the competence of the Senate
during the principate of Severus is restricted to the voicing of
acclamationes, of which one knows not whether to admire more
the servility or the insincerity.[4] In this Senate-crushing policy
Severus seems to have received no little assistance from the
consilium of jurists, who endeavoured to uphold the view that
the Senate had ceded rather than delegated its powers to the
emperor. The cosmopolitan spirit of the age, and of the
sovereign too, was not without its influence on the *curia*, and
from now we remark an ever-increasing number of non-Italians,
especially orientals, among the fathers. Dio expressly mentions
Coeranus as the first Egyptian to enter the Senate.[5] In only
one instance, perhaps, can we detect any favour shown by
Septimius to that body, that is the measure allowing rejected
members (*remoti*) to remain in Rome, and exempting them from
the usual *diminutio capitis* which attended that degradation.[6]

[1] See above, p. 68; Her. ii. 14. 3; Dio Cass. lxxiv. 2. 1; Vit. Sev.
vii. 5.

[2] 'Ηργυρολόγησέ τε δεινῶς says Dio (lxxiv. 8. 4); cf. Her. iii. 8. 2.

[3] 'Reddidit rationem suscepti imperii,' Vit. Sev. vii. 4.

[4] e.g. Lamp. Alex. Sev. vi, etc. Ceuleneer (p. 155) notes the peremptory
tone adopted by Septimius in certain of his rescripts, e. g. ' Praeterea,
P. C., interdicam ' (*Dig.* xxvii. 9. 1).

[5] Dio Cass. lxxvi. 5. 5; Ceuleneer, p. 243. For his fate cf. above,
p. 133.

[6] *Dig.* i. 9. 3. Schiller (p. 733) mentions a second instance of ' pro-

Innovations (other than the increase of the praetorian prefect's sphere of duties) in the magistrature, its personnel and its functions, are neither to be expected on *a priori* grounds, nor is their existence to be established by literary or inscriptional evidence. From the autocratic nature of Septimius' rule[1] we should imagine that the tendency would be towards the disappearance of office, though, with the exception of some minor posts of a religious or priestly character, this does not seem to have been the case.[2] On the contrary, it is at least possible that a new legal dignitary, the *praetor de liberalibus causis*, owes his existence to the law-loving Septimius.[3] New legal functions seem to have devolved, too, on the *praefectus vigilum*, who, as a knight, may have received some of the duties and privileges of the senatorial *praefectus urbi*.[4]

senatorialism' in the form of a senatorial *legatus* in Egypt. For this statement he gives no reference, nor can I find any justification. It is true that M. Aedinius Iulianus, mentioned above (p. 175, note 1) as the one case (besides that of Plautian) of a senatorial praetorian prefect, was *praefectus Aegypti* in, or shortly before, the year 223 (*Oxyrh. papyr.* i, n. 35), as it is also that in various Greek inscriptions found in Egypt the prefect is accorded not the equestrian title of διασημότατος (= *perfectissimus*) but the senatorial λαμπρότατος (Hirschf., p. 348). This evidence scarcely warrants the supposition of a senatorial legate.

[1] It is worth while noticing that the title *dominus* as applied to the emperor first comes into general use in Severus' reign. Cf. *CIL*. ii. 1085, iii. 5156. Tertullian's (*Apol.* 34) words show us that even the Christians did not scruple to use the term: 'plane dicam imperatorem dominum sed more communi sed quando non cogor, ut dominum dei vice dicam.' Further, that the emperor's court is now held within the palace walls is significant (Dio Cass. lxxvi. 17. 1; Her. iii. 10. 2).

[2] Ceuleneer, p. 244, notes the disappearance after 200 of the *praef. urb. feriar. latin.*, a religious office which had long been but nominal.

[3] Momm. *St.-R.* ii. 216, note 2. This office is first mentioned in an early third-century inscription (*CIL*. x. 5398); also in *Cod. Iust.* iv. 56. 1 (year 223).

[4] So Hirschfeld, p. 256, note 1. For the *praef. vigilum's* jurisdictional powers cf. *Dig.* i. 15. 5 ('cognoscit praef. vig. de incendiariis, effractoribus, furibus, raptoribus, receptatoribus'); *CIL*. vi. 266, with Mommsen's note; also Momm. *St.-R.* ii. 1011 (p. 1058) and notes. It is worthy of remark as against Hirschfeld's theory that from this reign dates the power of the *praefectus urbi* to sentence a criminal to deportation or to hard labour (i. e. work in the mines); *Dig.* xlviii. 19. 8. 5,

It is not to be supposed that, where so vast and complex a system for the administration of justice existed, the legislative side of the question would be lost sight of. In general we may notice the markedly milder character of the laws now framed; the growing feeling that human life is precious, as such, leads to a legislative humanitarianism, the more valuable in that it does not seem to degenerate into sentimentality. There is not the least need to see in Christianity the leaven of this movement towards mercy and toleration, and indeed the latter could scarcely be called the typical virtue of the early Church: the pagan Lucian could cry θεοῦ ἢ ἀνδρὸς ἰσοθέου ἐστι τὰ πταισθέντα ἐπανορθοῦν. From the principate of Severus, then, date the first laws against abortion,[1] laws protecting minors,[2] laws ensuring a wife's claim on the money she brings to her husband at the time of her marriage.[3] The rigour of certain enactments whereby the children suffered for the sins of the fathers was abated,[4] and a similar mitigation was introduced in the en-

xxxii. 1. 4, i. 12. 1, etc.; Momm. *St.-R.* ii. 947, etc. This last citation from the *Digest* (Ulpian) is curious. It runs: ' omnia omnino crimina praefectura urbis sibi vindicavit nec tantum ea quae intra urbem admittuntur, verum ea quoque quae extra urbem intra Italiam epistula divi Severi ad Fabium Cilonem praefectum urbi declaratur.' Relying on this and on the Maecenas passage in Dio (lii. 21), Mommsen (*St.-R.* ii. 1064-6) supposes the city prefect to have had judicatory power in all sorts of cases and over all degrees of persons—senators included. Wirth (p. 47) points out that Ulpian is here dealing with civil cases involving slaves and freedmen, and that there is no mention of criminal cases or of senators. He further shows that, there being an obvious bond of union between the Senate and this senatorial prefect, it is the pro-senatorial emperors who tend to increase his powers, not the anti-senatorial such as Septimius. Marcus, for example, the friend of the Senate, adds to the city prefect's authority (Vit. Marc. xi. 9): Hadrian curtailed that authority by his institution of *iuridici*, and the Senate in consequence tried to rescind his *acta*. Under the brief rule of the pro-senatorial Tacitus the city prefect's powers were again enlarged (Vit. Tac. xviii. 3, xix. 2), and in the fourth century his jurisdiction was made paramount (cf. note on p. 176).

[1] *Dig.* xlvii. 11. 4.
[2] Ulp. *Dig.* xxvii. 9—the Oratio Severi. Cod. iv. 26. 1.
[3] Cod. i. 5. 23. 1, v. 12. 1, v. 18. 1.
[4] *Dig.* l. 2. 2.

forcement of the *Lex Iulia maiestatis*.[1] On the other hand,
such laws as the *de adulteriis* and the *Papia Poppaea* were
administered with an increase of stringency.[2] The principle
that the law is no respecter of persons now comes clearly to
the fore: the use of torture in cases of *maiestas* is no longer
the exclusive fate of the lower classes.[3] The exact position
of the slave with regard to his master is decided and ensured,
though stringent measures are taken to prevent the latter's
'denouncing' the former.[4] The slave,[5] too, ceases to become
a mere chattel in the eyes of the law, and we find among the
statutes such a sentence as, for instance, 'Non offuisse mulieris
famae quaestum eius in servitute factum'.[6] The positive side
of the strict enforcement of the *Lex de adulteriis* is to be seen
in the privileges now extended to the fathers of numerous and
legitimate offspring.[7] On the more technical side may be
mentioned laws regulating inheritance,[8] laws fixing advocates'
fees,[9] the introduction of the principle that in the case of
disputed points custom and precedent should constitute a final
appeal.[10]

---

[1] *Dig.* xlviii. 4. 5.
[2] *Dig.* xlviii. 5. 14. 3, 8; Dio Cass. lxxvi. 16. 4 περὶ τῆς μοιχείας νομοθετῆσαί τινα.
[3] Paul. Sent. v. 29. 2.
[4] *Dig.* xlix. 14. 2. 6, xlviii. 18. 1. 16.
[5] *Dig.* iv. 4. 11 pr., xlviii. 18. 1. 16-18, xl. 4. 47.
[6] *Dig.* iii. 2. 24. The nature of the *quaestus* is unfortunately only too obvious.
[7] *Dig.* iv. 4. 20, 1. 5. 8. In Asia a father of five was excused the costly exercise of priesthood of his province—a principle soon extended to all provinces.
[8] *Cod. Iust.* ii. 18. 1, 2, xxxviii. 1, 1. 2. 9, xlvii. 19. 3, etc.
[9] *Dig.* l. 13. 1, 10, 12.
[10] *Dig.* i. 3. 38 'In ambiguitatibus quae ex legibus proficiscuntur consuetudinem aut rerum perpetuo similiter iudicatarum auctoritatem vim legis optinere debere.' I have made no attempt at exhaustiveness in this section on matters legal. The subject is well—though very diffusely—treated in Ceuleneer's fifth chapter, pp. 271-89. Schiller opines (p. 737) that Septimius' reign marks the cessation of the *quaestiones perpetuae*, though he produces no atom of justification for the statement.

In the history of imperial finance at least one important innovation dates from the reign of Septimius: that is, the growth of the *res privata,* the personal property of the emperor as opposed to the patrimonium or crown property. Thus from the beginning of the third century until Diocletian's time we get three financial departments, all separate and under separate management—the old *aerarium* or treasury of the Roman people, the *fiscus* probably including part of the *patrimonium,*[1] or property of the emperor *qua* emperor, and, including the rest of the *patrimonium,* the *res privata,* his private property as an individual. But in practice just as the *patrimonium* became overshadowed by the new *res* or *ratio privata,* so the old *aerarium* gave place to the *fiscus,* so that the *fiscus* and the *res privata* are the only two treasuries of any importance: the *aerarium* lapses into desuetude.[2] Spartian connects the institution of this new financial department with the enormous accumulation of wealth won by Severus at the conclusion of the civil wars, thanks to his systematic persecution of the supporters of his rivals, and

---

[1] The exact relationship between *patrimonium* and *fiscus* after the institution of the *ratio privata* forms a difficult problem. That the *fiscus* swallowed up part of the *patrimonium* seems almost certain, as we get no patrimonial officers in Rome or Italy mentioned in inscriptions after Caracalla's reign. The above-cited *CIL.* x. 6657 and *CIL* vi. 8498 are early examples, and Bormann has decided against the genuineness of *CIL.* vi. 3486* 'Achilles Gall(ieni) A(ugusti) l(ibertus) a rationibus patrimo(nii) '. On the other hand, there are plenty of instances of officials of the *res privata* in Italy, e. g. *CIG.* 6771 (regions 8 and 9); *CIL.* iii. 1464 (reg. 7 and 5); *CIL.* xi. 6337 (reg. 8), etc.; Hirschf., p. 44, note 2. Possibly, therefore, what was formerly patrimonial property in Italy went over partly into the *fiscus* and partly into the *res privata.* In the provinces we continue to find mention of *patrimonium,* though it looks as though, in the smaller provinces, both were taken together as = *res privata,* and as such managed by an official of that department; e. g. *CIL.* xiii. 1807 'proc. prov. Bithyniae Ponti Paphlagon(iae) tam patrimoni quam ra(tionum) privatar(um) '; *CIL.* viii. 11105 (a *proc. patrim.* in the region of Leptis and a *proc. ration. privatae* in that of Tripolis); cf. *CIL.* viii. 16542, 16543.

[2] In the *acta* of the saecular games for 204 (*CIL.* vi. 32326) we find the two expressions 'communi expensa' and 'ex aerario p. R.' *Communis* Mommsen holds to be the technical term for municipal, *publicus* for state property (*Eph. epigr.* viii, p. 297 ; cf. Ulp. *Dig.* l. 16. 15).

both Dio and Herodian bear witness to the amount of
money that found its way into the imperial coffers at that
time.[1] At the head of the fiscus had stood, up till the turn
of the second and third centuries, a *procurator a rationibus*,
but with the appearance of the new *procurator privatae* he
changes his title and becomes simply the *rationalis*.[2] The
official in charge of the *ratio privata* is known at first as the
procurator patrimonii privati, and soon as the *procurator rei
privatae, rationis privatae*, or *privatae* simply : his standing was
declared equal to that of the *rationalis*.[3]

---

[1] Vit. Sev. xii. 4; Dio Cass. lxxiv. 8. 4; Her. iii. 8. 2.

[2] Marini's view that the title *rationalis* is common to all higher
procurators in the third century is conclusively discredited by Hirschfeld
(p. 35). It is clear, however, that at any rate in the earlier years of that
century the two expressions *a rationibus* and *rationalis* occurred side by
side. There is, e. g., a dedication to Maximianus (*CIL.* vi. 31384) on
which is still found the title *a rationibus*, while *rationalis* occurs in the
second and even in the first century: *CIL.* x. 6092 (Flavian period);
CIL. xv. 7741, 7742 (Antonine age). Under Antoninus Pius we find the
same man referred to as *a rat. Aug.* (*CIL.* v. 867) and *rationalis* (*CIL.* xv.
7740). No distinction is drawn between the corresponding Greek terms
καθολικός and ὁ τοὺς καθολοῦ λόγους ἐπιτετραμμένος. Aelius Achilles and
Cl. Perpetuus Flavianus Eutychus, called *rationales* in *CIL.* vi. 1585
(year 193), are clearly respectively (1) the *procurator a rationibus*, (2) his
adiutor, whose full title was *proc. summarum rationum*.

[3] 'Quodcumque privilegii fisco competit hoc idem et Caesaris ratio
et Augustae habere solet,' Ulp. in *Dig.* xlix. 14. 6. 1. For the earlier
title see the Antium inscription (*CIL.* x. 6657) 'M. Aquilius Felix proc.
operum publicum (in 193) proc. hereditatium patrimonii privati . . .
proc. patrimonii bis '. Thus, after his procuratorship of public works he
looked after money left to the emperor—money which had previously
gone into the *patrimonium* and which now goes into the *patrimonium
privatum = res privata* (cf. Capit. Pii vii. 8 'patrimonium privatum in
filiam contulit'). This same Felix was one of the two patrimonial
procurators in Egypt in the year 201 (*BGU.* 156; cf. Rostowzew, *Diz.
epigr.* iii, p. 100). Incidentally the emperor may have found in the
imperial finance of Egypt the examples for his innovation, for in that
province a distinction had long been made between γῆ βασιλική—the
property of the emperor as successor of the Pharaohs—and γῆ οὐσιακή,
his private property. As an instance of the fully developed *privatae*
without the addition of *patrimonii* may be cited *CIL.* xv. 7333 (waterpipe
of Alexander Severus) 'stationis prop(r)iae privatae domini n(ostri)

A further advance in financial specialization is to be observed
in the reorganization of the *advocati fisci*—an office of which
Septimius had had personal experience.[1] From now dates the
subdivision of this department into different sections, each
dealing with some special point such as, for example, *bona
vacantia* or patrimonial property in any particular province.[2]
Whatever the machinery by which Septimius worked the
finances of the empire its excellence is sufficiently attested by
the flourishing state of that most important branch of the
government during his principate. On the murder of Commodus the empire had stood on the brink of bankruptcy. The
instigator of the *aureum saeculum* had, in the words of his
biographer, deplenished the *aerarium* 'luxuriae sumptibus ',[3] and
his luckless successor found but a beggarly million sesterces
left there, a sum to which the auction sale of Commodus' various
instruments of vice may have added a respectable amount.[4]
A cheese-paring policy may have enabled the *agrarius mergus*
considerably to better the state of the treasury, but that he
put it completely on its feet again is, in spite of the testimony
of Capitolinus, more than questionable. His goodwill at least

Alex. Aug.' He was a *trecenarius* (*CIL.* x. 6569), and his importance is
shown in that the next step in an official career could be *vice praefecti
vigilum* (*CIL.* viii. 822; ix. 12345), or even *praef. praetorio* (so Macrinus—
Capit. Macr. vii. 1, ii. 1). Hirschfeld (p. 20) with some reason doubts the
authenticity of *CIL.* viii. 3810, where apparently a 'procura(tor rationis)
privatae' of Pius' time is mentioned.

[1] Cf. p. 39. Another sceptic on this point is Domaszewski, who
remarks that for a senatorial such as Septimius to have held the post is
einfach sinnlos (*Rangord.*, p. 169, note 5). To what was said above we
may add that though the office belonged to the equestrian *cursus*
(cf. Capit. Macrin. iv. 4 ; Phil. Vit. Soph., p. 120 (ed. Kayser)), yet even
a born slave could hold it—Marcius Agrippa under Septimius himself
(Dio Cass. lxxviii. 13. 3). Besides, until he received the *laticlavus*,
Septimius would rank as equestrian (Vit. Sev. i. 2).

[2] *Bona vacantia*; cf. *CIL.* viii. 1439 ' fisci advocato cod(icil)lari stationis
hered(ita)tium et cohaerentium '. A patrimonial instance is to be seen
in *CIL.* v. 11341 'functo adv(oca)tione fisci Hispania(r)u(m, A)lpium,
(p)atrimoni tract(us) Karthaginis'. Schiller's statement (p. 736) that the
number of *advocati* was increased is a likely corollary.

[3] Lamp. Comm. xvi. 8.   [4] Capit. Pert. vii. 6, 8.

is proved by the apparent payment out of his own pocket of the
arrears of the Italian landowners in the department of alimentation.[1] Severus, on the other hand, at his death, left behind him
an almost incalculable fortune, and that too though he had spent
imperially.[2] Indeed, throughout his reign the openhandedness,
not to say the extravagance, of the emperor is little short of
amazing : not without justification did his coins celebrate him
as ' munificentissimus providentissimusque princeps '—a combination of epithets as fully merited in this instance as it is rare
in the generality of cases.[3] Coins show that between 193 and
208 occurred six *liberalitates*,[4] and a fourth-century writer as-
sesses their total sum at 220,000,000 denarii.[5] The expenses,
too, of the games given by Septimius must have been very
heavy. In the autumn of 202 were celebrated the Decennalia
in honour of the completion of ten years of his reign as of the
successful conclusion of the Eastern wars and the marriage
of Caracalla and Plautilla, where, not content with the exhibi-
tion of bears, lions, panthers, ostriches, and buffaloes, and the
introduction of the hyena to the people of Rome, the emperor
presented every praetorian with a gold piece for every year of
service.[6] Even more magnificent were the saecular games of
two years later. Domitian had last celebrated them in the year
88, and now Septimius was holding them for the eighth time
since their inauguration.[7] Mention has already been made of

---

[1] 'Aerarium in suum statum restituit,' Capit. Pert. ix. 2. Alimentation—ix. 3 'Alimentaria etiam compendia quae novem annorum ex instituto Traiani debebantur ... sustulit.' This might mean that he merely
refused to call in arrears without himself making good the deficit.

[2] Dio Cass. lxxvi. 16. 4 ; cf. 3 πάντα . . . τὰ ἀναγκαῖα ἐδαπάνα ἀφθονώτατα.
Her. iii. 15. 3.

[3] Eck. vii. 189, etc.

[4] Coh. iv, pp. 32–4. The fifth *liberalitas* (204) is celebrated on Syria-
minted coins (Eck. vii. 186).

[5] Philocalus (*CIL.* i, p. 378).

[6] Dio Cass. lxxvi. 1. Dio reckons that this munificence must have cost
him 50,000,000 drachmae. Eck. vii. 182 : coins showing a ship (cf. Dio
Cass. lxxvi. 1. 4) and a wild beast hunt in the circus. Her. iii. 10. 2.

[7] Her. iii. 8. 10 (out of chronological order) ; Zos. ii. 4. 3 ; Censorin. *de
die nat.* xvii. 11 ; Eck. vii. 185 ; Coh. Sev. 105–10, 623–5. Other lesser
public entertainments are mentioned by Dio (lxxv. 16. 5, lxxvi. 7. 5),

the free distribution of corn [1] and oil, and to this may be added the fact that in Severus' reign we come across the first clear instance of the 'dispensary' system, medicine being distributed free to the sick under the supervision of Galen.[2] The alimentary institutions also which had been stopped by Commodus were now restarted.[3] With yet another source of expense did the generous emperor burden himself—the imperial post. Although this department had been 'nationalized' since the reign of Hadrian [4] the various municipalities seem still to have found postal expenses a serious item : so much so that Antoninus Pius was obliged to introduce some alleviation into the system.[5] Severus, however, clinched the matter by paying everything connected with the service out of the *fiscus* [6]—a short-lived innovation, for we find the jurists of the third century including the obligation to supply post-horses and wagons among the duties of a provincial,[7] and the writers of the fourth century complaining bitterly of the imposition.[8]

It remains briefly to sum up the character and tendencies of

who does not distinguish between the saecular and decennalian games. Cf. *CIL.* vi. 32327 (April 15, 204) and address by the XV viri to Septimius and Caracalla as their colleagues. Mommsen, *Ludi Saeculares*, pp. 274 sqq.

[1] Yet such was the efficiency of the corn supply that at his death he left a seven years' supply in the public granaries (Vit. Sev. viii. 5, xxiii. 2 ; Lamp. Elagab. xxvii. 7)—the reading may be *canonem* or *annonam*, the text being faulty.

[2] Galeni, *de Antidot.* i. 3 ; *de Theriaca*, i. 2.

[3] One would imagine that alimentation was one of the things over which Commodus economized (Lamp. Comm. 16. 9). 'Alimentary' inscriptions begin again in Septimius' reign, e. g *CIL.* x. 3805 'Maecius Probus v. c. praef. alim.' For him cf. *Prosopograph.* ii, p. 320, n. 47 ; *CIL.* vi. 1634. Provincial governors were required to see to the organization and prosecution of this charity in their provinces (*Dig.* xxxv. 2. 89).

[4] Spart. Hadr. vii. 4. [5] Capit. Pii. xii. 3.

[6] Vit. Sev. xiv. 2.

[7] *Dig.* l. 4. 1. 1, l. 4. 18. 4, etc.

[8] Victor (Caes. xiii. 6) calls it a *pestem.* Ceuleneer (p 260) thinks that Severus merely extended to the provinces the privilege of freedom from postal obligations granted by Nerva to Italy, and that provincials continued to pay some counterbalancing tax.

Septimius' home administration. We notice first of all the waning importance of the senator whether as an individual or as a member of the *curia*, and we find his place in office usurped by the soldier and the *eques*. We observe the immense increase of power in the praetorian prefecture, its growing significance in the domain of law, and in general the heightened activity and wider field of jurisdiction. We mark the rapid advance in material prosperity of which an enlightened munificence is at once the cause and the effect.

Septimius had moulded the constitution to his hand: there was no department of government but bore his characteristic impress. Yet all cannot bend Odysseus' bow, and well might the Senate say of him 'aut nasci non debuisse aut mori'. A Phaethon was about to drive the horses of his father.

CHAPTER XII

THE PROVINCES UNDER SEPTIMIUS

ANY inquiry which has as its subject the provinces of the Roman Empire is bound to fall into a twofold division. The question, that is to say, must be examined from two points of view, viz. that of the home government and that of the provincials themselves. The first of these is clearly but one facet of the more general inquiry into the administration of the reign, and is complementary to the investigation of the methods of home government; the second, evidence for which must be almost entirely archaeological, belongs rather to the world's history of civilization and progress, and goes to justify or to condemn not an emperor but an empire for the furtherance or retardation of those beneficent forces.

We will examine the question in this order. Perhaps the most striking, if not the most important, feature of Severus' provincial administration is that tendency to break up big commands into smaller ones which characterized the policy of Domitian and his successors. Septimius' wars of accession had provided no uncertain testimony to the power of a provincial legate, and the founder of a dynasty had no wish to witness a re-enactment of his own success or even of the failures of Niger and Albinus. The province governed by the last-named legate was one of the first to experience the new treatment. The date of the division is uncertain, but it is no very hazardous supposition that it was made after the defeat of Albinus at Lyon, that is to say some time in the year 197.[1]

---

[1] So Ceuleneer (p. 244) and Wirth (p. 11). Schiller (ii, p. 731) says 'wahrscheinlich bereits 196', but refrains from advancing any support for the *Wahrscheinlichkeit*. Höfner (p. 326), also with little probability and slender evidence, supposes the division to date from Severus' arrival there: Herodian (iii. 8. 2) supports this latter view. We have inscriptions referring to the lower province (*CIL.* viii. 2766, 1578 b) and to the

The upper province comprised all the country in the south of
the island, but it is impossible to determine its northern boundary
with any certainty. All we can say is that Chester was in the
upper province, York the chief town of the lower. The presumption that the Mersey and the Humber formed the dividing
line is at least a likely one.[1] The military arrangements of the
province remained as before. The 2nd legion (Augusta) continued at Isca, the 20th (Valeria Victrix) at Chester, and the
6th (Victrix) at York. Now, however, the legate of the last-
mentioned legion was also propraetorian legate of the lower
province, and to him would therefore be answerable the com-
manders of the various auxiliary forces on the Wall. The title
of *praeses*, at least as an official designation, was probably not
given to either legate [2] until later. The titular use of the term
praeses, either alone or coupled with that of procurator, may, incidentally, be said to start from Severus' reign, and we notice
that in Macer's book, *De officio praesidis* (written in the reign of
Caracalla), this appellation is recognized as the *nomen generale*
for all governors except proconsuls. Properly speaking an
equestrian title, it gained its universal acceptance and employment owing to the elimination of senatorial governors.[3]

A twelvemonth or so later the other rebellious province, Syria,

upper (*CIL.* vii. 280, 281)—Alfenius Seneceo being the governor (205-8).
Little trust can be placed in the rescript (*Dig.* xxviii. 6. 2. 4) 'imperatoris
nostri (Caracallae) ad Virium Lupum Brittaniae praesidem', except as
making it probable that the governor of one or perhaps both provinces
later held the title of *praeses*. Lupus was legate in succession to Albinus ;
cf. Hübner, *Röm. Leg. in Brit. (Rhein. Mus.* xii, pp. 46–87).

   [1] So Oman, *England before the Norman Conquest*, p. 130.

   [2] For the question of the title see the last foot-note but one. Severus
was not without precedent in so dealing with Lower Britain (and, as we
shall see, with Syria Phoenice). To quote but two out of many instances,
Vespasian put Judaea under the legate of leg. X Fretensis, and Trajan
Arabia under that of leg. III Cyraenaica. Cf. Domasz., *Rang.*, p. 173 ;
Rhein. Mus. xlv, p. 208.

   [3] Macer; cf. *Dig.* i. 18. 1. Cf. Lamp. Alex. Sev. xxiv. 1 'Provincias
legatorias praesidiales plurimas fecit '. For inscriptional evidence cf.
'praes. Alp. Cott.', *CIL.* v. 7248, 7249, 7251, 7252 ; 'praes. Mauret.',
viii. 9002 ; 'praes. Sardiae ', vi. 1636, x. 8013 ; *CIG.* 2509 (ἡγεμὼν καὶ
δουκηνάριος). ' Proc. et prae[s, not *f*] Alp. Mar.', *CIL.* xii. 78 ; cf. xii. 7.

suffered a like fate, being, from the year 198, divided into Syria Maior (or Coele-Syria) and Syria Phoenice. This move, adumbrated nearly a century before by the Emperor Hadrian,[1] had the effect of separating most of the coast-line from the interior, Syria Phoenice having as its capital Tyre and extending from about Dora on the south to a little short of Laodicaea in the north. Its eastern boundary was probably not the Libanus range, as Heliopolis, Emesa, Damascus, and Palmyra, together with the districts of Auranitis, Batanea, and Trachonitis, fell under the jurisdiction of its governor. Coele-Syria was by far the larger and the more important of the two. Its capital was Antioch, recovered apparently from its punishment by Septimius for its championship of Niger and reinstated in imperial favour, while its territories comprised Commagene in the north. As in the case of Britain, so here, the legate of the one legion (III Gallica) stationed in the inferior province (Phoenice) became that province's praetorian legate.[2]

[1] Spart. Hadr. 14. 1 'Odio Antiochensium'.

[2] Geographically one would expect Libanus to separate the provinces, and most maps mark it so, e.g. that in Mommsen's *Provinces of the Roman Empire* (Eng. trans., vol. ii). We have, however, good enough evidence for the attachment of those Eastern districts to Phoenice: Heliopolis, *CIL*. iii. 202 (year 213). Hierocles mentions Emesa and Palmyra as in Phoenice; cf. Ulpian, *de censibus* (*Dig.* l. 15. 1 *passim*). Auranitis, etc., were not joined to the province of Arabia till Diocletian's reign. As to the date, Marquardt (*L'Organisation des prov.* ii, p. 374, note 2) rightly decides against the attribution to Hadrian of more than the intention: the passage in Justin Martyr (*Dial. c. Tryphon.* 78) which mentions Syrophoenicia must, like the New Testament passages, refer to the district, not the province. Tertullian (*adv. Marcionem*, iii. 13, written in 207) suggests that the change is a recent one. The earliest inscriptional evidence proving the split belongs to the year 198; *CIL*. iii. 205 'Q. Venidium Rufum leg. Augg. pr. pr. praesidem provinc. Syriae Phoenices'. The Coele-Syrian legateship of L. Marius Maximus (*CIL*. vi. 1450) is really undatable, though we may with some confidence suppose it to have followed not long after the Nigerian war, and to have been contemporaneous with the division of the province. Marquardt (*L'Organ. de l'emp.* ii, p. 376, note 1) suggests 194, but this rests on his assumption that Marius was consul in 195—an assumption which seems to me unwarranted. Marius was *cos. ii* in 223 (*CIL*. iii. 14565, vi. 32542, etc.) and possibly for the first time in 207 (*CIL*. xiii. 6623).

Yet a third province to undergo such a transformation was
Africa. Possibly in the year 198 what was, up to that date,
the *dioecesis* of Numidia, and held as such a position of equality
only with the other similarly organized dioeceses, now becomes
a province under a *praeses* who is at the same time the legate of
leg. III Augusta. That the two offices soon merge into one is
shown by his later title ' leg. Aug. pr. pr. provinciae Numidiae ',
or, more simply still, ' Numidiae legatus '.[1]

The financial management of the province is no longer entrusted
to the *quaestor Africae*, but becomes the special department of an
imperial procurator.[2]

There is no need, indeed it would be a mistake, to see in this
province-splitting policy a conscious and intentional anticipation
of the later Diocletianic system. Where a province was by
nature strong, large in extent, or possessed of extraordinary
resources, there the emperor was ready to dissipate possible seeds
of disruption and disturbance by dividing the administrative
power. On the other hand, where a province was, from a military
point of view, unimportant, Septimius did not hesitate to simplify
the machinery of government by attaching to it a neighbouring
district or even another province. This was certainly the case
in the third African province, that of Mauretania. Already, in
the course of the first century, the Emperor Claudius had divided
Mauretania into an eastern (Caesariensis) and a western (Tingi-

The statement of Malalas (p. 293) that Laodicea was made capital of
Syria instead of Antioch, in order to reward its faithfulness to Severus
in the Nigerian war, must be a mere exaggeration founded on such
passages as Herod. iii. 6. 10 ; Dio Cass. lxxiv. 8. 4, etc. It is true that the
city bears on its coins the title metropolis (Eck. iii. 317, 318), but that
is scarcely the same as capital.

[1] *CIG*. 6627 mentions as praeses Sextus Varius Marcellus, husband of
Iulia Soaemias, niece of Septimius. *CIL*. x. 6569 (cf. Eck. vii. 245). The
date 198 rests on *CIL*. viii. 2465, undoubtedly of that year, but of rather
doubtful import. It mentions a vexillatio of leg. III 'in procinctu':
cf. *CIL*. viii. 2392, 2615 for the title of legate. The mention of a 'consti-
tutio divi Pii ad Tuscium Fuscianum Numidiae legatum' must be an
anachronism by the editor Tryphonius, who wrote his *Disputationum
libri XXI* in 211.

[2] The earliest of whom we have evidence is one L. Iulius Victor
Modianus (*CIL*. viii. 7053). Later, *CIL*. viii. 8329.

tana) half, each being under the command [1] of a procurator, who was sometimes known as a *procurator pro legato*.[2] However, towards the end of Severus' reign we find one Diadumenianus who is a *proc. Augg. utrarumque Mauretaniarum*.[3] Whether or not some redistribution of districts in Asia Minor was effected during this reign is a matter of some dispute. It seems, however, at least possible that it was Septimius who subsumed Isauria and Lycaonia under the province of Cilicia : their previous connexion with Galatia had apparently not been of a very binding character.[4] Another instance of the shifting of a district from

---

[1] Dio Cass. lx. 9. 5 ; Plin. *H. N.* v. 2, 11 ; Aur. Vict. Caes. 4.

[2] So Marquardt, *L'Organis. de l'Emp.* ii, p. 481. There was one under Trajan (*CIL.* viii. 9990), another under Severus (*CIL.* xii. 1856)—the Hadrianic example cited by Marquardt (*CIL.* viii. 8813) is of doubtful interpretation. Hirschfeld, p. 386, thinks that these were procurators with some special command over legionary troops—the ordinary title of the ordinary governor of either Mauretania being simply *procurator*. He cites as a parallel instance of a procurator in extraordinary command of legionaries *CIL.* vi. 31856 '(proc.) Aug. et praep. vexil[la]tion.', etc.

[3] *CIL.* viii. 9366: date 209-11. It is true that this joining together of the two Mauretaniae is not originally or exclusively Severan. Tacitus (*Hist.* ii. 58) supplies us with an instance in the reign of Galba, and there is another ? in Caracalla's principate (*CIL.* viii. 9371). It is not necessary to suppose that the governor of the conjoined provinces received any special appellation. That he was called *praefectus* (Marquardt, *op. cit.* ii, p. 482) rests on what is probably a false reading in Spart. Hadr. vi. 7, while the passages in Capitolinus (Pii, v. 4 ; Marc. Ant. xxi. 2) mentioning *legati* can be supposed to refer to those of the proconsul of Africa; so too Spartian (Sev. ii. 6 ; cf. above, p. 41, note 3).

[4] So Marquardt (*L'Organisation des prov.* ii, p. 323) quoting an inscription of Tarsus (Waddington, vol. iii, no. 1480) as μ[ητρόπολις] τῶν γ' ἐπαρχιῶν [Κιλικίας] Ἰσαυρίας Λυκαονίας: and coins of Tarsus with the legend κοινὸς τῶν τρίων ἐπαρχιῶν (Mionnet, iii, p. 634, no. 478). But another inscription (Dittenberger, *Orientis Graeci inscr.*, no. 576) shows this threefold conjunction of provinces in existence under Antoninus Pius, which makes it seem as though the attachment of the two to Cilicia were contemporaneous with the re-establishment of the latter as an imperial province by Hadrian. But besides evidence of a separate κοινὸν Λυκαονίας (Eck. iii. 32) we have mention of an ἀνθυπάτου Λυκίας καὶ Παμφυλίας καὶ Ἰσαυρίας (*Bull. de corr. hell.* xi, 1887, p. 348, n. 5, 12, 13 ; cf. Prosop., vol. i, p. 305). From this M. Clerc argues that Isauria was joined to Lycia and Pamphylia by Commodus, but restored to the

the jurisdiction of one provincial governor to that of another is afforded by the region round Kanatha, which, originally Syrian and subsequently joined to the kingdom of Palestine, was perhaps under, and certainly not subsequent to, Severus' principate reattached to the province of Syria. It was not seemingly until the reign of Caracalla that the district was attached to Arabia.[1]

Besides these rearrangements of the old provinces Severus' reign saw the birth, or rather the rebirth, of a new one. Trajan it was who first made Mesopotamia a province. The retrenchment policy of his successor led to its abandonment by Rome, though Marcus Aurelius once more united it [2] to the empire.[3] Again Mesopotamia disappears from the list of provinces and once more reappears there in the reign of Septimius, being taken over, as we have seen, as a result of the successful termination of that emperor's Eastern wars.[4] The government of the new province was entrusted at first to a procurator,[5] and afterwards to an equestrian *praefectus*.[6] Under him, on the Egyptian model, were the two *praefecti* respectively of the first and third Parthian legions,[7] the latter of which was probably stationed at Rhesaena, a town which,[8] together with

governor of Cilicia by Septimius. For their connexion with Galatia cf. Dio Cass. xlix. 32. 3, liii. 26. 3; Strabo, xii, pp. 568, 569, 571; *CIG.* 3991. Even so late as Ptolemy Isauria counts as Galatian (v. 4. 12). But the detached nature of the two districts is shown by the fact that they seem to have been joined to Cappadocia by Trajan (Ptolem. v. 6; *CIL.* v. 8660).

[1] Kanatha attached to Coele-Syria (Joseph. *Bell. Iud.* i. 19. 2); to the Decapolis (Plin. *H. N.* v. 70); to Syria again under Marcus Aurelius (Waddington, no. 2331) and under Septimius (ibid., no. 2329). Under Caracalla we find legionaries of leg. III Cyr. stationed there (*CIG.* 4610). Ceuleneer (p. 246) wrongly puts its junction with Arabia in Severus' reign.

[2] Spart. Hadr. v. 3; Eutrop. viii. 6.   [3] So Rufus, Brev. 14.

[4] Rufus, Brev. 14, see above, p. 94.

[5] Dio Cass. lxxv. 3. 2; *CIL.* viii. 9760 'proc. sexagenarius prov. Mes.'

[6] Probably, however, post-Severan. The earliest regular epigraphic evidence belongs to the time of the Gordians; *CIL.* vi. 1638, etc. There is, however, a 'praef. Mesopot.' in *CIL.* vi. 1642, who was procurator Osrhoenae under Septimius.

[7] *CIL.* iii. 99.

[8] Eck. iii. 518; Mionnet, v. 630, etc.

Nisibis and Zaytha, received the *ius coloniae*[1] at the emperor's hands. The district of Osrhoene was at the same time detached from Mesopotamia proper and left under the rule of its native princes, whose capital was Edessa. It is true that immediately after the Eastern wars Severus preferred to put a procurator[2] in charge, but he soon gave the kingdom back to Abgarus,[3] its rightful ruler.

This may end our survey of administrative changes in the provincial government of Septimius' reign. There seems not the least reason to suppose with Ceuleneer that either Severus or his successor gave back the province of Bithynia to the Senate. Such a view is unlikely from *a priori* considerations and unsupported by any credible evidence.[4] It was in imperial hands as early as 165, and as late as 269.

Of the beneficent character of Septimius' provincial activities we do not need to look far for evidence. The granting of colonial rights to certain towns in Mesopotamia has already been mentioned, nor are these solitary instances of the bestowal of the same or similar privileges. In Dacia, for example, Apulum was granted the renewal or further ratification of municipal rights,[5]

---

[1] Rhesaena: cf. Eck. iii. 518; Mionnet, v. 630. Nisibis: Eck. iii. 517; Dio Cass. lxxv. 3. 2. Zaytha: Mionnet, suppl. 8, p. 418.

[2] C. Iulius Pacatianus (*CIL.* xii. 1856); *CIL.* ii. 4135, vi. 1644, mention procurators of Osrhoene, but are of uncertain date.

[3] Dio Cass. lxxvii. 12. 1, where Caracalla (? in 215) deprives Abgarus of his kingdom. Gordian the Third seems to have given it back: cf. Gutschmid, *Untersuch. über die Geschichte des Königreichs O.*, Petersburg, 1887, p. 34.

[4] Ceuleneer, p. 247. It is true that inscriptions occur mentioning proconsulship of Bithynia (e. g. *CIL.* xi. 1183, L. Coelius Festus), and the province certainly was in the hands of the Senate between the reigns of Hadrian and Pius (Marquardt, *L'Organ.* ii, p. 263). The remark of Capitolinus (Max. et Balb. v. 8) to the effect that Maximus 'proconsulatum Bithyniae egit' need not carry much weight. On the other hand, we get ample evidence for the existence of imperial legates of Bithynia until at least the second half of the third century: e.g. L. Fabius Cilo under Severus (*CIL.* vi. 1408, 1409); also M. Claudius Demetrius (*CIG.* 3771, 3773); L. Albinus Saturninus (? Cos. 264) (*CIL.* x. 4750); Velleius Macrinus in 269 (*CIG.* 3747, 3748) and as early as 165 (*CIG.* 4152 d).

[5] Municipium Septimium (*CIL.* iii. 976, 985, 1051). It is also

became the residence of the procurator, and a little later a *colonia iuris Italici*.[1] Potaissa, too, dates its colonial privileges from Septimius' reign.[2] In Thrace [3] we notice the elevation of Philippopolis to be the metropolis of the province, and, as such, the place of meeting for the κοινὸν Θρακῶν. From the province of Syria we have a long list of towns which from now took their rank as colonies: Laodicea, Tyre, Sebaste (Samaria), Heliopolis (Ba'albek),[4] and possibly, too, Palmyra.[5] In Cilicia a similar honour befell Olba, and perhaps Selinus.[6] As might be conjectured, the new African colonies are also numerous. We may mention Utica, Leptis Magna,[7] Thugga,[8] Cuicul,[9] and Vaga.[10]

Besides the gift of *ius coloniae* we find other privileges bestowed, less honorific perhaps if of more practical worth. Thus the small town of Tyras in lower Moesia, for instance, receives immunity from the *portorium Illyrici*, the vectigal in force over all the Danube provinces,[11] while Tarsus seems to have enjoyed the gift of perpetual *annona* as a result of the emperor's munificence: a similar donation was made to Laodicea.[12] Not even

referred to as 'municipium Aurelium', after Marcus (*CIL*. iii. 986, 1132).

[1] Date uncertain: Ulp. *de censibus*, l. 15. 1. 8, 9.

[2] Ulp. ibid.; cf. *CIL*. iii. 1030.

[3] Eck. ii. 44; Dumont, *Inscript. et monuments figurés de la Thrace* (in the *Archives des missions scientifiques et littéraires*, 3rd series, vol. iii, pp. 117–200), nos. 3, 42, 60. The κοινόν, Eck. ii. 43 (under Caracalla), and Dumont, no. 29.

[4] *Dig*. l. 15. 1. 3; prooem., § 7; Eck. iii. 319, 387, 440.

[5] Marquardt, *op. cit.* ii, p. 363.

[6] Olba: Mionnet, vii. 238. Selinus: *Dig*. l. 15. 1. 11; cf. Marquardt, *op. cit.* ii, p. 324.

[7] *Dig*. l. 15. 8. 11.   [8] *CIL*. viii. 1487; cf. 182.

[9] *CIL*. viii. 8318, 8326, 8329.   [10] *CIL*. viii. 1222, 1217.

[11] App. Illyr. 6 τὸ τέλος τῶνδε τῶν ἐθνῶν ἀπὸ ἀνίσχοντος Ἴστρου μέχρι τῆς Ποντικῆς θαλάσσης ... Ἰλλυρικὸν τέλος προσαγορεύουσιν. Cf. Cic. *pro Fonteio*, § 2. Customs frontier at Aquileia. Central bureau in Rome; cf. *CIL*. vi. 1921, a freedman of Claudius as '(tabularius vectigalis) Il(l)yrici'. Hirschf., pp. 78, 85, etc. The immunity of Tyras rests on the three inscriptions: *CIL*. iii. 12510 (cf. 13747 'tempori bono pro sal.'); *CIL*. iii. 781 (a letter of Feb. 17, 201, from the *praeses* L. Ovinius Tertullus); and *IGRR*. 598.

[12] Eck. iii. 78.

from the cities of the East who adhered to the cause of Niger
was the emperor's bounty and pardon withheld. Antioch, sub-
ordinated after the war to the city of Laodicea, soon won again
its title of metropolis,[1] and seems by the year 206 to have
enjoyed some amount of autonomy.[2] Even Byzantium, which
had been deprived of its rights as a city and reduced to the
position of a κώμη or, as it were, suburb of Perinthus,[3] was pardoned on the intercession of Caracalla, in whose honour it subsequently took the title of πόλις 'Αντωνινία.[4] A more practical
step was taken by Septimius himself in his rebuilding of the
city and construction of baths, a temple to Jupiter, and a
hippodrome.[5]

It yet remains briefly to notice the concession made by Severus
to the city of Alexandria, as mentioned in the pages of his
biographer. ' Deinde Alexandrinis ius buleutarum dedit,' says
Spartian. That is to say, the capital city of Egypt was allowed to
have its own Senate and so to enjoy a considerable measure of
self-government. That this arrangement restricted the sphere
of action of the *iuridicus Alexandrinus* is a fact which is commented upon by that author, though indeed it is self-evident.[6]

---

[1] Eck. iii. 302; Kuhn, *Städtische und bürgerliche Verfassung des röm.
Reichs*, ii. 192.

[2] *Dig.* xlii. 5. 37.

[3] Dio Cass lxxiv. 14. 3. B. loses its ἀξίωμα πολιτικόν.

[4] Spart. Car. i. 7: Antioch also received the favour of his intercession.
πόλις 'A. Cf. Hesych. Mil. *FHG.* iv, p. 153 (Müller). Cf. Eck. ii. 32 for
the festival 'Αντωνείνια Σεβαστά.

[5] Suid. ii. 2. 699; *Chron. pasc.* (Dindorf), p. 49; John Malal. xii,
p. 291.

[6] Vit. Sev. xvii. 2. There seems to me absolutely no justification for
Ceuleneer's presumption (p. 251) that the βουλή was accorded only to
the *Greeks* of Alexandria. His citation of the definitely Greek city of
Antinoe and its βουλή is no manner of proof. In the inscriptions which
deal with it we get mentioned specifically ἡ βουλὴ ἡ 'Αντινοέων νέων
'Ελλήνων (e. g. *CIG.* 4679), yet references in legal writers to the Senate
of Alexandria run simply 'curia Alexandriae' (cf. Gothofr., *Ad cod.
Theod.* xii. 1, Const. 192). Jouguet, *La Vie municipale dans l'Égypte
romaine*, pp. 346 sqq., thinks that other cities may have received a similar
right at the same time, e. g. the above-mentioned Arsinoe. Certainly
Oxyrhynchus had no βουλή in 201, as mention of the κοινόν is made in
that year (*P. Oxy.* i. 54). Hermopolis seems to have had a βουλή as

As a parallel may be cited the granting of a Senate to Sciathus, thus detaching it from the government of Athens, a city for which Septimius had but little affection.[1]

Up to this point our survey shows in general a mainly theoretic interest felt by the emperor in the provinces. The formation of new administrative areas, the redistribution of provincial commands, and even the honorific grants of the *ius coloniae*, might well exist side by side with the most selfish and short-sighted provincial policy in the wider sense of the term. Septimius was, however, eminently practical, and his care for the empire covered all those minutiae so important in the eyes of the historian because so often overlooked.

Inscriptional evidence—and all such evidence is bound to be almost exclusively of that nature—conclusively proves two things : first, that a great deal of practical work in the way of building was done during this reign, either at the instigation and possible expense of the emperor, or at that of the provincials ; secondly, that the provincials recognized the care and munificence of Severus, and were not slow to testify to their gratitude by raising statues and altars in honour of the royal family.

Of military buildings erected at this period we have already spoken, and we cannot do better than open our survey of other provincial *opera publica* than by glancing at that branch of constructive activity the *raison d'être* of which is, after all, mainly military—the imperial road system.

Road-making and restoration seem to have gone on fairly continuously throughout the reign, although it is a point worthy of remark that, especially in Gaul and Germany, the activity of Septimius in this line was less than that of Alexander : this is further the case in Africa, where most of the milestones bear the title ' divi Severi ', while Caracalla's name adorns no few.[2] Sitifis in Africa seems to have been a centre for Septimius' road-mending operations ; milestones of his reign are found on roads

early as 136 (*P. Amh.* ii. 97. 1).   Mommsen's view (*Hist. Rom.* v, p. 557) that this piece of generosity on Severus' part is due entirely to his wish to cause jealousy to the people of Antioch is hard to accept.

[1] *CIG.* 2154 ; Vit. Sev. iii. 7.

[2] e. g. *CIL.* viii. 10197, 10231, 10253, 10260, 10263, 10379.

leading east to Mons, west to Deheb[1]—the Cirta road[2]—and south to Meslug.[3] From Asia come many indications that means of communication were being improved. Tineius Sacerdos, proconsul of Asia towards the end of Severus' reign, seems to have done something towards the construction of roads in Pontus;[4] and in Phrygia we find milestones of this period on the road between Dorylaeum and Cotia,[5] Synnada, and Prumnessium.[6] Those connecting Cadyandria and Limyra in Pisidia and Hamaxia in Pamphylia with Olba in Cilicia may also be instanced:[7] also some work on the roads in the neighbourhood of Iconium by the legate Atticius Strabo.[8] Again, the road between Melitene and Comana in Cappadocia seems to have undergone a systematic restoration in the year 198 under the care of C. Julius Flaccus Aelianus.[9] Farther south the Syrian *praeses*, Venidius Rufus, was busy repairing the road that runs north and south through Sidon,[10] as well as that running east to Palmyra.[11] In the Danubian and east-European provinces road construction seems to have been confined mainly to Pannonia, Raetia, and Noricum, though we find traces of it in Dacia.[12] In Raetia the road

[1] *CIL.* viii. 8470, 10351, 10364.

[2] e. g. *CIL.* viii. 10353.

[3] *CIL.* viii. 10362. It will be understood that these few inscriptions are neither are, nor are intended to be, exhaustive. The other milestones are however of such diverse dates and provenances that no evidence of *consistent* road-making can be deduced from them: e. g. *L'Ann. Épigr.* 1904, no. 62.

[4] *IGRR.* iii. 82. For Tineius cf. Prosop. iii, p. 322, no. 170.

[5] *CIL.* iii. 7168, 7171.   [6] *CIL.* iii. 14200, 14201.

[7] *IGRR.* iii. 509, 730, 826 ; *CIL.* iii. 12120, 12123.

[8] *L'Ann. Épigr.* 1906, no. 21.

[9] *CIL.* iii. 12162, 12164, 12171, 12178, 12179, 12186, 12197, 12203, 12204.

[10] *CIL.* iii. 205, etc. Some five or six of these inscriptions are extant bearing the writing: 'vias et miliaria per Q. Venidium Rufum leg. augg. pr. pr. praesidem provinc. Syriae Phoen. renov(avit).' Cf. *L'Ann. Épigr.* 1910, no. 106.

[11] *CIL.* iii. 6723, 6725. For other Syrian, Palestinian, and Arabian milestones cf. *CIL.* iii. 13612, 14172, 14174, 13594, 12084 ; *L'Ann. Épigr.* 1904, no. 68 (Bostra: per Q. Scribonium Tenacem).

[12] e. g. a road running 'per ripam Alutae ', *CIL.* iii. 13802. This is probably the road leading to Sarmizegethusa. Schiller (p. 732) calls

between Augusta Vindelicum and Matreium occupied the con-
structor's attention from 195 to 201,[1] in which latter year the
roads and bridges between Pons Aeni and Arbor Felix were
taken in hand.[2] In Noricum the governor, M. Iuventius Surus
Proculus, repaired the roads round about Virunum,[3] besides
those connecting Iuvavum (Salzburg) with Teurnia (St. Peter-
im-Holz), Lauriacum (Lorch), and Pons Aeni.[4] There are at
Schloss Amras, near Innsbruck, nine very weatherworn Severan
milestones coming from the road over the Brenner, showing that
this road also received attention during the period.   In Pannonia
the road along the right bank of the Danube was restored
between the years 198 and 201 for almost its entire length.[5]
Besides the road connecting Vienna with Carnuntum the legate
of upper Pannonia mended that between Emona and Neviodunum,
rebuilding the bridges which had fallen.[6] The occurrence of
milestones in Italy and Gaul, though not uncommon, is nevertheless spasmodic, and affords but little evidence of any
systematic work.[7] With regard, however, to Gaul we may

Septimius the 'zweiter Begründer' of Dacia, and calls attention to the
roads built by the emperor in that province. However, he gives no
references.

   [1] *CIL.* iii. 5978, 5980, 5981, 5982. In the third of these inscriptions
Geta's name, almost invariably erased, is replaced by VIAS. PONT.

   [2] *CIL.* iii. 5987.

   [3] *CIL.* iii. 5712, 5704: the latter on the road from Aquileia.   The
work must have been finished under Caracalla (though no doubt begun
in Septimius' reign) as the former is referred to as Brit. Max.

   [4] *CIL.* iii. 5714, 5715, 5717, 5720, 5722, 5723, 5727 (in the Salzburg
Museum : some have been reused by Constantine) = Teurnia—Iuvavum ;
5745–7 = Iuvavum—Lauriacum ; 5750 = Iuvavum—Pons Aeni.

   [5] Vindobona—Carnuntum, *CIL.* iii. 4642 ('per leg. X curante Fabio
Cilone leg.'); Arrabona—Brigetio, 4638; Brigetio—Aquincum, 3745
('curante Tib. Claud. Claudiano', 198); Aquincum—Mursa, 3706, 3733
(199, 'curante L. Baebio Caeciliano').

   [6] *CIL.* iii. 4622, 4621, 4623, 4624, also 11320, probably earlier; for
other Pannonian roads cf. *CIL.* iii. 4650, 4654, Vienna—Scarabantia ;
5735, Celeia—Poetovio ; 10616, Sirmium—Taurunum.

   [7] For Italy cf. *CIL.* x. 6929, Puteoli—Naples ; 6908, Capua –Calatia
(on the Via Appia); 5909, at Anagnia ; ix. 6011, twenty-two miles from
Beneventum on the Via Traiana. Also the road out of Ostia called after

notice the not infrequent use of the Gallic *leuga* or league as a measure of distance instead of the more familiar Roman mile. Instances of its employment in Gaul do indeed go back to the reign of Pius: German examples are not pre-Severan.[1]

Somewhat strange is the comparative absence of Severan milestones in Spain, the only clear indication of work done to roads in the province being that afforded by some milestones in Lusitania on the road connecting Emerita with Salmantica.[2] In less important provinces, on the other hand, traces are far more frequent: we learn, for example, that Septimius and the royal household ' vias muniri iusserunt' in Sardinia,[3] and several bilingual inscriptions attest road-making in Cyprus.[4]

The construction of roads is of course a piece of governmental activity taken in hand for the good of the provincials. We now pass on to the consideration of buildings whose erection is owing to the goodwill, patriotism, and munificence of the provincials themselves. We notice first of all an astonishing number of triumphal arches in Africa:[5] it is as though a grateful province delighted to honour her imperial son.[6] Temples, too, seem to spring up all over Africa; nor are the other provinces so far

---

him the Via Severiana. For Gaul cf. xiii. 9031, Durocortorum—Samarobriva—Gesoriacum 'curante L. P. . . . . Postumo leg. Augg. pr. pr.'; 9033, Augusta Suessionum—Tarvenna; 8952, Lugdunum—Corallium; 9066, 9067, Lousonna—Eburodunum, etc.

[1] So Stuart Jones, *Companion to Rom. Hist.*, p. 48. Cf. Roth, *Geschichte der Leuga* (*Bonner Jahrb.* xxix, p. 9, etc.). For German instance cf. Narbonese Gaul, *CIL.* xii. 5518; *CIRh.* 1934. The mathematical relation between the Roman mile and the Gallic *leuga* is given in *Bonner Jahrb.* lvii. 39 as 1·4815 km. to 2·436 km.

[2] *CIL.* ii. 4650, 4655.

[3] *CIL.* x. 8010, 8022, 8025, Caralis—Turris.

[4] e.g. *CIL.* iii. 218; *IGRR.* iii. 967, Curium—Paphos ' "Ὀδίου Βάσσου " procos '. (For him see Prosop. i. 182, no. 1144.)

[5] e.g. at Ammaedara, *CIL.* viii. 306, 307; at Chidibbia, 1333; at Assuras, 1798; Vaga, 14395; Bondjem (erected by leg. III aug.), 10992, etc. As in the case of roads, so in this and the following sections inscriptions are cited merely *exempli gratia*: no attempt at an exhaustive enumeration is attempted.

[6] Septimius in a way returned the compliment by erecting a statue to Hannibal (Tzetzes, *Chil.* i. 27).

behind in their thanks to the gods for the blessings of a beneficent and, on the whole, a peaceful reign.[1]

In our own country, for example, Caerleon can boast the
restoration of a temple 'vetustate corruptum':[2] in Spain we
have traces of at least two temples.[3] Dacia supplies two others,[4]
Pannonia Superior and Pannonia Inferior a third and fourth,[5]
and Raetia a fifth.[6] Mention may also be made of a Mithraic
cave constructed in Palaeopolis (Andros) by some praetorians on
their way back from the Eastern wars.[7] Indeed, when we take
into consideration not only the foregoing but also the many
dedications by priests or priestly guilds we might not without
reason claim for Septimius' reign a religious as well as a military

---

[1] African temples: *CIL*. viii. 14465, temple of Saturn at Sûk-Tleta;
2557, cf. Aesculapius at Lambaesis camp, built by the cornicines of
leg. III aug. in 203 (Geta and Plautianus' names, as usual, erased).
Eight years later the city of Lambaesis built a temple to Aesculapius
and Salus 'pro salute et incolumitate dominorum nostrorum', 2585.
Calama, Sarra, and Thaca all provide instances (5329, 12006, 11194;
the latter bears the tribunician date 207, yet Severus is called Brit.
Max.). Such anomalies are by no means unknown on African inscriptions; cf. 4597, where cos. III (202) is coupled with trib. pot. IX (201):
also Septimius is referred to as *Germanicus maximus*, a title he never
bore; cf. *L'Ann. Épigr*. 1906, no. 10). As other instances may be cited
L'Ann. Épigr. 1904, no. 75 'templum victoriae' by 'Augustorum cultores'
at Henchir—R'mada (197), and ibid. 1907, no. 25, temple to Diana at
Bulla Regia (196).

[2] *CIL*. vii. 106. It must be confessed that the reading of this inscription
is somewhat uncertain.

[3] One at Olispo, 'soli aeterno lunae pro aeternitate', *CIL*. ii. 259;
the other at Ebora, 109. The interpretation of the latter is a little
questionable.

[4] One at Vicus Anartorum, *CIL*. iii. 7647; the other at Apulum, 1070
(193: Severus' name is not mentioned, only the consular date given.
This means that the vow to build the temple was taken in 193, but not
fulfilled until the next reign).

[5] *CIL*. iii. 11081, at Arrabona, 'victoriae Augg. . . . et leg. I. adi. P. F.'
(the ANTONINIANAE is a later addition, of course). *L'Ann. Épigr*. 1910,
no. 141, Temple 'deo soli Aelagabalo pro sal auggg.' at Dunapentele
restored 'sub Baebio Casciliano leg. augg.'

[6] *CIL*. iii. 5943 Regensburg).

[7] *L'Ann. Épigr*. 1911, no. 56.

revival, a conclusion which, as we have seen, we can draw on other grounds.[1]

Buildings of all kinds seem to have sprung into being with astonishing rapidity during these few years. Baths are built at Cemenelum in the Maritime Alps,[2] at Lanuvium,[3] at Olbia,[4] and at Choba in Africa;[5] many others fallen into disuse or disrepair are restored, often by a cohort stationed in the particular town.[6] Ruined aqueducts are rebuilt as at Carthage and Caernarvon,[7] fallen bridges replaced,[8] new stone quarries opened up,[9] not to mention less purely practical erections such as bull-baiting floors and androsphinges.[10]

Judging from archaeological evidence, then, the reign of Septimius seems to have formed an era of peace and prosperity for the provincials. One notices in particular what looks like a real anxiety on the part of the governors to act in the best interests of the governed, and an activity on their behalf which is altogether admirable. Nor must we see in this merely the finger of chance. No one could have shown a more meticulous care in his choice of *legati* than Severus. It was the emperor

---

[1] By priests, e. g. *CIL.* iii. 13805; *IGRR.* i. 577; *L'Ann. Épigr.* 1908, no. 263. By guilds, e. g. Bacchus cult at Heraclea in Thrace, *IGRR.* 787; by a 'corpus cannophorum' at Ostia, *CIL.* xiv. 116; by Dendrophori at Rome, *CIL.* vi. 1040.

[2] *CIL.* v. 7979.   [3] *CIL.* xiv. 2101.

[4] *IGRR.* 854.

[5] *CIL.* viii. 8375: for others cf. e. g. viii. 14457; ix. 2204; v. 7783.

[6] e. g. at Veczel in Dacia by coh. II Flav. Commag. (*CIL.* iii. 1374); also at Bowes, where a coh. I Thrac. restores baths 'dae (*sic*) Fortunae' (*CIL.* vii. 273).

[7] Carthage, *CIL.* viii. 891: borne out by the 'indulgentia in Carth.' coins, Eck. vii. 183, 204 (see above, p. 24). Caernarvon, *CIL.* vii. 142.

[8] e. g. near Beneventum, *CIL.* ix. 2122; another at the modern Kiachta in Syria 'sub Alfenium Senecionem . . . curante Mario perpetuo leg. augg. XVI F. F.' and done at the expense of 'quattuor civitates Commag.'

[9] *CIL.* iii. 75, Philae. It is worth remarking that Egyptian inscriptions of this reign are rare.

[10] The latter at Memphis, *IGRR.* 1113: the former at Oenoanda in Pisidia. The inscription refers to a βουκονιστήριον, a word used by Vitruvius (v. 11. 2) as equivalent to the Latin word *arena*.

who now nominated all provincial officials—'nec quicquam est in provincia quod non per ipsum expediatur', as Ulpian said.[1] No governor was allowed to extract presents from the provincials,[2] while the mercenary aims of officials were further checked by a law preventing any such official who had married a provincial heiress contrary to orders from becoming her legatee.[3] In the case of definite crime committed by a governor the emperor showed no mercy, and we hear of one case at least where a prefect of Egypt was convicted for embezzlement.[4] Two new ordinances affecting governors may be noticed in conclusion. The first forbids the sanction of any new municipal regulation or taxes without the closest scrutiny,[5] the second puts alimentary institutions run by private initiative into the governor's hands.[6]

How far, we must now ask, was all this care effective in the production of a generally good tone throughout the empire? In other words, was the state of the provinces really prosperous and peaceful? Evidence is scanty, but we may begin with summing up the result. When Septimius came to the throne there was undoubtedly a widespread feeling of unrest in all parts of the empire, and we should not be justified in showing surprise did history give us a record of provincial disturbances reaching far into the reign, if not coterminous with it. As a matter of fact we can find practically no evidence to show that any but the most desultory upheavals took place. Of course the mere absence of positive evidence is not in itself strong, and we have the example of the great and far-reaching Maternus revolt to remind us how little the imperial historian cared for provincial insurrections. Still, with the exception of a few back-washes, as it were, of the Niger and Albinus troubles, we may not unreasonably conclude that the state of

---

[1] *Dig.* i. 16. 9 ; cf. Mommsen, *St.-R.* ii. 887, note 4.

[2] *Dig.* i. 17. 6. 3.   [3] *Dig.* xxxiv. 9. 28.

[4] *Dig.* xlviii. 10. 1. 4.   Cf. Vit. Sev. viii. 4 'accusatos a provincialibus iudices probatis rebus graviter punivit'.

[5] *Cod. Iust.* iv. 62. 1 and 2.

[6] Marcian, *Dig.* xxxv. 2. 89; cf. xxxiv. 1. 14. 1; *Cod. Iust.* iv. 31. 3. One remembers the private alimentary institution of the younger Pliny (cf. Mommsen in *Hermes,* iii, p. 101). Schiller omits to notice (p. 736) that the reference of these laws is only to such *private* institutions.

the empire under Severus was one of even surprising peace-fulness. The statement of Ammianus [1] to the effect that con-spiracies were rife during the reign is to be taken rather as referring to that of Commodus : indeed the Plautianus con-spiracy is the only one he can adduce for Septimius' principate. We have, however, definite evidence of trouble in Africa, where certain native tribes seem to have needed drastic measures; [2] also we hear of an invasion of Baetica by the Moors. They laid siege to Singilia Barba, but were repulsed by the governor, C. Vallius Maximianus.[3] There appear also to have been in-cursions into Pannonia by trans-Danubian tribes, where the governor of the upper province, L. Equatius Victor Lollianus, was successful not only in beating back the barbarians but in carrying the war into their country.[4] Besides these outbreaks there seem at one time or another to have occurred attempts of private individuals on the emperor's life either in Rome or in the provinces. One such was the occasion of the erection of an altar at Sicca Veneria ' ob conservatam . . . salutem detectis insidiis hostium publicorum '.[5] Of a similar character is an Ephesian

---

[1] xxix. 1. 17 'Commodi et Severi quorum summa vi salus crebro oppugnabatur'.

[2] Vit. Sev. xviii. 3 'contunsis bellicosissimis gentibus' sounds, as Schiller suggests (p. 723, n. 5) as though taken from some inscription ; cf. Aurel. Vict. Caes. 20. Two inscriptions may refer to this outbreak, or rather series of outbreaks : *CIL*. viii. 2702, wherein is mentioned the 'familia rationis castrensis', an inscription which causes Ceuleneer (p. 133), I think unnecessarily, to suppose the presence of Severus in Africa in 203, the year of the inscription (see above, p. 134, note 1). The other is *CIL*. iii. 4364, which mentions a 'victoriae augg.' and is of the year 207, but the reference of this is entirely uncertain ; cf. above, p. 134, note 3.

[3] *CIL*. ii. 1120, 2015, if indeed these inscriptions refer to Severus' and not Marcus' reign.

[4] *CIL*. iii. 4364, vi. 1405. The first of these inscriptions may refer to the African trouble in which context it was quoted above (p. 205, note 2), for the mention of the 'I leg. adi.'—a Pannonian legion—does not prove that the action commemorated was performed by them. Inasmuch as the date is 207 it can scarcely refer to a British victory as Höfner would make out (p. 319).

[5] *CIL*. viii. 1628 ; cf. iii. 1174. Can we connect this with Dio's story of the bald-headed conspirator (Dio Cass. lxxvi. 8) ? Cf. 'pro in-

inscription recording the frustrated 'spes parricidales insidia-
torum': indeed the reference may be the same.[1] Of smaller
disturbances we naturally hear very little. From Gaul comes
an inscription recording the violent death of two wayfarers
at the hands of highwaymen,[2] and nearer home, in what may
now be called the province of Italy, a robber of the name of
Bulla seems to have held authority at bay for the space of two
years. According indeed to our authority for this,[3] Dio Cassius,
a general state of unrest had been caused in Italy by the drafting of foreigners into the praetorian guards, thus throwing a
number of Italians proper out of employment and forcing them
to have recourse to robbery.[4] Little store can be set by this
'little Roman' piece of criticism, though we do hear that the
emperor caused a sharper eye to be kept on *hetaeriae*, and indeed
that he disbanded many of them.[5] This may have been a pre-
cautionary measure. The same historian's account of Claudius,
the Jewish bandit who overran Judaea and Syria in the year
196, is one which belongs rather to the history of war than of
peace, and cannot be adduced in support of any contention to the
effect that the general state of the provinces was an unsettled
one.[6]

columitate', *L'Ann. Épigr.* 1906, no. 10 (Lambaesis), and *CIL.* viii. 7961
(Rusicade).

[1] *CIL.* iii. 427, *CIG.* 2971 (Ephesus). This may be connected with
the 'insidiatores' mentioned in Vit. Sev. xv. 4. Cavedoni (*Annali del-
l'Instituto*, 1859, p. 286) sees in this a reference to the bald Apronianus.

[2] *CIL.* xiii. 259 'c ... et s ... a [latron]ibus hi[c inte]rfecti V [? kal.]
iun. imp. Sept. Sev.'

[3] Dio Cass. lxxvi. 10.   [4] Dio Cass. lxxiv. ii. 5.

[5] Vit. Sev. xvii. 8 'delendarum cupidus factionum'. *Dig.* xlvii. 22. 1. 1,
i. 12. 1. 14.

[6] Dio Cass. lxxv. 2. 4. There can be little doubt but that the Claudius
episode is part and parcel of a larger Jewish disturbance of which we
catch the echoes in our secondary authorities. That Claudius, despite
his Roman name, was a Jew (a fact denied by Graetz, *Gesch. der Juden*,
iv. 253) is easy to understand when we remember the grecizing of Jewish
names, as, e.g., Jason for Joshua, and Alcimus for Eliachim (2 Macc. ii. 4
and 14). A war seems to have started in 193 between the Jews and the
Samaritans (so Gregorius Abulfaragius, quoting an older chronicle—
Hist. Dynastarum, 126; cf. *Chron. Syriac.* 60). At the commencement of

But perhaps the most convincing proof of the excellence of Septimius' provincial government is to be found in the amazing mass of inscriptions on what have been altars or statues erected in honour of the emperor and his family.   Here we find what we can only interpret as a genuíne expressing of thankfulness for favours received and recognized as such.   Most generally such erections are due to the admiration and loyalty of the army,[1] often of private individuals or of those in some public station, whether administrative or religious.[2]   But most curious and most instructive are those set up in honour of the emperor by a town or its council, and it is particularly interesting to note the distribution of such publicly erected monuments, not so much as showing the different degrees of popularity and esteem in which Septimius was held in the various provinces, but as indicative of the advance of local self-government in the different countries.   Naturally enough our longest list is the Italian and Sicilian one.   Benacus, Trebula, Mutuesca, Aecae, Ancona, Puteoli (2), Capua (2), Sinuessa, Suessa, Atina, Ferentinum, Anagnia (2), Formiae, Privernum, Panhormus (5), Gaulus Insula (2), Alsium, Camerinum, Clusium, Nepe, Capena may be mentioned as thus offering tokens of their respect to the

the Nigerian war the Samaritans espoused the cause of the Syrian legate, the Jews that of the emperor—hence the latter's destruction of Sichem (Spart. Nig. 7; cf. above, p. 92).   But just as the Adiabeni deserted the side of Severus so did the Jews, apparently.   Thus Orosius (vii. 17. 3) can write 'Iudaeos et Samaritanos rebellare conantes ferro coercuit'; cf. Jerome, 'Iudaicum et Samariticum bellum ortum' (year 196).   Jewish hostilities broke out again during the war with Albinus, so much so, indeed, that the emperor is said to have celebłated a triumph on the conclusion of peace (Vit. Sev. xvi. 7).

[1] This point has been so exhaustively treated by Ceuleneer (pp. 171-8) as to make it unnecessary for me either to give or to supplement his references.

[2] Reference has already been made to this latter class: other instances are *CIL*. iii. 154, by a priestess near Berytus; *IGRR*. 614, by δενδροφόροι at Tomi—a curious inscription calling Severus Μηδικός and Βριττ(ανικός), though belonging to the years 200-1, as is shown by the mention of Ovinius Tertullus, the governor.   An altar set up at Diana in Africa 'ob honorem IIviratus' (*CIL*. viii. 4583) is typical of the first-mentioned class.

emperor and his house.[1] More important is an inscription from Ricina,[2] where the Colonia Helvia Ricina erects a monument in 205 'conditori suo'. It seems to have been refounded by Septimius.

Compared with this list—and it is by no means exhaustive— the efforts of the provinces proper seem meagre indeed. Gaul and Germany only afford some six or seven instances;[3] Spain has scarcely more;[4] the Danubian provinces, considering their vast extent, are still further behindhand;[5] and it is not until we reach Asia or the islands of the eastern Mediterranean that we find urban dedications in any number : the cities of Gortyna and Itanus in Crete, for example, can both find money and enthusiasm enough to build some monument to Severus—τὸν τῆς πόλεως εὐεργέτην, as the latter city calls him.[6] In Asia Pisidia shows itself perhaps the most loyal district, Comana, Mulassa,

---

[1] The following references keep the order of the text: *CIL.* v. 4868, ix. 4880, 950, 5899, x. 1650, 1651, 3834, 3835, 4735, 4748, 5052, 5825, 5908, 8243, 6079, 6437, 7271-3 (respectively to Septimius, Julia Domna, and Caracalla by 'respub. Panhormitanorum', 195-6), 7274-5 (of 198-9 to Septimius and Caracalla), 7502, 7503, xi. 3716 (to Caracalla by 'Col. Alsiensis'), 5631, 2098, 3201, 3873 (these 'Capenates foederati' are guilty of a curious solecism in dedicating their (?) altar to 'omnium principi virtuiuum ').

[2] *CIL.* ix. 5747; cf. 5755. For some unexplained reason Septimius is referred to as the son of Lucius Verus in this inscription.

[3] e. g. Aventicum to Julia Domna, *CIL.* xiii. 5084; 'civitas Lingonum foederata,' xiii. 5681; (?) baths dedicated to Caracalla by r. p. Aquarum, xiii. 6300. Various *taurobolia*: e. g. Narbo, xii. 4323; Lyon, xiii. 1754 'inchoatum est sacrum IIII non. maias, consummatum nonis eisdem' of 197: clearly in connexion with the completion of the Albinus affair, see above, p. 111, note 7.

[4] Tucci, *CIL.* ii. 1669, 1670; Norba, 693; Malaca, 1969; Capera, 810; Regina, 1037. All these are in Baetica and Lusitania: in Tarraconensis only 'res pub. Vivatiensium' (Baënza), 3343.

[5] e. g. Tomi, in Moesia Inf., *IGRR.* i. 612; Brigetio, *CIL.* iii. 4309; Aquincum, 3518; Iuvavum, 5536; Nicopolis ad Istrum, *L'Ann. Épigr.* 1902, nos. 112, 105, 114; Sarmizegethusa (to Caracalla), 1432; Ampelum, 1308. This last inscription refers to the erection of an altar by the 'ordo Ampelensium'; the more usual form, at least out of Italy, is, e. g., 'Ampelenses publice'.

[6] Gortyna, *CIL.* iii. 12038; Itanus, *IGRR.* 1022.

Milyas, Osiena, Salagassum all supplying examples.[1] Greece, too, is well to the fore in adulation : most remarkable of Grecian inscriptions is that erected by Athens in the late autumn or winter of 209 in honour of Geta's elevation to the dignity of the Augustan title.[2] A statue was also set up at Magnesia in Lydia by the Athenians, though exactly why would be hard to say.[3] Sparta, Thespiae, Thebes, Troezen, and Megara honoured Caracalla in like manner.[4]

Two other localities demand at least a passing notice : these are Rome and Africa. Of the first we need say little : dedications to the emperor and his wife and children are no more than what we should expect in a capital city, and all the Roman monuments from the arch in the forum down to the altar given by the poorest citizen have but little value in the eyes of the historian.[5]

As might be expected the African inscriptions are the most numerous of all : yet even here we find the majority due to private enterprise and comparatively few to urban endeavour. Leptis itself, for instance, offers no example, though it was always careful to preserve the house in which the African emperor was born.[6] Mention has already been made of the various triumphal arches, and of them two certainly were erected at municipal expense—those of Assura and Ammaedara.[7] The

[1] *IGRR.* iii. 325, 384, 389, 418, 352. Adrianople in Galatia is another, ibid. 149.

[2] *CIG.* 353; *CIA.* iii. 10. The exact time is given by the mention of the month Poseideon : the archonship was that of Flavius Diogenes. For the historical bearing of this inscription see above, p. 137.

[3] *CIA.* 3407. For a native Lydian urban inscription cf. *L'Ann. Épigr.* 1909, no. 179.

[4] *CIG.* 1320, 1618, 1619, 1185, 1075. The islands are represented, among others, by Thera, *CIG.* 2456; Sciathos, 2154 (see above, p. 198); Mitylene, 2181.

[5] Naturally nearly all these dedications are personal ones: among those that are not may be mentioned the arch of the silversmiths, *CIL.* vi. 1053, built in 204 by the 'argentarii et negotiantes boarii'; and an inscription to Caracalla by the 'paedagogi caput Africesium' ('caput Africae' was in the 2nd *regio*), *CIL.* vi. 1052. For the palace cf. below, p. 212.

[6] The house was restored in 548 by order of Justinian (Procop. *de aed. Iustin.* vi. 4).

[7] *CIL.* viii. 1798: 306, 307 (A.D. 195). The arch in the forum of

Numidian examples, as Ceuleneer points out, seem to indicate
a deeper affection on the part of the people for Caracalla and
Julia Domna than for Septimius himself, both from the fact of
the greater frequency of inscriptions dedicated to Julia and from
the fact that in a great many instances her name precedes that
of her husband.[1]   As instances we may quote statues erected to
Caracalla by the town of Diana in 200 and to Julia by Sigus in
197, by Uzelis (Oudjel) in 201, and by Tiddis in 197.[2]   But on
the whole it is true to say that the African inscriptions, like
those of Germany and the few that are in Britain,[3] are assignable to the goodwill of private individuals, chiefly army officers,
or to bodies of soldiers. From this, as above suggested, we may
not unjustly infer that urban life was in a more flourishing condition and better recognized in the east of the empire than in
any other part.

Shortly to sum up the evidence to be got from inscriptions
as to the state of the provinces:—we find no lack of care and
attention bestowed by the emperor, and no stint of practically
expressed gratitude on the part of the provincials. The governors
seem to have been more than mere figure-heads, and the amount
of building both for military and civil purposes is distinctly
above the average. Trade seems to have been in a flourishing
condition[4] and an active frontier policy was pursued.[5] There are

Theveste was built by the legacy of one G. Cornelius Egrilianus, prefect
of leg. XIV gem., 1855, etc. The inscription from Thamugadi (203) may
refer to a triumphal arch publicly erected, 2368.

[1] e.g. on the public monuments of the pagus Phuensium, *CIL.* viii.
6306, and of the pagus Mercurialis veteranorum Medelitanorum, 885.
For two dedications to Julia cf. *L'Ann. Épigr.* 1908, no. 170 ('civitas
Ginfitana') and 1909, no. 159 ('civitas Sutunurcensis'). On the other
hand, the r. p. Uchitanorum erect a monument *pecunia pub.* to Severus
himself (*L'Ann. Épigr.* 1908, no. 263).

[2] *CIL.* viii. 4596, 5699, 6340, 6702.

[3] e.g. Netherby, *CIL.* vii. 963; Ithringum (Plautilla, erased), 875;
Chester (though the 'domin. nostr.' may refer to Diocletian and
Maximian), 167; Bremenium (Julia), 1047; Old Carlisle, 342, 343;
Greta Bridge (by Alfenius Senecio), 279.

[4] We notice the foundation of some trade suburb at Pizus in Thrace in
202 (*IGRR.* i. 766).

[5] The whole region round about Darmstadt and Stockstadt and else-

no indications of an approaching barbarism except such as may be seen in a few solecisms[1] and in the growing worship of deities with strange, outlandish names.[2] True, the use of Greek on public monuments even in the near East would have distressed the hearts of the reactionary Stoical party in the Senate—even now by no means a dead letter—but this was a tendency too long implanted in the empire to be easily eradicated: nor can it be called barbarism.[3] For the popular use of a language graffiti are of course the best evidence, but these are unfortunately rare— those, that is, with assignable dates. Still the two visitors to Memnon's statue, whoever they were, recorded their visits with the dates in good enough Latin.[4]

One sign there is of barbarism and that in plenty, but it is of a barbarism common in all periods of the empire, early as well as late—that is, the erasure from inscriptions of a disgraced (or unsuccessful) member of the imperial family. The names of Geta, Plautianus, and the luckless Plautilla have but seldom survived the ruthless vengeance of their quondam admirers. The removal of Geta's name belongs of course to the reign of Caracalla, that of the other two dates from the downfall of Plautianus early in the year 205. The method adopted was twofold: either a blank space was left where the name had been, or else, more commonly, that space was filled up by the insertion of further titles for Septimius or Caracalla, or by the introduction of some

where in the Neckar valley is particularly rich in inscriptions suggesting military building between the years 161–200, though most date from 180 to 190. See above, p. 170.

[1] Some have been mentioned. Add: *CIL.* viii. 2706 'fortissimique principi' at Lambaesis (but a second example of the same inscription is grammatically correct, 2707); viii. 2549 *matri* for *matris*; viii. 17259 *proadnepos*; xiv. 112, etc., etc. Cf. Momm. *CIL.* iii, p. 919; *Hermes*, xiv. 71; Friedl., iv, p. 26 (8th edit.).

[2] e.g. *CIL.* xiii. 6283 (A.D. 193) IN . . . DEANAE ABNOBAE; cf. 6356, 6357, at Arae Flaviae to the same goddess; xiii. 8162 'Ahveccanis Avehae et Hellivesae'; see above, p. 142.

[3] The number of Greek inscriptions dating from early in the second century A.D. in the museum at Sophia, for example, is remarkable.

[4] *CIL.* iii. 50, 51; respectively Mar. 9, 195, and Feb. 24, 196. 'Audi Memnona' say the old-world trippers—and they must have been nearly the last to do so; see above, p. 123.

such vague phrase as 'totiusque domus divinae'.[1]   Only in a few
out-of-the-way places do these hated names survive.[2]

A survey such as this, where the subject-matter is so diverse
in character and so scattered in extent, is of necessity not only
tedious but also defective.   Many points will escape notice: as
many, or more, must be purposely omitted.   No attempt, for
instance, has been made to deal at any length with Septimius'
buildings in Rome.   The remains of the gigantic palace on the
Palatine still stand for the tourist to marvel at: the Septizonium,
erection of a superstitious emperor, still offers us the puzzle of its
name, character, and use; while, in general, the vast amount of
building in the capital, necessitated by the great fire of 191,
is recalled to our memory by the marble plan set by Vespasian
on the east wall of the so-called Templum Sacrae Urbis and
restored after the fire by Septimius and his elder son.[3]

---

[1] It is unnecessary to quote many examples of so universal a custom.
An inscription from Corycus in Cilicia erected early in 211, Φιλαδελφίας
τῶν Σεβαστῶν, suffered the erasure of the first word in the following year
(*IGRR.* iii. 860).   The names of both Geta and Plautianus disappear
from the inscription on the temple of Aesculapius at Lambaesis camp
(*CIL.* viii. 2557).   In the arch in the Roman forum the third line
'optimis fortissimisque principibus' is an obvious substitution for the
name of Geta (*CIL.* vi. 1033).   Cf. *L'Ann. Épigr.* 1902, no. 105 (Nicopolis)
Geta erased: 1906, no. 24 (Bulla Regia) Plautianus do.; 1906, no. 34
(Lebda) Plautilla do., etc., etc.

[2] e. g. an inscription at Isgin near Melitene still reads 'Geta', while
an altar at Germisara bears the words 'fortunae pro sal. auggg.' (incidentally its date is 200, when Geta was not as yet Augustus).   Cf. *CIL.*
xii. 1745 for a similar instance from Valentia—a *taurobolium*: the last
g is uncertain.

[3] See Stuart Jones, *Companion to Rom. Hist.*, pp. 37, 38.   For the
repairing of the Aqua Claudia cf. *CIL.* vi. 1259.   All the building in
Rome would be done, as Hirschfeld (p. 481) remarks, by the *praefectus
urbi*, not by the Senate.   The so-called Capitoline city plan is published
by Jordan in *Aufträge der Berliner Akademie.*

The Palace contained a Labyrinth and a 'Memphis' (*CIL.* vi. 461,
Memphis; *CIG.* 5922 ὁ τόπος Λαβύρινθος) ; cf. Hadrian's Kanopus in his
villa at Tibur (Spart. Hadr. xxvi. 5).

The Septizonium was destroyed by Pope Sixtus V in 1586.   It seems
to have been reckoned a part of the palace, but to have stood apart from
the other buildings.   We possess only the sixteenth-century drawings,

now in the Uffizi Gallery at Florence and in the Vatican at Rome. Some (e. g. Lanciani) believe that there were originally seven stories, and that these drawings represent a mutilated Septizonium. Others (e.g. Hülsen) think that it never possessed more than the three stories. Cf. Hülsen, *Das Septizonium*, Berlin, 1886; Pelham, *Essays on Roman History*, p. 261.

BIBLIOGRAPHY

ORIGINAL SOURCES

AMMIANUS MARCELLINUS: Res gestae.
ANTONINI AUGUSTI Itinerarium.
AURELIUS VICTOR: Caesares.
———— ———— : Epitome.

CAGNAT: L'Année épigraphique.
CASSIODORUS: Chronicon.
CASSIUS DIO COCCEIANUS: Historiae Romanae.
Chronicon paschale.
Codex Iustinianus.
Corpus Inscriptionum Atticarum.
Corpus Inscriptionum Graecarum.
Corpus Inscriptionum Latinarum.

Digesta.
DITTENBERGER: Orientis Graeci inscriptiones.

Ephemeris epigraphica.
EUSEBIUS: Chronicon.
——: Historia Ecclesiastica.
EUTROPIUS: Breviarium.

GEORGE SYNCELLUS: Chronographia.
GRENFELL: Amherst papyri.
—— Greek papyri.
—— Oxyrhynchus papyri.
Griechische Urkunden = BGU.

HERODIANUS: Historiae.

Inscriptiones graecae ad res romanas pertinentes.
IOHANNES ANTIOCHENSIS: Historia chronica.
IULIANUS: Caesares.

LACTANTIUS: De orig. error.

MOSES CHORENAZI.

Notitia Dignitatum.

ORIGENES: Contra Celsum.
OROSIUS: Historiae contra paganos.

PHILOSTRATUS: Vit. Apolloni.
——: Vit. Soph.
PORPHYRIUS: Vita Plotini.

Scriptores Historiae Augustae.
SUIDAS: Lexicon.

TERTULLIANI opera.

VEGETIUS: de re militari.

ZONARAS: Epitome.
ZOSIMUS (ed. MENDELSSOHN): Historiae.

LATER WORKS

ASHBY: Recent Discoveries at Ostia. (In *Journal of Roman Studies*, vol. ii.)

BAAZ: De Herodiani fontibus, et auctoritate.
BAYER: Historia Osrhoëna et Edessena.
BECK: de Orosii fontibus et auctoritate.
BEUCHEL: De legione rom. I. Ital.
BOISSEVAIN: article on a fragment of Dio in *Hermes*, xxv.
BORGHESI: Œuvres complètes.
BÜDINGER: Untersuchungen zur röm. Kaisergeschichte.

CAGNAT: L'armée rom. d'Afrique.
—— 'Légion' in Daremberg et Saglio.
—— Les deux camps de lég. III aug. à Lambèse.
—— 'Limes imperi' in Daremberg et Saglio.
—— article Peregrini in Daremberg et Saglio.
CEULENEER: Essai sur la vie et le règne de Septime Severe.
CHEESMAN: Auxilia of the Roman Imperial Army.
CLINTON: Fasti Romani.
COHEN: Médailles impériales, ed. 2.
CREES: Emperor Probus.
CUMONT: Textes et monuments figurés relatifs aux mystères de Mithra.

DAREMBERG ET SAGLIO: various articles.
DE BOZE: Essai sur les médailles de Pescennius Niger (*Acad. des inscript. anc. coll.* xxiv).

216 SEPTIMIUS SEVERUS

DE ROSSI: L'horrea sotto l'Aventino. (In *Annali dell' Instit. archeol.*, 1885.)

DE SANCTIS: article on S.H.A. in *Rivista di Storia antica*, 1895.

DESJARDINS: Voyage archéologique et géographique dans la région du Bas-Danube.

DESSAU: articles on S.H.A. in *Hermes*, 1889 and 1892.

DOMASZEWSKI: Geschichte des röm. Reiches.

—— Magna Mater in Latin Inscriptions. (In *Journal of Roman Studies*, vol. i.)

—— Rangordnung des röm. Heeres. (*Bonner Jahrb.* 1908.)

ECKHEL: Doctrina nummorum.

ENMANN: article on S.H.A. in *Philologus*, 1884.

FIELD, M.: Iulia Domna.

FILOW: Die Legionen der Provinz Moesia.

FRIEDLÄNDER: Darstellungen aus der Sittengeschichte Roms. 8th edit.

FUCHS: Geschichte des Kaisers L. Septimius Severus.

GIBBON: Decline and Fall of the Roman Empire, ed. Bury.

GRAETZ: Geschichte der Juden.

GUTSCHMID: Untersuchungen über die Geschichte des Königreichs Osrhoëne.

GWATKIN: Church History.

HAVERFIELD: Britain, in Mommsen's *Provinces*.

—— chapter xiii (Roman Britain) in *Cambridge Mediaeval History*.

—— Roman London. (In *Journal of Roman Studies*.)

HEER: Der historische Wert der Vita Commod. (In *Philologus*, Supplementband ix.)

HASSEBRANK: Geschichte des Kaisers L. Septimius Severus.

HIRSCHFELD: Die kaiserlichen Verwaltungsbeamten, ed. 2.

HÖFNER: Untersuchungen zur Geschichte des Kaisers L. Septimius Severus.

HOPKINS: Alexander Severus.

HÜBNER: Die röm. Legionen in Brit. (*Rhein. Mus.* xx.)

HÜLSEN: Das Septizonium.

JOUGUET: La vie municipale dans l'Égypte romaine.

JÜNEMANN: De Legione rom. i adi. (*Leipziger Studien*, 1894.)

JUNG: Die röm. Provinzen.

—— Fasten der Provinz Dacien.

KÖCHER: De Iohannis Antiocheni aetate, fontibus, auctoritate.

KREUTZER: De Herodiano rerum romanarum scriptore.

KUHN: Städtische und bürgerliche Verfassung des röm. Reiches.

LÉCRIVAIN : Études sur l'hist. aug.
LETRONNE : Rech. pour servir à l'hist. de l'Egypte pendant la domination des Grecs et des Romains.
LIEBENAM : Fasti consulares.
LONGPÉRIER : Rois Parthes Arsacides.
LUMBROSO : L'Egitto al tempo dei Greci e dei Romani.

MARQUARDT : Le Culte chez les Romains.
—— L'Organisation de l'emp. romain.
—— L'Organisation financière.
—— L'Organisation militaire.
MARTIN : De fontibus Zosimi.
Mélanges d'archéologie et d'histoire, articles in.
MEYER : Heerwesen der Ptolemäer und Römer.
MILNE : Egypt under Roman Rule.
MINNS : Scythians and Greeks.
MIONNET : Description de médailles antiques.
MOMMSEN : article on S.H.A. in *Hermes*, 1890.
—— Die röm. Lagerstädte. (In *Hermes*, vii).
—— Ludi saeculares.
—— Provinces of the Roman Empire.
—— Staatsrecht, 3rd edit.

NEWBOLD : Excavations on the Line of the Roman Wall in Cumberland.
—— Excavations on the Roman Wall at Limestone Bank. (In *Arch. Ael.*, 3rd ser., vol. ix.)
Numismatic Chronicle.

OCCO : Imp. rom. numismata.
OMAN : England before the Norman Conquest.

Pauly-Wissowa, articles in.
PELHAM : Essays on Roman History.
PETER : article on S.H.A. in *Jahresbericht*, 1906.
—— article on S.H.A. in *Philologus*, 1884.
—— Historia critica scriptor. hist. aug.
PFITZNER : Geschichte der röm. Kaiserlegionen.
PHYTHIAN-ADAMS : The Problem of the Mithraic Grades. (In *Journal of Roman Studies*, vol. ii.)
PLEW : De diversitate auct. hist. aug.
—— Kritische Beiträge zu den S.H.A.
PREMERSTEIN : Untersuchungen zur Geschichte des Kaisers Marcus (in *Klio*, 1913).
Prosopographia imp. romani.

RAWLINSON: The Sixth Great Oriental Monarchy.
RÉVILLE: Die Religion der röm. Gesellschaft im Zeitalter des Synkre-
    tismus (German trans.).
ROTH: Geschichte der Leuga. (*Bonner Jahrb.* xxix.)

SAUVAGE: De Orosio.
SCHILLER: Geschichte der röm. Kaiserzeit.
SCHULTE: De imperio Sept. Sev.
SCHULZ: Beiträge zur Kritik unserer litterarischen Überlieferung für
    die Zeit von Commodus' Sturze bis auf den Tod des M. Aurelius
    Antoninus.
—— Kaiserhaus der Antonine.
SCHWARTZ: article Cassius Dio in Pauly-Wissowa.
SEECK: article on S.H.A. in *Neue Jahrb. für Philologie und Paedagogik*,
    1890.
—— 'Comites' (in Pauly-Wissowa).
SIEVERS: Über das Geschichtswerk des Herodianus.   (In *Philologus*,
    xxvi.)
STOUT: Governors of Moesia.
STUART JONES: Companion to Roman History.
—— The Roman Empire.

THIELE: De Severo Alexandro imperatore.
TILLEMONT: Histoire des empereurs.
TOUTAIN: Les cultes païens dans l'empire romain.
TROPEA: article on S.H.A. in *Rivista di Storia antica*, 1897.

VAN DE WEERD: Trois légions rom. du Bas-Danube.

WIRTH: Quaestiones Severianae.

INDEX

Abgarus, 115, 279.
Adiabeni, 93.
advocati fisci, 185.
Aelian, 144.
Aelius Julius Cordus, 18.
Aelius Maurus, 18.
Aemilius Saturninus, 131.
aerarium, 183, etc.
Aetius, 11, 12.
Africa, 35, 192.
Albano, camp at, 161, 162.
Alexander of Aphrodisias, 145.
Alexandria, 122, 197.
Alfenius Senecio, 134.
alimentation, 186, etc.
Antipater, 17, 144.
Anullinus, 88, 94.
Apuleius Rufinus, 47.
Arabia, 2 *n.*, 194.
Arabs, 93.
Arch of Severus, 125, 162.
Arche, 94.
Armenia, 118.
Arval brothers, 147.
Ascanius, Lake, 86.
Asellius Aemilianus, 76, 80, etc.
Astarte, 29, 152.
Athenaeus, 147.
Aurelius Victor, 19.

Babylon, 116.
Barbarisierung theory, 164, etc.
Barsemius, 80.
Bellona, 142.
Bithynia, 195.
Bona Dea, 142.
Britain, division of, 190.
Britannicus Maximus, 35, 136.

building in Rome, 212.
Bulla, 206.
Byzantium, 61, 81, etc., 96, 197.

Caeonius Rufinus Volusianus, 13.
Caesar worship, 148, etc.
Caledonii, 194, etc.
Capitolinus: *see* Scriptores.
Caracalla, 48–53, 103, 124.
Carthage, 24, 29.
castra peregrina, 160.
castra Severiana, 160.
Cervidius Scaevola, 39.
Christianity, 152, etc.
Cilicia, arrangements of, 193.
Cilician gates, 87, etc.
Claudius Attalus, 81.
Claudius Candidus, 86, 94, 111.
Claudius Pompeianus, 56, 57, 64.
Cleander, 44, 46.
Clodius Albinus, 31, 61, 83, 99, etc.
Coeranus, 133, 179.
colonial rights, granting of, 195, etc.
comites Augusti, 174.
Commodus, 45, 54.
corn supply, 177, etc.
Ctesiphon, 116.
Cybele, 142.
Cyzicus, 85.

Dacia, division of, 72.
Decennalia, 125, 186.
dedicatory inscriptions, 207, etc.
Dexippus, 20.
Didius Julianus, 39, 56, 58–65.
Dio Cassius, 3, 4.
Diogenes Laertius, 144.